Beautiful Northern California

Colorful
Northern
California,
Volume II

Text by William Curran

Library of Congress Cataloging in Publication Data
Curran, William, 1921-
Colorful Northern California, Volume II

    1. California—Description and travel—1951-
—Views. I. Title.
F862.C87   979.4'05   78-9901
ISBN 0-915796-87-2
ISBN 0-915796-86-4 pbk.

Published by Beautiful America Publishing Company
4720 S.W. Washington, Beaverton, Oregon 97005
Robert D. Shangle, Publisher

First Printing

Copyright © 1978 by Beautiful America Publishing Company
Printed in the United States of America

PHOTO CREDITS

MARGARET ANNALA—*Page 57, below; page 60, below; page 64.*

ROY BISHOP—*page 18; page 19, below; page 22, below; page 25, below; page 50; page 55; page 61.*

BOB CLEMENZ—*page 11, below; pages 12-13; page 14, below; pages 16-17; pages 44-45; page 60, above.*

ED COOPER—*page 9; page 19, above; page 24; page 40, above; page 42; page 54, below; page 65, below.*

JOHN GRONERT—*pages 20-21; page 37; page 33; page 32; page 28, below; page 28, above; page 46, below; page 51, below; pages 52-53; page 68, below.*

TOM MYERS—*page 40, below.*

ROBERT SHANGLE—*Page 11, above; page 14, above; page 36, below; page 36, above; page 29; page 25, above; page 41; page 43, above; page 46, above; page 47; pages 48-49; page 54, above; page 56; page 57, above; page 65, above.*

BRUCE AND SAM WHITE—*page 10; page 15; page 22, above; page 23; page 43, below; page 51, above; page 68, above; page 69; page 72.*

CONTENTS

Introduction 7

The Mountains 26

The Coast 31

The Lakes 39

The Valley 63

San Francisco and the Bay Area 67

Enlarged Prints

of most of the photography
in this book
are available.
Send self-addressed,
stamped envelope
for information.
Beautiful America Publishing Company
4720 S.W. Washington
Beaverton, Oregon 97005

INTRODUCTION

CALIFORNIA! The name has probably stirred more emotion in the breasts of Americans than has any other except "America" itself. For almost a century and a half those emotions have been largely positive, pleasurable excitement at the thought of a land wholly new, beautiful, and rich. Such feelings gave birth to epithets like El Dorado and the Golden State. In recent decades some of the feeling about California has turned to denigration and hostility. Concerning California, it seems, neutrality is impossible.

The promise of California has not been the same for everyone. To the pretty, unemployed Chicago typist in the 1920s, the Oklahoma farmer in the 1940s, and the restless Brooklyn war veteran in the late 1940s, it almost certainly meant the Los Angeles basin, with its plentiful sunshine, its beaches, its citrus groves, its 20th-century industries like motion pictures, aircraft construction, electronics. To the Ohio farm boy of the 19th century, however, California could only have meant the mother lode country of the Sierra foothills or a slower kind of riches drawn from the warm soil of the central valley.

People within the state have long recognized two Californias. Geologically, it may be argued that Northern California extends as far south as Point Conception and the entrance to the warm Santa Barbara Channel. On the other hand, social attitudes associated with Southern California are readily observed as far north as Carmel and Fresno. Although this book is intended as a record of the beauties of Northern California, it does not claim to define exact boundaries between the two.

People in the north charge that Southern Californians are insensitive to the beauties of nature, that they are wanton despoilers of the environment. Such a sweeping indictment is unfair and almost certainly untrue. What is true is that in Northern California, nature lovers and conservationists have been visible, vocal, and well organized for more than a century. There should be nothing surprising in this, since few people in history have had so much worth preserving. From the once heavily-timbered coast to the deep blue bowl of Lake Tahoe, from Shasta's peak to the Monterey Peninsula, the California first seen by Americans must have been a land of heart-stopping beauty. The settlers have taken their toll of this beauty, it is true, but thanks to the foresight and selflessness of a few, many natural treasures have survived, as the photos in the book illustrate.

Intoxicated by life in a demi-paradise, some Northern Californians early developed an Arcadian mentality and a consequent fear that coarse and insensitive newcomers could bring a swift end to the good life. The roots of this feeling can be seen in the reported reluctance of Captain John Sutter to disclose that gold had been discovered at his mill and the private revelation in his diary that "At once...the curse of the thing burst upon my mind." Sutter did eventually lose all his land to gold-crazed intruders and died penniless. His tragic history has not been lost on later generations of Northern Californians. And so the dream of Arcadia persists, fueled by the undeniable fact that Northern California has the natural wealth to go it alone.

As recently as 1975, Ernest Callenbach of Berkeley published an utopian novel, *Ecotopia,* about a secessionist republic of that name, embracing Northern California, Oregon and Washington. The major, and virtually the sole, national policy of Ecotopia is to maintain a society living in harmony with nature and dedicated to the perpetuation of natural beauty. Significantly, when Callenbach's Ecotopians revolt from the U.S., they covet no territory south of Monterey.

Visions of Ecotopias notwithstanding, the two Californias are, in the words of the marriage ceremony, joined together "for better or for worse." They have no choice but to face the future together and like George and Martha in the play, they may come to agree that they wouldn't have it any other way.

In this book, the contributions of several photographers sum up the prodigious and infinitely varied beauty of the region. Brilliant as they are, photos can offer but a suggestion of actuality. But there should be in this record a note of reassurance for us all, Californians and visitors alike. Whatever course the state's political and economic history may take, much of her natural beauty is likely to remain. It may prove the most enduring capital.

W.C.

(Preceding page) Autumn's colors and a light dusting of snow suggest winter is not far away in the Mt. Shasta area.

(Opposite) The broad, shallow expanse of Tule Lake offers food and shelter to migratory waterfowl.

(Right) Roses thrive in the mild climate of Northern California.

(Below) Emerald Bay is a peaceful, sheltered inlet on the California side of Lake Tahoe.

(Preceding pages) Spectacular Yosemite Falls seems to dissipate into mist as it spends its power against the stone cliff.

(Left) Barrel cactus blossoms brighten the Northern California desert.

(Below) Rainbow Falls is one of many cascades in the High Sierras.

(Opposite) Winter's snows are slow to melt from the banks of Long Lake, in Plumas National Forest.

(Following pages) Almost bereft of snow in this summertime scene, Mt. Shasta basks in late afternoon sun while an evening breeze ripples the waters of Lake Shasta.

(Preceding full page) Redwoods reach for the sky in Rockefeller Grove, Humboldt Redwoods State Park.

(Preceding page, above) Springtime brings a riot of color to the slopes of Poppy Hill, in Solano County.

(Preceding page, below) Yosemite's Cathedral Rocks are reflected in the clear waters of the Merced River.

(Left) Twisted by its struggle to survive against the harshness of the elements, a lone pine stands silhouetted against the Northern California sky.

(Left) The tiny snowplant offers a surprising splash of color in the volcanic soils of Lassen National Park.

(Below) The autumn stillness of the placid Merced River accents the towering ruggedness of Cathedral Rocks in this view of Yosemite.

(Opposite) The towering grandeur of Castle Crags seems aptly named, though it is doubtful that any man-made castle could be so magnificent.

(Following full page) The massive rock face of El Capitan is perhaps the most popular of Yosemite's scenic attractions.

THE MOUNTAINS

Northern California is a land of mountains. In reasonably clear weather, there is probably no spot in the region outside of visible range of a peak, a ridge, a rounded headland. In poetic terms, Northern California is a child of its mountains. Without them, it might be another Libya, with 100,000 square miles of desert sands continuing to the edge of the sea.

On the coast north of Eureka, rainfall is heavy. The central valley, on the other hand, doesn't get nearly enough. It remains for the tall peaks of the Cascades and the High Sierras to wring additional moisture from the winds in the form of snow. Later, this water finds its way back to the valley through the mountain streams and the river system. Since they also shield California from the frigid winter winds of the continental interior, the high mountains prove a double blessing.

Mountain ranges in Northern California generally run north-south, the prevailing pattern in the Western Hemisphere. At the northern end of the state, small transverse ranges like the Salmon Mountains link the larger chains.

The Coast Range, or more accurately ranges, extend as far north as the Olympic Peninsula of Washington and could be described in Northern California as the "habitable mountains." Most of the population — and this includes that of San Francisco — already lives within the limits of the range. With elevations averaging 2,000 feet, the coastal mountains are suitable for farming, cattle grazing, winemaking, dairying, and — growing in importance — outdoor recreation.

South of San Francisco, agriculture along the coast is in slow retreat. Fields that once produced artichokes, broccoli, or Brussels sprouts are giving way to golf courses and housing developments. North and south of the Bay Area, the premium wine country is still holding its own. It remains to be seen whether Californians will ever be ready to sacrifice good wine for row houses.

Estimates are that by the year 2000, the state's population may be 40 million or more. Most of these millions are likely to be within the coastal mountains. The region may begin to resemble Italy. That's not an unpleasant prospect.

(Preceding page, above) Wildflowers and occasional outcroppings of stone punctuate the green smoothness of a Northern California hillside.
(Preceding page, below) Wedding Rock takes a relentless pounding from the powerful breakers at Patricks Point State Park.

In contrast to the populated Coast Range, the Warner Mountains in the northeast corner of the state are in part a wilderness area. For backpackers, the Warners may well offer the maximum solitude possible within the state borders.

The photogenic peaks of the Cascade Range stretch as far north as the Canadian Border. They don't occupy much of Northern California but they are important. The 14,000-foot, double-peaked Mount Shasta is very nearly the tallest peak in the range, and one of the showiest. For sheer spectacle, it rivals Alaska's Mt. McKinley, a much bigger mountain. With five living glaciers clinging to its sides, Shasta's snowy top dominates the skyline north of Redding. Beyond its beauty, Shasta is important as the keystone of a vast watershed, whose water is impounded fifty miles to the south at Shasta Lake.

Smaller than Shasta, and perhaps not so striking, Mount Lassen brings its own kind of fame to the Cascades. It is the only volcano in the coterminous forty-eight states to erupt in the 20th century. Its 1915 eruption was enough to win it the 100,000-acre Lassen Volcanic National Park in which to show off its lava fields and steaming fissures.

South and east of Lassen begin the Sierra Nevada, a very different kind of mountains. In simplest geological terms, the Sierras are block mountains (in a sense *one* mountain) formed millions of years ago when the earth bulged to a height of 14 thousand feet and the bulge split at the top. The eastern portion slipped thousands of feet, exposing a wall of rock 300 miles long, now known as the eastern escarpment. On the western side, the slope of the Sierras is so gentle that in places it is scarcely perceptible.

The Spanish, who named ''the great snowy ridge'' probably never explored it. It was 1844 before Fremont led the first wagon train of Americans over the range, and it remained something of a barrier to immigration until the coming of the railroad in the 1860s. Even today there are only five roads through the Sierras, and most are closed by snow in winter.

Mark Twain, who as a young man explored the Sierras, observed, ''There are just two seasons in the region—the breaking up of one winter and the beginning of the next.'' But the vast amount of snow is now looked upon with joy, not only for its beauty and the precious water it stores but also for its contribution to winter recreation areas like Squaw Valley and Echo Summit near Lake Tahoe.

The natural beauty of the Sierras and its preservation is inevitably linked with the name of John Muir, the great naturalist and founder of the Sierra Club. Muir was

(Following page, above) Winter's snows cover the upper reaches of Yosemite.
(Following page, below) Autumn-tinted foliage provides a colorful foreground along the banks of this lake in the Central Cascades.

brought to California from Scotland as a child and spent most of his long life exploring and living in the Sierras, which he called "the range of light." It was largely through his efforts that vast areas in the range have come under federal protection as national parks, national forests, and wilderness areas. Muir's creed was simple. "Everyone," he said, "needs beauty as well as bread."

One of Muir's early homes, and apparently his favorite, was Yosemite Valley, where he settled in 1860. Using this as a base, he explored places like King's Canyon and the Sequoia forests and published their existence to the world. Partly because of Muir's zeal of a century ago, the Sierras have become one of the most heavily-used recreations areas in the country. It is estimated that in summer alone between eight and ten million persons visit and enjoy the parks and other public lands.

Muir spent a lifetime in the Sierras and never ran out of new things to see. In anyone's language the range is a wonderland of natural beauty, jagged granite peaks, and glacier-sculptured rock; forests of sequoia, lodgepole pine, red fir; thousands of deep blue lakes from big Tahoe down to nameless ponds; falls and torrents; deep-walled canyons; whole meadows of shooting star, lupine, larkspur; ouzels and hawks; ground squirrels and bighorn sheep; and, finally, the benign mountain light that moved Muir so deeply.

If the Sierras harbored nothing more than the great sequoias (*Sequoiadendron giganteum*), cousins of the coast redwoods, they would be worth crossing a continent to visit. The big trees are the earth's largest living things, some measuring 40 feet in diameter and up to 300 feet in height.

Many Americans think of the destruction of natural beauty as a 20th century phenomenon. In the Sierras most of the damage was done in the last century, by hydraulic mining for gold in the foothills, grazing of sheep and cattle, clear cutting of forests. The Wilderness Act of 1964 should insure that these activities have ended forever on many public lands.

Today's young nature lover will be shocked to learn that the rock walls around Yosemite Falls were once painted with commercial advertising. His next trip to the falls may convince him that despite the crush of visitors, the lot of the nature lover has probably improved in the past century.

Across the Owens Valley from the Sierra Escarpment, in the Inyo National Forest, are the White Mountains which also reach a height of 14,000 feet. Here grow the mysterious bristlecone pine, the oldest living things on earth. Some of the bristlecones in the Inyo Forest are thought to be 4,000 years old. The mountains themselves, at a mere 180 million years, are considered young. Nature has no limit of paradoxes.

(Preceding page) Wildflowers of early spring add a touch of color to this placid Northern California scene.

THE COAST

VIEWED from the sea, the coast of Northern California appears remarkably undomesticated. Except at San Francisco, it is not a coast of snug harbors, broad estuaries, or navigable rivers—those deep and quiet backwaters which invite heavy human settlement and commerce. A great wall of rock rises from the ocean; hills and peaks glimpsed through breaks in the fog confirm that the wall is backed by a mighty continent. At scattered offshore rookeries, seals and sea lions define their turf with croaks and barks. Sea birds fly their tireless patrols in search of fish. Nature seems everywhere in command.

From driftwood-strewn Pelican Beach south to the jutting headlands of Big Sur, roughly 500 miles, there are only three significant breaks in the coastline: Humboldt Bay, Golden Gate, and Monterey Bay. It is not a coast that navigators are drawn to hug. Thousands of sharp rocks and a large, angry surf have claimed more than their share of imprudent or just plain unlucky mariners.

To describe a surf as *angry* is to seize upon a shop-worn metaphor. But, in this case, nothing else seems quite accurate. Robert Frost, a native Northern Californian, lived most of his adult life within a short distance of the Atlantic Ocean, and never seemed moved to draw upon it for imagery. But he retained from his childhood an image of the Northern California surf which symbolized for him nothing less than divine anger:

> The shattered water made a misty din.
> Great waves looked over others coming in,
> And thought of doing something to the shore
> That water never did to land before. *

Inland, Northern California could scarcely offer a more pleasant contrast to the forbidding aspect of the coastline. High above ragged headlands on gently rolling brown hills, beef cattle graze on chapparal and woodland grass and seek shade in stands of live oak. California poppies, violets, and lupine color hillside meadows. On neat seaside farms, furrows run to the cliff's edge. Regions of lush dairy farms and

*From "Once the Pacific" by Robert Frost, *West-Running Brook,* New York, Henry Holt, 1928.

(Following page) Changing maples signal the approach of autumn to the California Coast Range.

pampered vineyards produce bucolic landscapes to rival Europe's. And in higher elevations of the Coast Range, herds of Roosevelt elk disregard both man and his works.

Most of California's coastline is privately owned and not accessible to the public. But state and federal governments have been able to salvage a few enclaves for public use. South of Crescent City for about 30 miles stretches the shore of Redwood National Park, the last sizeable stand of the tall Coast Redwoods *(Sequoia sempervirens),* which once dominated this coast from Southern Oregon to Big Sur. Nowhere is the voice of man so small and muffled as beneath these 300-foot giants. Visitors have long commented on the silence in the groves and perhaps only acoustics engineers can explain the cause. But just to stand under a living tree which may have been a thousand years old in the time of Christ seems reason enough for silence.

South of Cape Mendocino is the experimental King Range National Conservation Area. In this part of the state Highway 101 has carried the stream of commerce 20 miles inland through the Humboldt Redwoods. From Ferndale to Rockport is the most sparsely populated section of the north coast. In the King Range, the Bureau of Land Management is trying to determine whether a near wilderness area can sustain itself when limited recreational and commercial use is permitted.

From an elevation of four thousand feet, the land drops steeply through thick second-growth woodlands and grassy meadows. The absence of roads helps to isolate beaches. There is some belief that in the forested canyons, cadres of mountain lions and black bears are busily regaining their lost numbers. It looks as though wilderness is taking hold again, but only time will tell.

About thirty miles north of San Francisco, Point Reyes juts out sharply from suburban Marin County. It is the most distinct point of land on the entire coast and the federal government has designated the entire peninsula a National Seashore. The eastern edge of this 64,000-acre preserve is defined by the San Andreas Fault. Beyond this point, the fault disappears beneath the ocean. Broad beaches, busy tidal pools, lonely dunes, and grass-covered headlands create a seascape that might look familiar to Sir Francis Drake. Drake is believed to have moored his ship *The Golden Hind* in Drake Bay, a few miles northwest of San Francisco Bay.

In addition to the extensive seashore, Point Reyes encompasses a large forest, where the Douglas fir of the north country and the Bishop pine of the south meet and flourish. The forest has helped turn the area into an important wildlife sanctuary. More than 300 species of birds and dozens of mammals have been identified within

(Preceding page) Redwood trees stand tall and straight in Lady Bird Johnson Grove, Redwood National Forest.

the park. Looking at Point Reyes today, it is hard to believe that less than 25 years ago housing developers were poised with their bulldozers ready to level the place.

With a decline in logging and fishing over the decades, the coast north of the Golden Gate has lost some of its former commercial importance, although tourism and recreation bid fair to take up that slack. Eureka, a town of only 25,000 on Humboldt Bay, is still one of the chief ports between San Francisco and the Columbia River. In the late 19th century, when logging dominated the economy of the north coast, Eureka was a boom town. It is still a busy port for its size, but an atmosphere of past glory is evident. In fact, the town is developing the aura of an historic landmark. The Victorian mansions built by lumber barons are now the subject of a guided tour.

The tiny port of Mendocino, one of the oldest towns on the north coast, also grew rich exporting lumber in the 19th century and then almost faded from existence. In recent years it has enjoyed a renaissance as an art colony and popular location for shooting Hollywood movies.

South of San Francisco the coast is more heavily populated. In suburbs like Pacifica, promontories are virtually covered with development housing. At Half Moon Bay the crowding diminishes and agriculture again dominates the landscape.

Broad curving Monterey Bay with its many beaches is one of the most popular vacation areas in California. At the south corner of the bay, the Monterey Peninsula has been attracting tourists — usually affluent ones — since the last century. Robert Louis Stevenson was one of the first to sing the praises of the Peninsula in the 1880s, and visitors have been coming to see for themselves ever since. But not even this heavy stream of human traffic has been able to obscure the beauty and charm of the place.

Monterey was California's first capital and so can claim legitimate historic importance. Until the decline in sardine runs, it was also an important fishing port. The vestiges of Cannery Row, immortalized in the fiction of John Steinbeck, still get attention from tourists.

Carmel, at the other side of the Peninsula, has cultivated a kind of chic to supplement nature as a tourist draw. The presence of "colonies" of artists and writers has strengthened the image. Carmel's most conspicuous attraction is the Carmel Mission, a well-preserved example of the 18th-century Spanish missions which stretched almost the length of California. The famous missionary and explorer, Father Junipero Serra, who founded many of them, is buried here.

(Following page, above) Mission San Carlos Borromeo de Carmelo, the mission at Carmel, is one of the most picturesque of the California missions.
(Following page, below) San Francisco presents its magnificent skyline from this viewpoint near the Bay Bridge.

There is a state preserve at Point Lobos and here nature comes into her own again. Below Point Lobos begins the famous Big Sur coast. When the poet, Robinson Jeffers, first came to this area with his bride in 1914, they had to travel the last forty miles by horse-drawn mail stage, since no motor vehicle of that day could have negotiated the post road. In the half century since then, man has brought many changes to the coast and may even have done some damage. But despite man's intrusion, the fundamental majesty of this part of the coast has not been diminished.

The overpowering surf continues its slow task of wearing away the headlands. The redwoods stand tall and straight; the graceful cypress yields and grows as the wind directs. Pelicans and cormorants fish from offshore rocks, and the bull sea lion keeps an eye on his hard-won harem. In spring the wildflowers — violets, roses, creamcups, poppies — envelop whole acres of Point Lobos.

Looking at all this Jeffers drew comfort from the smallness and impotence of man.

> ... we know
> that the enormous invulnerable beauty of things
> Is the face of God, to live gladly in its presence, and die without
> grief or fear knowing it survives us.*

*From "Nova" by Robinson Jeffers, *The Selected Poetry of Robinson Jeffers*, New York, Random House, 1937.

(Preceding page) A young aspen tree provides colorful contrast to the massive Ponderosa pines.

THE LAKES

Northern California is not usually associated with lakes as Minnesota or Wisconsin might be. Yet, it can claim some of the most beautiful mountain lakes in the country. Some of the largest and most striking have been man made through the damming of rivers; a few natural lakes have been enlarged by the same means. But even these man-made bodies of water seem to blend well with their setting and enhance the beauty of the landscape.

Traditionally, lakes in California are treated with care by government and citizen alike. It is a state with chronic water problems, and many of its major lakes were created principally to impound the lifegiving water.

Lakes are among the most short-lived and delicate of natural land features. Limnologists tell us, in fact, that lakes are supposed to disappear in the course of time, silting up and giving way to forests. Geological evidence suggests that Yosemite Valley was once covered by a large lake. The Mojave Desert in Southern California is checkered with the beds of quite large lakes which dried up in the unknown past. If interfered with by man, even a large lake can sometimes disappear within the span of a human lifetime, as has Tulare Lake in Kings County.

Though there are lakes in all parts of Northern California, most, as might be expected, are to be found in the Cascade and Sierra Nevada ranges, and this includes some of the largest artificial ones. Lake Tahoe, which extends into Nevada, is certainly the best known of California lakes and perhaps the most beautiful, if such things can be measured. If we may judge from the written comments of visitors from Mark Twain onward, this must be so.

Tahoe is a natural lake and the prototype of a high mountain lake. At 6,000 feet elevation, it rests in a ring of forested mountains. It is 23 miles long, 13 miles wide, and more than 1,500 feet deep in places. It it extraordinarily blue in all seasons. Tahoe's great depth may account for its not freezing over in winter.

The explorer John Fremont first named it Bonpland in the 1840s to honor a French botanist. In 1852, it was renamed Lake Bigler to honor California's governor. But during the Civil War the governor proved to be a Copperhead, and an angry mapmaker on his own initiative again renamed the lake. He chose the Washoe Indian word for "big water," and so it became Tahoe, a major improvement in both significance and euphony.

> *(Following page, above) Oaks are the predominant trees in the hills above Suisan Valley, Solano County.*
>
> *(Following page, below) This peaceful stream is in Russian Gulch State Park, on the northern California coast.*

(Preceding page) Evening fog adds an eerie feeling to a sunset at Pigeon Point Lighthouse.
(Opposite) The yellow leaves of the oak indicate that winter is one the way to the Mt. Shasta area.
(Right) Brightly-colored impatiens grow in shaded areas of Northern California gardens.
(Below) Yellows and purples of wildflowers sweep across Grass lake, near Klamath National Forest.
(Following pages) Snow dusts the craggy faces of stone in Yosemite.

(Left) California coastal flora comes in a variety of shapes and colors.

(Below) Rugged cliffs of Carpenteria face the endless waves of the Pacific.

(Opposite) A peaceful stream highlights this meadow near Mariposa.

(Following pages) A rare moment of stillness hangs over San Francisco as the sun's first rays waken the sleeping city.

(Preceding full page) Fog drifts through the forest in Del Norte Redwoods State Park, where the moist coastal environment provides almost rainforest conditions for plant life.

(Preceding page, above) A drier kind of landscape is seen in this view of the Coast Range from Pinnacles National Monument.

(Preceding page, below) Dogwood blooms amid forest greenery in Northern California.

(Left) The setting sun washes Midway Point with color while sturdy cypress trees make their stand against the prevailing ocean winds.

(Left) Foxglove enjoys the moist environment of the coast range.

(Below) This green-and-gold grove of oak trees is in the southwest foothills of the Sierra Nevada.

(Opposite) Higher Cathedral Spire towers over the Yosemite Valley.

(Following page) The City's light start twinkling on as the sun sets behind the hills.

The discovery of the Comstock Lode in nearby Nevada resulted in a stampede of gold prospectors through the area in the mid-19th century and they seriously threatened the ecology. The mountains on the Nevada side were stripped of their forests to supply timbers for the mines at Virginia City. Once the mining had declined, however, the forests began to grow back.

Today, Tahoe faces another threat: urbanization. Carson City, Nevada, has stretched out westward to envelop the eastern shore of the lake with condominiums and night clubs. Since Tahoe is one of the most popular recreation centers in the West, summer and winter, there is much concern about pollution of the natural environment. On the California side, a National Forest offers some measure of protection and the great depth of the lake, too, may help it survive the impact of modern American life.

Clear Lake, the largest natural lake lying entirely within California, is not in the western mountains as might be expected but in the Coast Range north of Santa Rosa. About 100 square miles in area, it may have been two lakes in prehistoric times. The presence of hot springs in the area suggests that volcanic activity may have played a role in the lake's formation.

For more than a century agricultural activity has been heavy at Clear Lake, with both grazing and farming. By the 1940s, the accumulation of insecticides and fertilizers in the lake had dangerously affected its ecological balance. Prompt action by the state, especially the introduction of fresh-water smelt, has reversed the decline and the lake is rapidly regaining its former vigor. It is a major recreation area.

Lake Shasta, north of Redding, is the largest man-made lake in California. It was created by the damming of the powerful Upper Sacramento River and covers an area of 30,000 acres. The lake is also fed by the Pit and McCloud Rivers. Lake Shasta is the pivot of the Central Valley project for flood control, irrigation, and water conservation. It has also developed into one of the largest and most popular recreation areas in the state. Lake Shasta is so large that even in heavily-populated California, it does not appear crowded with vacationers. Among sportsmen, Shasta is perhaps best known for its great variety of game fish, some 16 in all.

Among the other major man-made lakes are Oroville, Clair Engle, Lewiston, Berryessa, Folsom, Almanor, McClure, and Isabella. The waters of Lake Oroville are held by the country's highest dam, and one of the world's highest, at 770 feet. The lake is fed by the three branches of the Feather River, the greatest water flow out of the Sierra Nevada.

(Preceding page, above) The waters of the Upper Merced River are startlingly clear in the area of Yosemite.
(Preceding page, below) Vineyards like this are a familiar sight in Northern California's wine country.

Lake Berryessa in Napa County is close to the Bay area and is much used by city people. Its relatively warm waters support year-round fishing. Folsom Lake, made by damming the American River, is relatively new. It is close to Sacramento and is a popular recreation spot for people from the capital city. Almanor was once California's largest man-made lake.

Mono lake, at the foot of the Sierra Escarpment and bordered by Highway 395, is probably not an American's idea of a lake. Its mineral-heavy waters support no fish, and its barren shore area, with its curious tufa towers, evokes a vision almost otherworldly. Evaporation has reduced its extent and further concentrated its mineral content. Now deprived of the fresh water streams which used to feed it, Mono Lake, still close to 100 square miles in area, will continue to evaporate until it becomes a dry lake bed like those in the Mojave.

Another shallow lake but of a very different sort is Tule Lake in the extreme north end of the state. Tule is very shallow and is what would be called in Central Europe a steppe lake. It used to be much larger than its present 12,000 acres, but ill-conceived federal land reclamation projects early in the century caused a sizeable portion of it to be drained and put to the plow. Fortunately the drainage schemes were halted and the area was designated a National Wildlife Refuge. Each year, Tule witnesses the largest gathering of migratory waterfowl in the world. Two neighboring lakes, Clear and Lower Klamath, are also National Wildlife Refuges.

For all its present beauty and serenity, Tule Lake has known some unpleasant history. In the 19th century, it was the setting for the bloody Modoc Wars, when the Modoc Indians resisted being driven from their homeland. Again in 1942, Tule came to national attention. Because of anti-foreign sentiment at the height of World War II, thousands of Japanese-Americans were herded into a concentration camp at nearby Newell.

Within the Lassen Volcanic Park are many small- and medium-sized lakes formed when glacier-gouged depressions filled with runoff. They are known collectively as the Lassen Lakes though a few like Manzanita, Juniper, and Snag are distinct enough to have established their own reputations. Some of the Lassen Lakes are fed by hot springs or heated by subterranean volcanic activity. Others are glacier-cold. Few of the lakes have natural outlets and they do not reliably support fish populations. However, the lakes do provide a striking setting for the volcanic peak.

Eagle Lake, east of Mount Lassen, is the second largest natural lake within the state's borders and something of an ecological curiosity. At 5,000 feet above sea

(Following page, above) California poppies cover this hillside along the Merced River.
(Following page, below) These smooth, rolling hills make good pastureland in the early spring.

level, Eagle is nevertheless a vestige of a prehistoric inland sea that once covered this part of Lassen County. Its slightly alkaline waters will not support most fish, either game or coarse, though it has been stocked many times. Inexplicably, the only game fish that can survive in its waters is the resident Eagle lake trout, which can be found nowhere else in the world. There is some evidence to suggest that the Eagle Lake trout may be a prehistoric species. One of the few other creatures to flourish in the lake is a sea snail which can clearly be traced to prehistoric times. Unique species of reptiles and small mammals have been found around the shores of the lake. Like Tule Lake, Eagle has been the victim of crackpot drainage schemes in years past and as a consequence has lost some of its size.

The most mysteriously misnamed lake is Honey, a large lake in southeast Lassen County. Its bitter waters support no life, and the name may even have been some pioneer's idea of a joke. Honey Lake is broad but very shallow. In periods of drought it has been known to dry up completely.

Donner Lake, northwest of Tahoe, is well-known primarily because of its associations with the ill-fated Donner Party. It lies in a beautiful forested basin, scoured by the glacier, just east of 7,000-foot Donner Pass. In 1846, the stranded Donner Party camped for months in the deep snow around its shore. Little more than half the group survived.

Big Lagoon and its fellows, Stone and Freshwater, border Highway 101 along the coast north of Arcata. Their principal charm is their proximity to the Pacific surf. No more than a sand spit separates Big Lagoon from the ocean, not unlike the ponds on Cape Cod in Massachusetts. The lagoons may have been formed when the surf pushed a high sand spit into the path of freshwater streams pouring out of the coastal forests. In the 1850s, this area became the object of a hysterical gold rush when it was announced in San Francisco that the sands of the beach were laced with gold. The sands do in fact contain gold but in such small quantities that it cannot be extracted economically. After the gold rush, the lagoons and adjacent beaches settled back to the tranquility that they enjoy to this day.

(Preceding page) The Carson home, in Eureka, is understandably one of the most photographed buildings in the state.

THE VALLEY

The great Central Valley, 450 miles long and an average of forty miles wide, lies mostly in Northern California. It is the world's richest agricultural area, and its diversity of crops—fruit, vegetables, grain, grapes, cotton, and more—is unmatched. The valley is protected by a continuous mountain wall, broken only by San Francisco Bay. In contrast to the mountains, scenic beauty in the valley is mostly man-made. It is a carefully tended, giant garden.

The northern section, drained by the Sacramento River, is properly named the Sacramento Valley, and the southern end, the San Joaquin Valley. Sacramento, the state capital, owes its place of honor to its proximity to the first goldfields in mother lode country of the Sierra foothills to the east. In fact, the city was founded by Captain John Sutter in 1839, and, in effect, this is where the history of modern California began.

With an assist from the engineers Sacramento, and Stockton on the San Joaquin River, have become deep-water ports. Since the end of World War II, both cities have moved to diversify their economies, which had been totally bound to agriculture, and some light industry has sprung up. But it will always be agriculture that makes the wheels turn in the valley.

The most glamorous product of the valley, and probably the biggest money maker, is wine. The vineyards are concentrated in the San Joaquin, and the towns of Lodi, Modesto, Madera, and Fresno have become major centers of winemaking and distribution. The new mass production methods used by big wineries like A. & J. Gallo, United Vintners, and Guild would turn the hair of a vineyard master in France. But the methods have paid off in millions of gallons of good bulk table wines at low prices.

Most visitors agree that the meticulously ordered vineyards stretching for miles across the floor of the San Joaquin are one of the scenic treats of California. To further cheer the tourist, most wineries maintain tasting rooms, where guests are invited to sample the wines. Many of the wineries offer guided tours, as well.

Seen from the air, the central valley is a mammoth tapestry of green and brown geometric patterns, groves, vineyards, and fields, bordered by rivers, irrigation canals, highways, and fences. From Red Bluff to Visalia, the sun-baked towns are laid

(Following page) Grizzly Giant is one of Yosemite's redwoods, big enough to make a name for itself.

out on a north-south axis along Interestate 5 and old U.S. 50 like the vertebrae of a gigantic spine, the backbone of Northern California. The central valley cannot rival the infinite and spectacular beauties of a Point Lobos or a Tuolumne Gorge. Still, it has its own kind of glamour.

(Preceding page, above) A variety of springtime flowers brighten this meadow near Sacramento.
(Preceding page, below) Wild lupine on the hillsides contrasts with the orderly rows of orchards on the Suisun Valley floor.

SAN FRANCISCO AND THE BAY AREA

San Francisco and the dozen or so cities that ring San Francisco Bay are known collectively as the Bay Area. These include San Mateo, Palo Alto, Hayward, Alameda, Oakland, Richmond, Berkeley, and others. They share one of the largest landlocked harbors in the world—and one of the most beautiful. Actually, there are three bays: San Francisco, San Pablo, and Suisun, which add up to 450 square miles. Originally the bay was larger than this, but it is constantly being reduced by landfill. Richly endowed by nature to satisfy the needs of trade, the Bay Area has become, inevitably, a major center of population.

Built on twenty-nine small hills at the end of a peninsula, San Francisco has dominated the area since the Spanish established its predecessor, Yerba Buena, on the site. It has been called the city that everyone loves. That is sweeping praise, but it is truly hard to find a person who doesn't love the place.

San Francisco has been much admired by some Americans for not seeming like an American city at all. But this curious compliment has less to do with the city's rich ethnic mix than with its incomparable physical setting, the broad bay, the brown hills, blue Pacific to the west, and the Golden Gate itself. All in all, a tough act for Kansas City and Indianapolis to try to match.

This world city has kept size and distance manageable. The land area is less than forty-five square miles, as compared to Chicago's 228 or New York's 320. It can't be much more than a mile from Fisherman's Wharf to the Trans-America Pyramid, incomparably different worlds. Chinatown is a five-minute walk from Nob Hill. In spite of the presence of tall buildings and the two great bridges, the city conveys a feeling of being committed to the human scale. That's why the few remaining cable cars make sense, even though they may function mainly as tourist attractions.

Officially, San Francisco's climate is described as temperate, a subtle way of saying that it never gets warm. Fogs are frequent and notorious, especially in

(Following page, above) Mt. Lassen's peak catches the last of the day's sunlight from this viewpoint in Lassen Volcanic National Park.
(Following page, below) Young maples and vine maples are well into their autumn change in this Coast Range scene.

summer. Winds can spring up without warning and turn a sunny August day into a bone-chiller. Then they will die down as suddenly as they came. Residents insist that it's all very invigorating.

San Francisco is a center of intellectual and cultural life. Its people take pride in their sophistication and artistic taste, and they can be brutally patronizing toward those Southern Californians whom they view as non-cerebral, sun-and-surf-struck Angelenos. But along with the sophistication comes a kind of fatalism, and not without reason. Anyone old enough to read knows that the city sits atop the San Andreas Fault and that tension in the fault has already reached maximum levels. It is a matter of *when* rather than *if* it is to generate a major earthquake. The local attitude seems to be, "we may have only one day to live, but at least we will live it in San Francisco."

Many writers have celebrated the virtues and even confessed the vices of the city. Among them are Charles Caldwell Dobie, George Sterling, Jack London, Herbert Asbury, Gertrude Atherton, Lawrence Ferlinghetti, and Herb Caen. San Franciscans love their city with a quiet determination, and they are possessive of her beauty. The truncated Embarcadero Freeway is a monument to their will to preserve as much of it as they can.

Geographically, the Bay Area is more intimately linked with the central valley than with other places along the coast. Through the great delta, where the Sacramento and San Joaquin rivers meet, the entire drainage of the interior empties into the Bay. In turn, the wind tunnel of the Golden Gate helps to air-condition parts of the interior. The cooling ocean winds which reach into the Sonoma and Napa Valleys make possible the kind of climate needed for the production of premium table wines.

Recently the federal government established the Golden Gate National Recreation Area, a unique park facility which is still in development. It comprises miscellaneous former federal military reservations, beaches, islands in the bay, museums, and some state and county lands, in all about 35,000 acres. Included in the preserve is some undeveloped coastline in Marin County, across the Golden Gate and only minutes from downtown San Francisco. The Golden Gate Recreation Area is the first of its kind in the country and may prove to be a blueprint for the development of recreational lands close to big cities.

(Preceding page) Snow melt in the Plumas National Forest adds chill and strength to small creeks like this one.

Beautiful America Publishing Company

The nation's foremost publisher of quality color photography

CURRENT BOOKS	FORTHCOMING BOOKS IN 1979	1979 CALENDARS
Utah	Massachusetts	Texas
Ohio	North Idaho	Hawaii
Texas	Pennsylvania	Illinois
Detroit	New Mexico	Florida
Alaska	Mississippi	Oregon
Georgia	New York	Colorado
Hawaii	Wisconsin	California
Arizona	Kentucky	Michigan
Portland	Maryland	Washington
Montana	Vermont	Western America
San Francisco	Virginia	
British Columbia	Illinois	
Oregon, Volume II	Idaho	
Southern California		
Western Impressions		
California, Volume II		
No. California, Volume II		
Washington, Volume II		
Lewis & Clark Country		

Send for complete catalog, 50 ¢

Beautiful America Publishing Company
4720 S.W. Washington
Beaverton, Oregon 97005

(Following page) Sunset shows a silhouette of Black Butte in this scene from the Shasta-Trinity National Forest.

The Complete Ninja Foodi

Cookbook for Beginners

1500-Day Simple, Affordable, and Delicious Ninja Foodi Recipes for Your Ninja Foodi XL Pressure Cooker Steam Fryer with SmartLid

Janice Sottile

© Copyright 2022 – All Rights Reserved

This document is geared towards providing exact and reliable information with regards to the topic and issue covered. The publication is sold with the idea that the publisher is not required to render accounting, officially permitted, or otherwise, qualified services. If advice is necessary, legal, or professional, a practiced individual in the profession should be ordered. - From a Declaration of Principles which was accepted and approved equally by a Committee of the American Bar Association and a Committee of Publishers and Associations. In no way is it legal to reproduce, duplicate, or transmit any part of this document in either electronic means or in printed format. Recording of this publication is strictly prohibited and any storage of this document is not allowed unless with written permission from the publisher.

All rights reserved. The information provided herein is stated to be truthful and consistent, in that any liability, in terms of inattention or otherwise, by any usage or abuse of any policies, processes, or directions contained within is the solitary and utter responsibility of the recipient reader.

Under no circumstances will any legal responsibility or blame be held against the publisher for any reparation, damages, or monetary loss due to the information herein, either directly or indirectly. Respective authors own all copyrights not held by the publisher.

The information herein is offered for informational purposes solely, and is universal as so. The presentation of the information is without contract or any type of guarantee assurance. The trademarks that are used are without any consent, and the publication of the trademark is without permission or backing by the trademark owner.

All trademarks and brands within this book are for clarifying purposes only and are the owned by the owners themselves, not affiliated with this document

CONTENTS

Introduction 1

Fundamentals of Ninja Foodi Smart XL Pressure Cooker Steam Fryer ... 2

4-Week Diet Plan 7

Chapter 1 Breakfast Recipes 9

Chapter 2 Snack and Appetizer Recipes 23

Chapter 3 Chicken and Poultry Recipes 36

Chapter 4 Beef, Pork and Lamb Recipes 48

Chapter 5 Fish and Seafood Recipes 64

Chapter 6 Vegetable Recipes 78

Chapter 7 Dessert Recipes 95

Conclusion 107

Appendix 1 Measurement Conversion Chart 108

Appendix 2 Air Fryer Cooking Chart 109

Appendix 3 Recipes Index 110

Introduction

Just when you think that Ninja Foodi can't amaze you with any more of its innovation, the company releases an amazing product to surprise you with its latest kitchen technology. Yes, Ninja Foodi has managed to again dazzle its customers with yet another kitchen miracle, which has made pressure cooking, baking, air frying, steam crisp, sous vide, dehydrating, and broiling easier than ever before. The Ninja Foodi Smart XL Pressure Cooker Steam Fryer is the innovation of today that has successfully brought a variety of cooking functions into a single appliance. Imagine, instead of having a steamer, crisper, air fryer, and an oven separately lying on your kitchen shelf, you will have one single appliance which can do all of that with much efficiency. This 14-in-1 multipurpose Ninja Foodi Smart XL Steam Air Fryer is extremely user-friendly and gives its users complete control over both the cooking time and temperature. This Ninja Foodi Steam Air Fryer cookbook is designed to introduce all its readers to this digital pressure cooker, its features, and its better use. There is a range of recipes all cooked in an air fry oven, accompanied by a 21 days meal plan for all beginners.

Fundamentals of Ninja Foodi Smart XL Pressure Cooker Steam Fryer

What is Ninja Foodi Smart XL Pressure Cooker Steam Fryer?

The newest electric pressure cooker designed by Shark Ninja is the 14-in-one Ninja Foodi Smart XL Pressure Cooker Steam Air Fryer. There is presently only an 8-quart size available. A ceramic cooking pot, a cook-and-crisp basket, and a reversible rack are all included

in the box. With an extra-large, family-sized capacity and the ability to pressure cook, air fry, and Steam Crisp all under one Smart Lid, the Ninja Foodi Smart XL Pressure Cooker Steam Fryer is able to do all the cooking for you. With this smart lid's sliding feature, you can access all 14 cooking settings and 3 cooking modes from one lid.

Benefits of Using Ninja Foodi Smart XL Pressure Cooker Steam Fryer

The device has a touchscreen and dial combination, which makes the control panel look neater and make it simpler to use. In other words, it lacks the confusing number of buttons that prior models do. Additionally, the slider makes switching between settings simple (which also neatly organizes the cooking functions). The "smart" apps' trademark default settings also remove the element of guesswork for a simpler experience.

The smart lid enhances both your recipes and the machine's overall usability. There are separate lids on another pressure cooker/air fryer combination. You must pressure cook and air fry separately to replicate steam frying. You don't even need to swap out the cover with the Ninja Foodi Smart XL Pressure Cooker Steam Fryer, and you can utilize both the steam and air fry functions.

The majority of cooking features are self-explanatory. It functions, in essence, like a convection oven with a powerful fan and great air circulation for consistent cooking. More importantly, you may have healthier and less expensive fried dishes because you just require little to no oil (compared to deep-frying). Second, the Ninja Foodi Smart XL Pressure Cooker Steam Fryer can be used as a proofer. In essence, this equipment makes baking simpler because you can control the temperature and time. Additionally, after proving, you can use the steam directly to bake rather than moving it around. There will be less cleanup to do later. (Applicable to the sear/sauté function as well.) The sous vide program is also available in this cooker. By doing this, you may make the inexpensive meals taste more upscale.

Cooking Functions and Features

It has great flexibility and toughness. In comparison to other cooking techniques, it cooks food much faster. As an environment fryer, it also cooks food without the need for oil, resulting in lower-calorie and healthier meals. Ninja Foodi Smart XL Pressure Cooker Steam Fryer has all these cooking features that you can use with the help of user-friendly control.

   Pressure: Keep food soft while cooking it quickly.
   Steam & crisp: Create one-touch whole meals, juicy and crisp vegetables and proteins, and handmade artisan bread with Steam & Crisp.
   Steam & bake: Quickly and with less fat, bake fluffier cakes and quick bread.
   Air fry: With little to no oil, air frying adds crispness and snap to food.
   Broil: To caramelize and brown the tops of your meal, use strong heat coming from above.
   Bake/roast: Use the appliance as an oven for a variety of baked goods, tender meats, and more.
   Dehydrate: Dehydrate fruits, vegetables, and meats for wholesome snacking.
   Proof: Provide a space for the dough to rest and rise.
   Sear/sauté: Use the device as a cooktop to cook a variety of foods, including meats, vegetables, and sauces.
   Steam: Cook delicate items at a high temperature while using steam.
   Sous vide: Sous vide, which is French for "under vacuum," is a feature that uses a precisely controlled water bath to slowly cook food that is sealed in a plastic bag.
   Slow cook: Cook your meal for a longer amount of time at a lower temperature.
   Yogurt: Pasteurize milk and allow it to ferment to make creamy homemade yogurt.
   Keep warm: The appliance will switch to keep warm at the conclusion of the cycle when steam, slow cooking, or pressure is being used. Once the function has begun, press the keep warm button to stop the automated transition.

Operation Keys

   Smart lid slider: As you slide the slider, the features that are available in each mode will light up.
   Dial: Use the dial to cycle among the available functions once

you've selected a mode using the slider until your desired function is highlighted.

Left arrows: To change the cooking temperature, use the "up/down" keys to the left of the display.

Right arrows: To change the cooking time, press the "up/down" keys next to the display.

Hit the "start/stop" button to begin cooking. The current cooking function will be stopped if the button is pressed while the appliance is cooking.

Power: The power button turns off the appliance and ends all cooking settings.

Ninja Smart XL Steam Fryer OL 601 Vs OL 701

Ninja Foodi Smart XL Pressure Cooker Steam Fryer is mainly available in two different variations, the OL 600 series and the OL 700 series. Since I have personally used the OL601 and OL701 versions I will draw a little comparison of those two models to help you decide which one to bring home. First of all, if you choose the OL701 over the OL601, you won't lose any functionality because the OL701 has the same appearance, accessories, and features as the OL601. When using any mode that requires water, which is most of them, water will drip from the lid to the counter on both models.

The pressure release on the OL601 is the same as it was on earlier models. By adjusting the valve, you can release pressure slowly or quickly. You can digitally select the release you want on the OL701. Natural Release is the cooker's default setting, but you can also select Quick Release or Delayed Release, and it will be carried out automatically. This doesn't bother me personally because I don't mind opening the valve quickly to relieve pressure or allowing the cooker naturally release for around 10 minutes before opening the pressure release valve to release any remaining pressure.

Unlike the OL601, which lacks a probe, the OL701 has a probe that connects to the underside of the lid. This is the OL701's main selling factor in my opinion. They refer to the "Smart Cooking" feature of the OL701. The pressure cooker's side has a holder for the probe. You can select the meat, poultry, or fish you're cooking using the probe and choose a preset temperature or manually set it. This, in my opinion, is the OL701's greatest advantage.

When pressure cooking, it's usually preferable to hazard a guess as to when the meat will be the required doneness and temperature. You may pressure cook roasts, chicken, etc. to the desired internal temperature using the probe. You can select beef, pig, or chicken in the pressure cooking mode for presets, and you can also select between well and shred. You can specify the internal temperature at which the meat should be cooked if you select manually. The guidebook provides temperature recommendations for various levels of doneness and permits carryover cooking. You can select presets for beef, chicken, pig, and fish in the steam and crisp mode, as well as your preferred level of doneness (rare, med. rare, medium, medium well, and well). For a manual setting, you can choose the preferred temperature. The steam and bake mode does not support the probe.

Step-By-Step Ninja Foodi Smart XL Pressure Cooker Steam Fryer

Take off and throw away any packaging, stickers, and tape from the appliance. Pay close attention to operational guidelines, precautions, and warnings to prevent harm or property damage. Warm, soapy water should be used to wash the silicone ring, removable cooking pot, Cook & Crisp Basket, deluxe reversible rack, and condensation collector. Rinse and dry everything well afterwards. NEVER use a dishwasher to clean the cooker base.

The silicone ring can be put in either direction and is reversible. On the underside of the lid, insert the silicone ring around the outside of the silicone ring rack. Make certain it is completely inserted and flatly rests beneath the silicone ring rack. High (Hi) pressure will be the unit's default setting. To change the time to 2 minutes, press the right-down arrow. To start, hit the "start/stop". The progress bars and the letter "PrE" on this display signal that the device is developing pressure. The timer starts to tick when the device is fully pressurized. The appliance will beep and show "End" when the cooking time has expired before manually quickly releasing the pressured steam. When the pressure release valve is about to open, a warning bell will ring. Steam will flow from the pressure release valve as it opens. Slide the slider towards the right side to open the lid once the display says "OPN Lid." Next, remove the cover. Depending on the amount, temperature, and chosen pressure level of the materials, the time to pressure will change.

Water Test

It is advised that new users perform a water test to get comfortable with pressure cooking. 3 cups of room temperature water should be added to the pot before placing it in the cooker base. Close the lid and slide the lever to PRESSURE. Ensure that the seal position is selected on the pressure release valve.

Natural Pressure Release VS. Quick Pressure Release

Natural Pressure Release: As the appliance cools down after pressure cooking is finished, steam will naturally escape from it. Depending on the volume of liquid and food in the pot, this could take up to 20 minutes or longer. The appliance will enter Keep Warm mode during this period.

If you want to exit Keep Warm mode, press the KEEP WARM button. The display will read "OPN Lid" when the unit has finished its natural pressure release. Only use a quick pressure release if your recipe specifies it. Rotate the pressure release valve handle to the VENT position to immediately release pressure via the valve once pressure cooking is done and the keep warm light is on. Some steam will still be present in the appliance after pressure has been released naturally or by using the pressure release valve; this steam will escape when the lid is opened.

Steps for Pressure Cooking

The control panel display will show PrE and progress bars as the pressure inside the unit increases. The liquid in the pot, the number of components, and their temperature all affect how long it takes to reach pressure. The lid will lock for safety as the unit builds pressure and will unlock as the pressure is released. Cooking will start once the appliance reaches full pressure, and the timer will start to clock down. Press the button after inserting the power cord into a wall outlet to turn on the device. Fill the pot with the ingredients, at least 1 cup of

liquid, and any other required equipment. Past the PRESSURE MAX line, DO NOT continue to fill the pot. Put the lid on. The pressure release valve is then turned to the SEAL position. The slider moved to PRESSURE. To choose Hi or LO, use the "up and down" keys to the left of the display.

To change the cooking time, move the "up and down" keys to the right of the display in one-minute increments up to 1 hour, then for 1 hour to 4 hours you can increase the value in 5-minute increments. To start or stop cooking, hit the "start/stop". Pressure will start to build in the unit. "PrE" and progress bars will be seen on the display. When the appliance is fully pressurized, the timer will start to run out.

Rotate the pressure release valve to the VENT position when the cooking time reaches zero minutes. The device will beep, go into Keep Warm mode automatically, and start counting down. It has depressurized when the device shows "OPN Lid," at which point you can adjust the slider towards the right side to open the lid.

Steps for Steam & Crisp

Add the ingredients as directed by the recipe instructions. Now move the Slider to Steam & Crisp. Steam & Crisp will be the default choice for the function. The time and temperature settings will automatically display. Use the "up and down" keys to the left of the display to select a temperature between 300°F and 450°F in 5-degree increments. The cook time can be changed using the "up and down" keys to the right of the display in minute increments up to an hour.

Hit the "start/stop" to start or stop cooking. The progress bars and "PrE" indicator on the LCD demonstrate that the device is generating steam. The number of ingredients in the pot determines how long it will take to steam. The display panel will show the set temperature and the timer will start counting down when the unit reaches the proper steam level. The appliance will beep and display "End" for five minutes when the cooking time reaches zero. Use the "Up" key to the right of the display to add more time if your cuisine needs it. The appliance will not pre-heat.

Steps for Steam & Bake

Set the multipurpose pan in the lower position on the rack. After that, insert the rack and accessories into the pot. Move the slider to Steam & Crisp, then choose Steam & Bake with the dial. It will show the current temperature setting. With the "up and down" keys to the left of the display, you can select a temperature between 225°F and 400°F in 5-degree increments. The cook time can be changed in one-minute increments up to one hour and fifteen minutes by using the "up and down" keys to the right of the display. Hit the "start/stop" to start the stove. As the unit builds steam, the display panel will show "PrE" and progress bars. It takes 20 minutes to steam.

The temperature will be displayed on the display and the timer will start to count down after preheating is finished. The appliance will beep and display "End" for five minutes when the cooking time reaches zero. Use the "Up" key to the right of the display to add more time if your cuisine needs it. The appliance will not pre-heat.

Steps for Air Frying

Steps for Broiling

Alternatively, you can follow the instructions in your recipe and place the premium reversible rack in the pot on the higher broil setting. Arrange the ingredients on the rack, then cover. The slider should be set to AIR FRY/STOVETOP, and the dial should be set to BROIL. Adjust the cooking time up to 30 minutes using the "up and down" keys on the right side of the display. To start or stop cooking, hit the "start/stop". The device will beep and "End" will flash three times on the display when the cooking time reaches zero.

Steps for Baking or Roasting

Add any necessary ingredients and accessories to the pot. Put the lid on. The slider should be set to AIR FRY/STOVETOP, then BAKE/ROAST should be chosen with the dial. It will show the current temperature setting. With the "up and down" keys to the left of the display, you may select a temperature between 250°F and 400°F in 5-degree increments. The cook time can be changed by using the "up and down" keys to the right of the display in minute increments up to 1 hour. To start or stop cooking, hit the "START/STOP". The device will beep and "End" will flash three times on the display when the cooking time reaches zero.

Steps for Dehydrating

Lower the deluxe reversible rack into the pot, then arrange some ingredients on top of the rack. Lay the deluxe layer over the reversible rack as shown below, holding it by its handles. Then top the deluxe layer with a layer of ingredients and secure the lid. The slider should be moved to AIR FRY/STOVETOP, then select DEHYDRATE on the dial. It will show the current temperature setting. With the "up and down" keys to the left of the display, you can select a temperature between 80°F and 195°F in 5-degree increments.

To change the cooking time from one hour to twelve hours, use the "up and down" keys to the right of the display. To start or stop cooking, hit the "START/STOP". The device will beep and "End" will flash three times on the display when the cooking time reaches zero.

Steps fot Sear/Sauté

Fill the pot inside the Ninja Foodi Smart XL Pressure Cooker Steam Fryer with the ingredients. Open the lid or move the slider to AIR FRY/STOVETOP, then with the help of the dial select Sear/Sauté. It will show the current temperature setting. To choose "Lo1," "2," "3," "4", or "Hi5", use the "up and down" keys to the left of the display. To start or stop cooking, hit the "Start/Stop".

To switch off the Sear/Sauté feature, hit the "start/stop". Hit the "start/stop" to stop the current cooking function, then with the help of the slider and dial pick the next function you want to use. When using a cooking pot, ALWAYS use nonstick utensils. A nonstick coating on the pot will be scratched if metal utensils are used.

NOTE: For "4" and "Hi5", Sear/Sauté will automatically shut off after an hour, and for "LO1," "2," and "3," it will do so after four hours.

How to Proof a Dough?

Add the dough and secure the lid of the pot or Air Fry Basket. The slider should be set to AIR FRY/STOVETOP, then PROOF should be chosen using the dial. It will show the current temperature setting. The temperature ranges from 75°F to 95°F, and you may adjust it in

5-degree increments by using the "up and down" keys to the left of the display. To change the proof time between 20 minutes and 2 hours, use the "up and down" keys to the right of the display. To start or stop cooking, hit the "START/STOP". The device will beep and "End" will flash three times on the display when the cooking time reaches zero.

Tips for Using Accessories

Besides the 14 amazing cooking functions, what makes this steam fryer special are the different accessories that come along with it. You can use those accessories to cook all sorts of food. Here is how you can use its accessories:

Deluxe Reversible Rack

Set the Deluxe Reversible Rack's bottom layer in the lowest position. Put the ingredients on the rack's lowest layer. The Deluxe layer should then be slid through the handles of the bottom layer. Add the remaining ingredients to the Deluxe layer to enhance the amount of food you can prepare.

Cook & Crisp Basket

Pull the two diffuser fins out of the groove on the basket to remove the diffuser for cleaning. Then, firmly pull the diffuser down. Place the Cook & Crisp Basket on top of the diffuser and firmly press down.

The Smart Lid with Slider

You may switch between cooking modes by using the slider, which also notifies the lid of your current function.
 Pressure
 Steam Crisp
 Air Fry/Stovetop

To open and close the lid, always use the handle that is situated above the slider. When the slider is set to Steam & Crisp or AIR FRY/STOVETOP, you can open and close the lid. The lid cannot be opened when the slider is in the PRESSURE position. Slide the slider to the "Steam & Crisp" or "AIR FRY/STOVETOP" position to open the device if there is no pressure within.

The Anti-Clog Cap

The anti-clog cap shields users from potential food splatters and prevents the inner valve of the lid from clogging. After each use, it should be cleaned using a cleaning brush. Holding the anti-clog cap between your thumb and bent index finger, turn your wrist in a clockwise direction to remove it. Put it in place and press down to reinstall. Before operating the device, check if the anti-clog cap is in the proper position.

Ensure the silicone ring is securely mounted in the ring's grove and the anti-clog cap is securely fastened to the pressure release valve before each usage. After cooking, be sure to remove any extra water that accumulated in the condensation collector. This collector can only be used with a silicone ring made specifically for Ninja Foodi Smart Lid models. No other Ninja Foodi silicone rings or rings made by other companies may be worn.

Special Tips to Use Ninja Foodi Smart XL Pressure Cooker Steam Fryer

Make sure the ingredients are layered evenly and without overlap in the cooking pot for uniform browning. Make sure to shake halfway through the designated cook time if the ingredients overlap. I advise first wrapping smaller items in a parchment paper or foil pouch if they might fall through the premium reversible rack. After cooking, keep food at a warm mode, safe temperature by using the Keep Warm option. I advise keeping the lid on and using this feature right before serving to avoid food drying out. Use the Reheat function to reheat food.

Cleaning

After each usage, the appliance needs to be completely cleaned. Before cleaning, unplug the appliance from the wall outlet. Use a moist towel to clean the control panel and the base of the stove. The Cook & Crisp Basket, detachable diffuser, luxury reversible rack, silicone ring, and cooking pot can all be cleaned in the dishwasher. The anti-clog cap and pressure release valve can be cleaned with water and dish soap.

Cooking pots, deluxe reversible racks, and Cook & Crisp Baskets should be filled with water and given time to soak before being cleaned if food residue is stuck to them. AVOID using scouring pads. If scrubbing is required, use a nylon pad or brush with liquid dish soap or non-abrasive cleaner.

After each use, let all pieces air-dry. Taking off and replacing the Silicone Ring. Pull the silicone ring from the metal ring rack slowly outward, part by section. Either side of the ring can be mounted facing upward. To reinstall, carefully insert the silicone ring piece by piece into the rack while making sure the metal ring rack is visible. Remove

any food particles from the silicone ring and anti-clog cap after use. To prevent odor, keep the silicone ring clean.

Odors can be eliminated by washing them in the dishwasher or warm, soapy water. It is however typical for it to take in the aroma of some acidic foods. It is advised to keep several silicone rings on hand. Additional silicone rings are available on ninjaaccessories.com. NEVER use too much force to remove the silicone ring, as this could damage the rack and compromise the pressure-sealing mechanism. Replace any silicone ring that has cracks, cuts, or other damage right away.

Prior to using any "wet cooking functions," such as Pressure, Steam, Sous Vide, Slow Cook, Sear/Sauté, and all Steam & Crisp functions, I advise checking the interior of the lid. I advise steam cleaning the appliance if you see any food leftover or oil buildup on the heating element or fan. After that, wipe down the interior of the lid.

Steam Cleaning

Pour about 2-3 cups of water into the pot. Move Smart Slider to AIR FRY/STOVETOP. Set the timer to 30 minutes and choose STEAM. Hit the start/stop button. Use a lightly damp cloth or sponge to clean

the interior of the lid once the clock hits zero and the device has cooled. WARNING: Avoid touching the fan when cleaning the inside of the lid.

Frequently Asked Questions & Notes

Why does it take my unit so long to reach pressure? How long does it take for pressure to build?

Depending on the chosen temperature, the cooking pot's current temperature, and the temperature or quantity of the contents, cooking times may vary. Verify that the silicone ring is flush with the lid and fully seated. If placed properly, you should be able to rotate the ring by giving it a small tug. When pressure cooking, make sure the lid is completely secured and the pressure release valve is in the "SEAL" position. If there is not enough liquid, the unit won't pressurize.

Why does the clock go so slowly?

Instead of setting minutes, you might have done such. When adjusting the time, the display will read HH: MM and the time will change in minute steps.

How will I know when the machine starts to pressurize?

To show that the unit is developing pressure, a progress bar will load as the building animation plays. When employing the Pressure, Steam, or any other Steam & Crisp function, "PrE" and moving lights appear on the display screen.

When utilizing STEAM or PRESSURE, this shows that the unit is preheating or creating pressure. Your designated cook time will start to run out once the machine has finished creating pressure. When activating the Steam function, the appliance emits a lot of steam. When cooking, steam should normally escape through the pressure release valve.

Why am I unable to lift the lid after pressuring?

As a security measure, the lid won't open until the appliance has entirely lost pressure. To quickly discharge the pressurized steam, rotate the pressure release valve to the VENT position. Steam will suddenly erupt from the pressure release valve. The apparatus will be prepared to open once all of the steam has been discharged.

Is a loose pressure release valve normal? Yes. The loose fit of the pressure release valve is deliberate; it makes it simple to switch from SEAL to VENT and helps regulate pressure by releasing a tiny quantity of steam while cooking to produce excellent results. For pressure cooking, please check to see if it is turned completely towards the SEAL position, and for quick releasing, check to see if it is turned completely towards the VENT position. The appliance hisses and cannot build pressure.

A pressure release valve should be turned to the SEAL setting, so double-check this. When you've done this and the silicone ring is still making a loud hissing noise, it might not be entirely in place. To halt cooking, hit the "start/stop", then VENT if necessary, then open the lid. Make sure the silicone ring is properly placed and flatly underneath the ring rack by applying pressure on it. Once everything is put in place, you ought to be able to rotate the ring by giving it a gentle tug. Instead of counting down, the device is counting up. The appliance is in Keep Warm mode once the cooking cycle has finished.

How much time does it take the unit to depressurize?

The amount of food in the unit and the recipe can affect how long it takes to release pressure. Unplug the appliance and wait until all the pressure has been released before opening the lid if it is taking longer than usual for the appliance to depressurize.

Troubleshooting

The error message "ADD POT" displays on the monitor. The cooker base does not contain the cooking pot. Every function requires a cooking pot.

The error message "SHUT LID" shows on the monitor. The selected function cannot begin because the lid is open.

When using the Steam or Pressure function, an "ADD WATER" error message shows on the display screen.

The water is not deep enough. To keep the device functioning, add extra water.

When using the Pressure function, a notice saying "NO PRESSURE" shows on the screen. Before starting the pressure cook cycle again, add more liquid to the cooking pot. Ensure that the seal position is selected on the pressure release valve. Verify that the silicone ring is properly fitted. The error message is displayed. The device is not operating correctly.

The error message "SLIDE" displays on the monitor. The slider should be moved to a position that corresponds to the desired cooking function.

The error message "LOCK LID" displays on the monitor. To lock the lid, slide the knob to the PRESSURE position.

4-Week Diet Plan

Week 1

Day 1:
Breakfast: Vanilla Banana Bread
Lunch: Pomegranate Radish Mix
Snack: Ninja Foodi Banana Cookies
Dinner: Spicy Crispy Shrimp
Dessert: Mocha Cake

Day 2:
Breakfast: Deviled Eggs
Lunch: Potatoes and Lemon Sauce
Snack: Nutmeg Peanuts
Dinner: Stuffed Whole Chicken
Dessert: Air Crisped Cake

Day 3:
Breakfast: Cowboy Casserole
Lunch: Creamy Kale
Snack: Herbed Cauliflower Fritters
Dinner: Roasted Lamb
Dessert: Blueberry Buttermilk Cake

Day 4:
Breakfast: French Toast Bites
Lunch: Chives, Beets, and Carrots
Snack: Instant Cheesy Broccoli
Dinner: Mongolian Beef
Dessert: Raspberry Cobbler

Day 5:
Breakfast: Broccoli Egg Scramble
Lunch: Italian Potatoes
Snack: Tortilla Crackers
Dinner: Panko Crusted Cod
Dessert: Double Chocolate Cake

Day 6:
Breakfast: Ninja Foodi Arugula Omelet
Lunch: Broccoli Cauliflower
Snack: Ninja Foodi Spicy Peanuts
Dinner: Bacon Strips
Dessert: Crispy Apple Delight

Day 7:
Breakfast: Eggs in Avocado Cups
Lunch: Cabbage with Bacon
Snack: Roasted Chickpeas
Dinner: Adobo Steak
Dessert: Honey Almond Scones

Week 2

Day 1:
Breakfast: Spinach Casserole
Lunch: Sesame Radish
Snack: Pork Shank
Dinner: Sweet and Sour Fish
Dessert: Banana Bread

Day 2:
Breakfast: Fruit Pancakes
Lunch: Leeks and Carrots
Snack: Cashew Cream
Dinner: Braised Lamb Shanks
Dessert: Pineapple Chunks

Day 3:
Breakfast: Ninja Foodi Hard-boiled eggs
Lunch: Carrots Walnuts Salad
Snack: Garlicky Tomato
Dinner: Pork Meatballs
Dessert: Rocky Road Fudge

Day 4:
Breakfast: Breakfast Oats Bowl
Lunch: Ninja Foodi Roasted Red Pepper Gazpacho
Snack: Cheese Stuffed Dates
Dinner: Pineapple Chicken
Dessert: Ninja Foodi Banana Custard

Day 5:
Breakfast: Swiss Bacon Frittata
Lunch: Buttered Cabbage
Snack: Buttery Potatoes
Dinner: Ninja Foodi Beef Casserole
Dessert: Ninja Foodi Blackberry Crumble

Day 6:
Breakfast: Nut-Packed Porridge
Lunch: Seasoned Beets
Snack: Coated Onion Rings
Dinner: Fish Broccoli Stew
Dessert: Chocolate Walnut Cake

Day 7:
Breakfast: Western Omelet
Lunch: Gluten-free Taco Beans
Snack: Chicken Wings
Dinner: Spicy Indian Shrimp Curry
Dessert: Strawberry Crumble

Week 3

Day 1:
Breakfast: Ham Breakfast Casserole
Lunch: Steak and Veggie Bowl
Snack: Ninja Foodi Herb Crackers
Dinner: Ninja Foodi Beef Chili
Dessert: Lemon Cheesecake

Day 2:
Breakfast: Ninja Foodi Baked Eggs
Lunch: Garlic Red Bell Pepper Mix
Snack: Air Crisped Chicken Nuggets
Dinner: Chicken Potato Stew
Dessert: Mini Chocolate Cheesecakes

Day 3:
Breakfast: Bell Pepper Frittata
Lunch: Crispy Balsamic Cabbage
Snack: Loaded Zucchini Chips
Dinner: Taco Meatballs
Dessert: Blackberry Cake

Day 4:
Breakfast: Nutmeg Pumpkin Porridge
Lunch: Black-Eyed Peas
Snack: Air Crisped Chicken Nuggets
Dinner: Ninja Foodi Minced Beef with Tomatoes
Dessert: Chocolate Lava Cake

Day 5:
Breakfast: Apricot Oatmeal
Lunch: Saucy Kale
Snack: Ninja Foodi Spicy Cashews
Dinner: Air Fried Scallops
Dessert: Yogurt Cheesecake

Day 6:
Breakfast: Ninja Foodi Ham Muffins
Lunch: Balsamic Cabbage with Endives
Snack: Dried Tomatoes
Dinner: Lamb Curry
Dessert: Chocolate Cheesecake

Day 7:
Breakfast: Ninja Foodi Broccoli Pancakes
Lunch: Okra Stew
Snack: Japanese Eggs
Dinner: Roasted BBQ Shrimp
Dessert: Mini Vanilla Cheesecakes

Week 4

Day 1:
Breakfast: Almond Quinoa Porridge
Lunch: Kale and Parmesan
Snack: Ninja Foodi Spiced Almonds
Dinner: Honey Garlic Chicken
Dessert: Chocolate Blackberry Cake

Day 2:
Breakfast: Chicken Omelet
Lunch: Air Crisped Brussels Sprouts
Snack: Zucchini Egg Tots
Dinner: Corned Cabbage Beef
Dessert: Lime Blueberry Cheesecake

Day 3:
Breakfast: Spinach and Turkey Cups
Lunch: Mac & Cheese
Snack: Ninja Foodi Cod Sticks
Dinner: Bay Crab Legs
Dessert: Ninja Foodi Yogurt Cheesecake

Day 4:
Breakfast: Omelets in the Jar
Lunch: Zucchini and Spinach Mix
Snack: Breadsticks
Dinner: Mexican Chicken Soup
Dessert: Mocha Cake

Day 5:
Breakfast: Ninja Foodi Pancakes
Lunch: Maple Dipped Kale
Snack: Zucchini Muffins
Dinner: Beer Battered Fish
Dessert: Chocolate Walnut Cake

Day 6:
Breakfast: Glazed Carrots
Lunch: Flavored Fries
Snack: Avocado Deviled Eggs
Dinner: Garlicky Pork Chops
Dessert: Pineapple Chunks

Day 7:
Breakfast: Cauliflower Meal
Lunch: Pumpkin Chili
Snack: Ninja Foodi Spicy Popcorns
Dinner: Coconut Curry Salmon with Zucchini Noodles
Dessert: Raspberry Cobbler

Chapter 1 Breakfast Recipes

10	Spinach and Turkey Cups	16	Cauliflower Meal
10	Spinach Casserole	16	Fruit Pancakes
10	Ninja Foodi Arugula Omelet	17	Ham Breakfast Casserole
11	French Toast Bites	17	Omelets in the Jar
11	Eggs in Avocado Cups	17	Glazed Carrots
11	Cowboy Casserole	18	Swiss Bacon Frittata
12	Broccoli Egg Scramble	18	Chorizo Omelet
12	Deviled Eggs	18	Avocado Cups
12	Vanilla Banana Bread	19	Pepperoni Omelets
13	Nut-Packed Porridge	19	Ninja Foodi Coconut Cereal
13	Crispy Spiced Broccoli	19	Ninja Foodi Hard-Boiled Eggs
13	Chicken Omelet	20	Ninja Foodi Ham Muffins
14	Western Omelet	20	Ninja Foodi Cinnamon Tea
14	Bell Pepper Frittata	20	Ninja Foodi Baked Eggs
14	Nutmeg Pumpkin Porridge	21	Ninja Foodi Broccoli Pancakes
15	Apricot Oatmeal	21	Ninja Foodi Pancakes
15	Spinach Turkey Cups	21	Egg Bites
15	Almond Quinoa Porridge	22	Breakfast Oats Bowl
16	Flaxseeds Granola		

Spinach and Turkey Cups

Prep Time: 15 minutes | Cook Time: 23 minutes | Serves: 4

Ingredients:

- 1 tbsp unsalted butter
- 1 lb. fresh baby spinach
- 4 eggs
- 7 oz cooked turkey, chopped
- 4 tsp unsweetened almond milk
- Salt and ground black pepper, as required

Directions:

1. Add the butter into the Ninja Foodi cooking pot. Select the Sear/Sauté setting at MD on the Ninja Foodi to heat the butter for about 2–3 minutes. 2. Add the spinach and cook for about 2–3 minutes or until just wilted. 3. Press Start/Stop to stop cooking and drain the liquid completely. 4. Transfer the spinach into a bowl and set it aside to cool slightly. 5. Arrange the Cook & Crisp Basket in the Ninja Foodi cooking pot. 6. Close the Ninja Foodi with the Crisping Lid and select Air Crisp. 7. Set the temperature to 355°F for 5 minutes. Press Start/Stop to begin preheating. 8. Divide the spinach into 4 greased ramekins, followed by the turkey. 9. Crack 1 egg into each ramekin and drizzle with almond milk. Sprinkle with salt and black pepper. 10. After the appliance has preheated, open the lid, and place the ramekins into the Cook & Crisp Basket. 11. Close the Ninja Foodi with the Crisping Lid and select Air Crisp. 12. Set the temperature to 355°F for 20 minutes. Press Start/Stop to begin cooking. 13. When done, open the lid and serve hot.

Nutritional Information Per Serving: Calories: 200; Fat: 10.2g; Carbs: 4.5g; Protein: 23.4g

Spinach Casserole

Prep Time: 10 minutes | Cook Time: 5 minutes | Serves: 4

Ingredients:

- 4 whole eggs
- 1 tbsp milk
- 1 tomato, diced
- ½ cup spinach
- ¼ tsp salt
- ¼ tsp black pepper

Directions:

1. Take a baking pan small enough to fit Ninja Foodi and grease it with butter. 2. Take a medium bowl and whisk in eggs, milk, salt, pepper, add veggies to the bowl and stir. 3. Pour egg mixture into the baking pan and lower the pan into the Ninja Foodi. 4. Close the unit with Crisping Lid and Air Crisp for 325°F for 7 minutes. 5. Remove the pan from eggs, and enjoy hot.

Nutritional Values Per Serving: Calories: 78; Fat: 5g; Carbs: 1 g; Protein: 7 g

Ninja Foodi Arugula Omelet

Prep Time: 10 minutes | Cook Time: 5 minutes | Serves: 4

Ingredients:

- 6 eggs
- 2 tbsp unsweetened almond milk
- 2 cups fresh arugula, chopped
- 4 scallions, chopped finely
- 2 tbsp olive oil
- Salt and black pepper, to taste

Directions:

1. Add everything except olive oil in a bowl. Whisk well. 2. Now, heat olive oil in the Ninja Foodi cooking pot and add in egg mixture. 3. Close the unit with Pressure Lid and turn the pressure release valve to VENT position. Select the unit on Steam function. 4. Cook for about 5-minutes on LO. 5. Open the Pressure Lid and take out. 6. Serve and enjoy!

Nutritional Values Per Serving: Calories: 163; Fat: 13.8g; Carbs: 2.1g; Protein: 8.9g

French Toast Bites

Prep Time: 10 minutes | Cook Time: 15 minutes | Serves: 1

Ingredients:

¼ loaf of French bread
2 eggs
2 tbsp milk
Topping
1 tbsp brown sugar
1 tbsp honey

½ tsp cinnamon
1 mashed banana

½ tsp cinnamon

Directions:

1. Cut the French bread into cubes and add it to a container. 2. In a separate small bowl, combine eggs, milk, mashed banana, vanilla, and cinnamon. 3. Pour mixture over the bread cubes and mix it all well till it's equally coated. 4. In a greased Ninja Foodi, add bread pieces in a single layer. 5. Sprinkle brown sugar and cinnamon on top of it. 6. Then select Air Crisp at 390° F for 10 minutes. Keep tossing or mixing halfway through. 7. When the golden-brown color appears, drizzle the honey, bites are ready to be served!
Nutritional Values Per Serving: Calories: 302; Fat: 6g; Carbs: 21g; Protein: 13g

Eggs in Avocado Cups

Prep Time: 10 minutes | Cook Time: 12 minutes | Serves: 2

Ingredients:

1 avocado, halved and pitted
Salt and ground black pepper, as required
2 eggs

1 tbsp parmesan cheese, shredded
1 tsp fresh chives, minced

Directions:

1. Arrange a greased square piece of foil in the Cook & Crisp Basket and place the basket in the Ninja Foodi cooking pot. 2. Close the Ninja Foodi with the Crisping Lid and select Bake/Roast. 3. Set the temperature to 390°F for 5 minutes. Press Start/Stop to begin preheating. 4. Carefully scoop out about 2 tsp of flesh from each avocado half. 5. Crack 1 egg in each avocado half and sprinkle with salt, black pepper, and cheese. 6. When the appliance has preheated, open the lid. 7. Place the avocado halves into the Cook & Crisp Basket. 8. Close the Ninja Foodi with the Crisping Lid and Select Bake/Roast. 9. Set the temperature to 390°F for 12 minutes. 10. Press Start/Stop to begin cooking. 11. When done, open the lid and transfer the avocado halves onto serving plates.
Nutritional Information Per Serving: Calories: 278; Fat: 24.7g; Carbs: 9.1g; Protein: 8g

Cowboy Casserole

Prep Time: 30 minutes | Cook Time: 30 minutes | Serves: 4

Ingredients:

1 lb. ground beef
1 bag frozen tater tots
1 small onion, chopped
1 can black beans
1 cup corn
1 can Ro-Tel tomatoes with chilies

1 tsp cumin
1 tsp chili powder
1 cup sour cream
1 cup cheddar cheese, shredded
3 slices cooked bacon
Green onions, for topping (optional)

Directions:

1. Turn your Ninja Foodi on to Sear/Sauté mode. Cook the ground beef on HI until no longer pink. 2. Add the onions and cook until they are soft, about 1–2 minutes, and then add the seasonings. 3. Stir in the beans, corn, and sour cream. Stir until well combined. 4. Top with the frozen tater tots. 5. Adjust the setting to Air Crisp and place the Crisping Lid on the Foodi. Cook at 390°F for 20 minutes. 6. Remove the lid and place the cheese on top. Place the Crisping Lid again, select Air Crisp at 390°F, and cook for an additional 5 minutes.
Nutritional Information Per Serving: Calories: 500; Fat: 30g; Carbs: 24g; Protein: 34g

Broccoli Egg Scramble

Prep Time: 10 minutes | Cook Time: 5 minutes | Serves: 4

Ingredients:

1 pack, 12 ounces frozen broccoli florets
2 tbsp butter
Black pepper and salt, to taste
8 whole eggs
2 tbsp milk
¾ cup white cheddar cheese, shredded
Crushed red pepper to taste
Optional bacon strips

Directions:

1. Open your Ninja Foodi lid and add butter and broccoli, and stir. 2. Season the mix with black pepper and salt, adjust according to your taste. 3. Lock the unit with Pressure Lid, turn the pressure release valve to SEAL position, and then cook on "HI" pressure for 10 minutes. 4. Release pressure naturally. 5. Take a medium-sized bowl and crack an egg, beat well, add milk to the eggs and stir. 6. Add egg mixture into the Ninja Foodi over the broccoli mix, gently stir. 7. Set your pot to "Sear/Sauté" mode at MD and let it cook for 2 minutes. 8. Once the egg has settled in, add cheese, sprinkle red and black pepper. 9. Season with salt. 10. Serve and enjoy with some bacon.

Nutritional Values Per Serving: Calories: 184; Fat: 12g; Carbs: 5 g; Protein: 12 g

Deviled Eggs

Prep Time: 10 minutes | Cook Time: 10 minutes | Serves: 4

Ingredients:

8 large eggs
1 cup of water
Guacamole
Sliced Radishes
Mayonnaise
Furikake

Directions:

1. Add water to the Ninja Foodi cooking pot. 2. Place the deluxe reversible rack inside the pot and set the eggs on top of the rack. 3. Lock pressure lid, turn the pressure release valve to SEAL position, and cook on "HI" pressure for 6 minutes. 4. Release pressure naturally over 10 minutes and transfer the eggs to a suitable full of icy water. Peel after 5 minutes. 5. Cut in half and decorate with guacamole, sliced radish, and mayo, and enjoy.

Nutritional Values Per Serving: Calories: 70; Fat: 6g; Carbs: 1g; Protein: 3g

Vanilla Banana Bread

Prep Time: 10 minutes | Cook Time: 50 minutes | Serves: 8

Ingredients:

2 cups flour
1 tsp baking powder
½ cup erythritol
½ cup butter softened
2 eggs
1 tbsp vanilla extract
4 bananas, peeled and mashed

Directions:

1. Grease a 7-inch springform pan. 2. In a suitable bowl, mix flour and baking powder. 3. In another bowl, add erythritol, butter, and eggs and beat until creamy. 4. Add the bananas and vanilla extract and beat until well combined. 5. Slowly add flour mixture, 1 cup at a time, and mix until smooth. 6. Place mixture into prepared loaf pan evenly. 7. In the Ninja Foodi cooking pot, place 1 cup of water. 8. Set the "Reversible Rack" in the Ninja Foodi cooking pot. 9. Place the pan over the "Reversible Rack." 10. Close the Ninja Foodi with the pressure lid and place the pressure valve to the "Seal" position. 11. Pressure Cook the bread at HI for 50 minutes. 12. Switch the pressure valve to "Vent" and do a "Quick" release. 13. Cut into desired sized slices and serve.

Nutritional Values Per Serving: Calories: 336; Fat: 13.1 g; Carbs: 50.4 g; Protein: 5.4g

Nut-Packed Porridge

Prep Time: 10 minutes | Cook Time: 10 minutes | Serves: 6

Ingredients:

1 cup porridge
1 cup roasted pecans, halved
1 cup roasted cashew nuts, unsalted
4 tsp coconut oil, melted
2 cups water
Fresh mix berries (optional)

Directions:

1. Add 2 cups water along with 1 cup porridge with coconut oil in the Ninja Foodi cooking pot. 2. Close the pressure lid, turn the pressure release valve to SEAL position, pressure cook for 4 minutes on HI. 3. Quick-release the pressure. 4. Open the lid and mix the nuts in the porridge.
Nutritional Information Per Serving: Calories: 70; Fat: 6g; Carbs: 1g; Protein: 3g

Crispy Spiced Broccoli

Prep Time: 5-10 minutes | Cook Time: 10 minutes | Serves: 4

Ingredients:

2 heads broccoli, cut into florets
4 tbsp soy sauce
2 tbsp canola oil
4 tbsp balsamic vinegar
2 tsp maple syrup
Red pepper flakes and sesame seeds, to garnish

Directions:

1. In a mixing bowl, whisk together the soy sauce, balsamic vinegar, oil, and maple syrup. Add the broccoli; toss well. 2. Take the Ninja Foodi, place it on your kitchen countertop, and open the top lid. Arrange the broccoli over Cook & Crisp Basket in the Ninja Foodi cooking pot. 3. Arrange the Cook & Crisp Basket in the pot and close the unit with Crisping Lid. Select Air Crisp and then the temperature to 350°F. Adjust the timer to 10 minutes and then press Start/Stop. 4. Allow the broccoli to cook until the timer reads zero. 5. Divide the broccoli among serving plates.
Nutritional Information Per Serving: Calories: 141; Fat: 7g; Carbs: 14g; Protein: 4.5g

Chicken Omelet

Prep Time: 10 minutes | Cook Time: 16 minutes | Serves: 2

Ingredients:

1 tsp butter
1 small yellow onion, chopped
½ jalapeño pepper, seeded and chopped
3 eggs
Black pepper and salt, as required
¼ cup cooked chicken, shredded

Directions:

1. Select the "Sear/Sauté" setting of Ninja Foodi at MD: HI and place the butter into the cooking pot. 2. Heat for about 2-3 minutes. 3. Add the onion and cook for about 4-5 minutes. 4. Add the jalapeño pepper and cook for about 1 minute. 5. Meanwhile, in a suitable bowl, add the eggs, salt, and black pepper and beat well. 6. Press the "Start/Stop" button to pause cooking and stir in the chicken. 7. Top with the egg mixture evenly. 8. Close the Ninja Foodi with Crisping Lid and select "Air Crisp." 9. Set its cooking temperature to 355°F for 5 minutes. 10. Press the "Start/Stop" button to initiate cooking. 11. Open the Ninja Foodi's lid and transfer the omelet onto a plate. 12. Cut into equal-sized wedges and serve hot.
Nutritional Information Per Serving: Calories: 153; Fat: 9.1g; Carbs: 4g; Protein: 13.8g

Western Omelet

Prep Time: 10 minutes | Cook Time: 35 minutes | Serves: 4

Ingredients:

- 3 eggs, whisked
- 3 oz chorizo, chopped
- 1 oz feta cheese, crumbled
- 5 tbsp almond milk
- ¾ tsp chili flakes
- ¼ tsp salt
- 1 green pepper, chopped

Directions:

1. Add all the listed ingredients to a bowl and mix well. Take an omelet pan and pour the mixture into it. 2. Preheat your Ninja Foodi on Bake/Roast mode at 320°F for 10 minutes. 3. Transfer the pan with the omelet mix to your Ninja Foodi and bake for 30 minutes, or until golden and the egg has set properly.

Nutritional Information Per Serving: Calories: 426; Fat: 38g; Carbs: 7g; Protein: 21g

Bell Pepper Frittata

Prep Time: 15 minutes | Cook Time: 18 minutes | Serves: 2

Ingredients:

- 1 tbsp olive oil
- 1 chorizo sausage, sliced
- 1½ cups bell peppers, seeded and chopped
- 4 large eggs
- Black pepper and salt, as required
- 2 tbsp feta cheese, crumbled
- 1 tbsp fresh parsley, chopped

Directions:

1. Select the "Sear/Sauté" setting of Ninja Foodi at MD and place the butter into the pot. 2. Press the "Start/Stop" button to initiate cooking and heat for about 2-3 minutes. 3. Add the sausage and bell peppers and cook for 6-8 minutes or until golden brown. 4. Meanwhile, in a suitable bowl, add the eggs, salt, and black pepper and beat well. 5. Press the "Start/Stop" button to pause cooking and place the eggs over the sausage mixture, followed by the cheese and parsley. 6. Close the Ninja Foodi with Crisping Lid and select "Air Crisp". 7. Air crisp the frittata at 355°F for 10 minutes. 8. Open the Ninja Foodi's lid and transfer the frittata onto a platter. 9. Cut into equal-sized wedges and serve hot.

Nutritional Information Per Serving: Calories: 398; Fat: 31g; Carbs: 8g; Protein: 22.9g

Nutmeg Pumpkin Porridge

Prep Time: 15 minutes | Cook Time: 5 hours | Serves: 8

Ingredients:

- 1 cup unsweetened almond milk
- 2 pounds pumpkin, peeled and cubed into ½-inch size
- 6-8 drops liquid stevia
- ½ tsp ground allspice
- 1 tbsp ground cinnamon
- 1 tsp ground nutmeg
- ¼ tsp ground cloves
- ½ cup walnuts, chopped

Directions:

1. In the Ninja Foodi cooking pot, place ½ cup of almond milk and remaining ingredients and stir to combine. 2. Close the Ninja Foodi with Pressure Lid, turn the pressure release valve to VENT, and select "Slow Cook". 3. Slow cook on "LO" for 4-5 hours. 4. Open the Ninja Foodi's lid and stir in the remaining almond milk. 5. With a potato masher, mash the mixture completely. 6. Divide the porridge into serving bowls evenly. 7. Serve warm with the topping of walnuts.

Nutritional Information Per Serving: Calories: 96; Fat: 5.5g; Carbs: 11.2g; Protein: 3.3g

Apricot Oatmeal

Prep Time: 10 minutes | Cook Time: 8 hours | Serves: 8

Ingredients:

2 cups steel-cut oats
⅓ cup dried apricots, chopped
½ cup dried cherries
1 tsp ground cinnamon

4 cups milk
4 cups water
¼ tsp liquid stevia

Directions:

1. In the Ninja Foodi cooking pot, place all ingredients and stir to combine. 2. Close the Ninja Foodi with Pressure Lid, turn the pressure release valve to VENT position, and select "Slow Cook." 3. Slow cook the oatmeal on "LO" for 6-8 hours. 4. Open the Ninja Foodi's lid and serve warm.

Nutritional Information Per Serving: Calories: 148; Fat: 3.5g; Carbs: 4.2 g; Protein: 5.9 g

Spinach Turkey Cups

Prep Time: 15 minutes | Cook Time: 23 minutes | Serves: 4

Ingredients:

1 tbsp unsalted butter
1-pound fresh baby spinach
4 eggs

7 ounces cooked turkey, chopped
4 tsp unsweetened almond milk
Black pepper and salt, as required

Directions:

1. Select the "Sear/Sauté" setting of Ninja Foodi at MD and place the butter into the cooking pot. 2. Heat for about 2-3 minutes. 3. Add the spinach and cook for about 3 minutes or until just wilted. 4. Press the "Start/Stop" button to pause cooking and drain the liquid completely. 5. Transfer the spinach into a suitable bowl and set aside to cool slightly. 6. Set the Cook & Crisp Basket in the Ninja Foodi cooking pot. 7. Close the Ninja Foodi with Crisping Lid and select "Air Crisp." 8. Air Crisp at 355°F for 5 minutes. 9. Divide the spinach into 4 greased ramekins, followed by the turkey. 10. Crack 1 egg into each ramekin and drizzle with almond milk. 11. Sprinkle with black pepper and salt. 12. After preheating, open the lid. 13. Place the ramekins into the Cook & Crisp Basket. 14. Close the Ninja Foodi with Crisping Lid and select "Air Crisp." 15. Set its cooking temperature to 355°F for 20 minutes. 16. Press the "Start/Stop" button to initiate cooking. 17. Open the Ninja Foodi's lid and serve hot.

Nutritional Information Per Serving: Calories: 200; Fat: 10.2g; Carbs: 4.5g; Protein: 23.4g

Almond Quinoa Porridge

Prep Time: 10 minutes | Cook Time: 1 minute | Serves: 6

Ingredients:

1¼ cups water
1 cup almond milk
1½ cups uncooked quinoa, rinsed

1 tbsp choc zero maple syrup
1 cinnamon stick
Pinch of salt

Directions:

1. In the Ninja Foodi cooking pot, add all ingredients and stir to combine well. 2. Close the Ninja Foodi's pressure lid and place the pressure valve in the "Seal" position. 3. Select "Pressure Cook" mode and set it to "Hi" for 1 minute. 4. Press the "Start/Stop" button to initiate cooking. 5. Now turn the pressure valve to "Vent" and do a "Quick" release. 6. Open the Ninja Foodi's lid, and with a fork, fluff the quinoa. 7. Serve warm.

Nutritional Information Per Serving: Calories: 186; Fat: 2.6 g; Carbs: 4.8 g; Protein: 6 g

Flaxseeds Granola

Prep Time: 15 minutes | Cook Time: 2½ hours | Serves: 16

Ingredients:

- ½ cup sunflower kernels
- 5 cups mixed nuts, crushed
- 2 tbsp ground flax seeds
- ¼ cup olive oil
- ½ cup unsalted butter
- 1 tsp ground cinnamon
- 1 cup choc zero maple syrup

Directions:

1. Grease the Ninja Foodi cooking pot. 2. In the greased cooking pot, add sunflower kernels, nuts, flax seeds, oil, butter, and cinnamon and stir to combine. 3. Close the Ninja Foodi with Pressure Lid and turn the pressure release valve to the SEAL position. 4. Slow cook on "HI" for 2½ hours. 5. Stir the mixture after every 30 minutes. 6. Open the Ninja Foodi's lid and transfer the granola onto a large baking sheet. 7. Add the maple syrup and stir to combine. 8. Set aside to cool completely before serving. 9. You can preserve this granola in an airtight container.

Nutritional Information Per Serving: Calories: 189; Fat: 10 g; Carbs: 7.7 g; Protein: 4.6 g

Cauliflower Meal

Prep Time: 10 minutes | Cook Time: 4 minutes | Serves: 4

Ingredients:

- 1 cauliflower head, florets
- ½ cup vegetable stock
- 2 garlic cloves, minced
- Black pepper and salt to taste
- ⅓ cup grated parmesan
- 1 tbsp parsley, chopped
- 3 tbsp olive oil

Directions:

1. Take a suitable bowl and add oil, salt, pepper, garlic, and cauliflower, and toss well. 2. Transfer the mix to Ninja Foodi cooking pot. 3. Add stock and stir. 4. Lock and secure the Ninja Foodi's pressure lid, turn the pressure valve to SEAL position. Set the unit to Pressure Cook mode. Then cook on "HI" pressure for 4 minutes. 5. Add parsley and cheese, and toss to combine well. 6. Serve and enjoy a healthy breakfast.

Nutritional Information Per Serving: Calories: 120; Fat: 2g; Carbs: 4g; Protein: 3g

Fruit Pancakes

Prep Time: 7 minutes | Cook Time: 20 minutes | Serves: 2

Ingredients:

- ½ cup pancake mix oats
- 2 eggs
- ¼ cup regular milk
- 1 tsp melted butter
- 2 drops of Vanilla essence
- 1 date
- ½ tsp cinnamon
- ½ cup any fresh fruit of your choice

Directions:

1. In a mixing bowl, mix together the pancake mix oats, eggs, melted butter, cinnamon, dates, vanilla essence, and milk until a thick batter is prepared. 2. Gently mix in available fresh fruit, it can also be any thawed fruit. 3. Spray the Ninja Foodi cooking pot with spray oil. Non-sticky canola spray could also be the best option. 4. Preheat your Ninja Foodi at 375°F on the Bake/Roast option. 5. After that, pour in the batter and it should be spread with even consistency throughout the Ninja Foodi. 6. Close the Ninja Foodi with Crisping Lid and bake at 375°F for 12 to 15 minutes. 15 minutes are considered ideal for a perfect turnout of the pancake. 7. Lastly, serve it with any fruit or toppings of your choice.

Nutritional Information Per Serving: Calories: 227.5; Fat: 8.5g; Carbs: 18.5 g; Protein: 10.5 g

Ham Breakfast Casserole

Prep Time: 10 minutes | Cook Time: 10 minutes | Serves: 4

Ingredients:

- 4 whole eggs
- 1 tbsp milk
- 1 cup ham, cooked and chopped
- ½ cup cheddar cheese, shredded
- ¼ tsp salt
- ¼ tsp black pepper

Directions:

1. Take a baking pan small enough to fit into your Ninja Foodi Cook & Crisp Basket, and grease it well with butter. 2. Take a medium bowl and whisk in eggs, milk, salt, pepper and add ham, cheese, and stir. 3. Pour mixture into the baking pan and lower the pan into your Ninja Foodi. 4. Set your Ninja Foodi on Air Crisp mode and Air Crisp for 325°F for 7 minutes. 5. Remove pan from eggs and enjoy.

Nutritional Information Per Serving: Calories: 169; Fat: 13g; Carbs: 1g; Protein: 12g

Omelets in the Jar

Prep Time: 10 minutes | Cook Time: 8 minutes | Serves: 5

Ingredients:

- 10 eggs
- ⅓ cup heavy cream
- ⅔ cup shredded cheese
- 1 green pepper, chopped
- 1 ham steak, chopped
- ½ lb. bacon, cooked and chopped
- 5 mason jars or other jars

Directions:

1. Grease the mason jars with canola spray. 2. Whisk 2 eggs with 1 tbsp cream in a bowl and then pour it into a jar. 3. Add 1 tbsp of ham, green peppers, and cheese to the same jar. 4. Repeat the same steps to fill remaining jars. 5. Pour 1 cup of water in the Ninja Food cooking pot and place a reversible rack over it. 6. Set all the mason jars over the rack. 7. Secure the Ninja Foodi with Pressure Lid and turn its pressure release valve to 'SEAL' position. 8. Select Pressure Cook mode for 8 minutes at HI. 9. Once done, release the steam naturally then remove the lid. 10. Drizzle bacon and cheese over each jar. 11. Serve fresh.

Nutritional Information Per Serving: Calories: 111; Fat: 8.3 g; Carbs: 1.9 g; Protein 7.4 g

Glazed Carrots

Prep Time: 10 minutes | Cook Time: 4 minutes | Serves: 4

Ingredients:

- 2 pounds carrots, washed, peeled and sliced
- Pepper, to taste
- 1 cup water
- 1 tbsp butter
- 1 tbsp choc zero maple syrup

Directions:

1. Add carrots and water to the cooking pot. 2. Lock and secure the Ninja Foodi with Pressure Lid, then cook on "HI" pressure for 4 minutes. 3. Quick-release Pressure. 4. Strain carrots. 5. Add butter and maple syrup to the warm mix, stir it gently. 6. Transfer strained carrots back to the pot and stir. 7. Coat well with maple syrup. 8. Sprinkle a bit of pepper and serve. 9. Enjoy.

Nutritional Information Per Serving: Calories: 358; Fat: 12g; Carbs: 20g; Protein: 2g

Swiss Bacon Frittata

Prep Time: 10 minutes | Cook Time: 30 minutes | Serves: 6

Ingredients:

1 small onion, chopped
½ lb. raw bacon, chopped
1 lb. frozen spinach
10 eggs
1 cup cottage cheese
½ cup half and half cream
1 tsp salt
1 cup shredded Swiss cheese

Directions:

1. Preheat your Ninja Foodi for 5 minutes at MD: HI on Sear/Sauté Mode. 2. Add bacon, and onion to the Foodi and sauté for 10 minutes until crispy. 3. Stir in spinach and stir cook for 3 minutes. 4. Whisk eggs with cottage cheese, salt, and half and half cream in a bowl. 5. Pour this mixture into the Ninja Foodi cooking pot. 6. Drizzle Swiss cheese over the egg mixture. 7. Secure the Ninja Foodi with Crisping Lid and switch the Ninja Foodi to Bake/Roast mode for 20 minutes at 350°F. 8. Serve warm.

Nutritional Information Per Serving: Calories: 139; Fat: 10.1g; Carbs: 2.3g; Protein: 10.1g

Chorizo Omelet

Prep Time: 10 minutes | Cook Time: 30-35 minutes | Serves: 4

Ingredients:

3 eggs, whisked
3 ounces chorizo, chopped
1-ounce Feta cheese, crumbled
5 tbsp almond milk
¾ tsp chili flakes
¼ tsp salt
1 green pepper, chopped

Directions:

1. Add listed ingredients to a suitable bowl and mix well. 2. Take an omelet pan and pour the mixture on it. 3. Preheat your Ninja Food on "Bake/Roast" mode at 320°F for 5 minutes. 4. Transfer pan with omelet mix to your Ninja Foodi and cook for 30 minutes, or until the surface is golden and the egg has set properly. 5. Serve and enjoy.

Nutritional Information Per Serving: Calories: 426; Fat: 38g; Carbs: 7g; Protein: 21g

Avocado Cups

Prep Time: 10 minutes | Cook Time: 12 minutes | Serves: 2

Ingredients:

1 avocado, halved and pitted
Black pepper and salt, as required
2 eggs
1 tbsp Parmesan cheese, shredded
1 tsp fresh chives, minced

Directions:

1. Set a greased square piece of foil in Cook & Crisp Basket. 2. Set the basket in the cooking pot. 3. Close the Ninja Foodi with Crisping Lid and select "Bake/Roast". 4. Set its cooking temperature to 390°F and cook time for 5 minutes. 5. Press the "Start/Stop" button to initiate preheating. 6. Carefully scoop out about 2 tsp of flesh from each avocado half. 7. Crack 1 egg in each avocado half and sprinkle with salt, black pepper, and cheese. 8. After preheating, open the lid. 9. Place the avocado halves into the Cook & Crisp Basket. 10. Close the Ninja Foodi with Crisping Lid and Select "Bake/Roast." 11. Set its cooking temperature to 390°F and cook time for about 12 minutes. 12. Press the "Start/Stop" button to initiate cooking. 13. Open the Ninja Foodi's lid and transfer the avocado halves onto serving plates. 14. Top with Parmesan and chives and serve.

Nutritional Information Per Serving: Calories: 278; Fat: 24.7g; Carbs: 9.1g; Protein: 8.4g

Pepperoni Omelets

Prep Time: 10 minutes | Cook Time: 5 minutes | Serves: 4

Ingredients:

- 4 tbsp heavy cream
- 15 pepperoni slices
- 2 tbsp butter
- Black pepper and salt to taste
- 6 whole eggs

Directions:

1. Take a suitable bowl and whisk in eggs, cream, pepperoni slices, salt, and pepper. 2. Set your Ninja Foodi to "Sear/Sauté" mode at MD and add butter and egg mix. 3. Sauté for 3 minutes, flip. 4. Lock and secure the unit with Crisping Lid and Air Crisp for 2 minutes at 350°F. 5. Transfer to a serving plate and enjoy.

Nutritional Information Per Serving: Calories: 141; Fat: 11g; Carbs: 0.6g; Protein: 9g

Ninja Foodi Coconut Cereal

Prep Time: 5 minutes | Cook Time: 8 hours 3 minutes | Serves: 3

Ingredients:

- ½ cup unsweetened coconut, shredded
- 1 cup water
- ¼ tsp ground cinnamon
- ⅛ tsp liquid stevia
- 1 cup unsweetened almond milk
- ¼ cup coconut flour, divided
- ¼ tsp vanilla extract

Directions:

1. Add shredded coconut, almond milk, half of the coconut flour, water, and cinnamon in the pot of Ninja Foodi. Mix well. 2. Close the Pressure Lid, turn the pressure release valve to VENT position, and select "Slow Cook". 3. Slow cook the cereal on LO for 8 hours. 4. Open the lid and add in the remaining coconut flour, stevia, and vanilla extract. Mix until well combined. 5. Close the Pressure Lid and cook for 3 minutes. 6. Open the lid and take out. 7. Serve and enjoy!

Nutritional Information Per Serving: Calories: 102; Fat: 6.6g; Carbs: 9.6g; Protein: 2.1g

Ninja Foodi Hard-Boiled Eggs

Prep Time: 8-10 minutes | Cook Time: 15 minutes | Serves: 6

Ingredients:

- 12 eggs
- 1 cup water

Directions:

1. Place the multi-purpose pan filled with one cup of water inside Ninja Foodi. 2. Be very careful while placing the eggs in the Ninja Foodi. 3. Secure the pressure lid and turn the valve to Seal. Set the Ninja Foodi to High Pressure for 5 minutes. Press Start/Stop. 4. While the eggs are being done, take a bowl, add ice cubes and water. 5. After 5 minutes, turn valve for Quick Pressure Release. Then take eggs out. 6. After taking out the eggs, put them in that ice bath for 5 minutes at least. 7. Peel and serve, the eggs are ready. They can also be stored in the fridge for up to a week!

Nutritional Information Per Serving: Calories: 155; Fat: 11g; Carbs: 1g; Protein: 6g

Ninja Foodi Ham Muffins

Prep Time: 10 minutes | Cook Time: 20 minutes | Serves: 4

Ingredients:

- 4 eggs
- ½ cup cooked ham, crumbled
- ½ cup red bell pepper, seeded and chopped
- 1 tbsp water
- Salt and black pepper, to taste

Directions:

1. Add eggs, salt, pepper, and water in a bowl. Mix well. 2. Now, add in red bell pepper and crumbled ham. Mix well and set aside. 3. Pour the mixture in greased muffin-tins and place them in Ninja Foodi cooking pot. 4. Close the unit with Crisping Lid and select the unit on Bake/Roast mode. 5. Bake for 20 minutes at 350°F. 6. Take out, serve and enjoy!

Nutritional Information Per Serving: Calories: 95; Fat: 5.9g; Carbs: 2.1g; Protein: 8.5g

Ninja Foodi Cinnamon Tea

Prep Time: 5 minutes | Cook Time: 12 minutes | Serves: 2

Ingredients:

- 1 cup water
- 1 tsp black tea
- 2 cinnamon sticks
- 4 black peppercorns
- ½ cup fat-free cream

Directions:

1. Add water, peppercorns, and cinnamon in the Ninja Foodi cooking pot. Close the Ninja Foodi with Pressure Lid and turn the pressure release valve to VENT position. Select the Ninja Foodi on Steam function. 2. Boil for about 10 minutes and add in cream. 3. Close the pressure Lid, turn the pressure release valve to SEAL position, and select the unit on Pressure Cook function. 4. Pressure cook for about 2 minutes at LO. 5. Open the lid and strain the tea. 6. Serve hot and enjoy!

Nutritional Information Per Serving: Calories: 62; Fat: 0.8g; Carbs: 5.4g; Protein: 8.5g

Ninja Foodi Baked Eggs

Prep Time: 12 minutes | Cook Time: 9 minutes | Serves: 3

Ingredients:

- 3 eggs
- 3 tbsp low-fat parmesan cheese, shredded
- ½ cup fresh spinach, chopped finely
- 3 tbsp heavy cream
- 3 tbsp olive oil
- Salt and black pepper, to taste

Directions:

1. Grease three muffin tins with olive oil and add spinach in them. 2. Add in eggs and top them with heavy cream, parmesan cheese, salt, and pepper. 3. Place the muffin tins in the Ninja Foodi cooking pot. Close the unit with Crisping Lid and select "Bake/Roast" function. 4. Bake for 9 minutes at 400°F and open the lid. 5. Take out, serve and enjoy!

Nutritional Information Per Serving: Calories: 326; Fat: 29.9g; Carbs: 2g; Protein: 15g

Ninja Foodi Broccoli Pancakes

Prep Time: 5 minutes | Cook Time: 20 minutes | Serves: 2

Ingredients:

¼ cup chopped broccoli
¼ cup low-fat cheddar cheese, shredded
½ tsp dried onion, minced
1 egg
½ tsp garlic powder
Salt and black pepper, to taste

Directions:

1. Add everything in a food processor and pulse until a smooth mixture is formed. 2. Pour the mixture in the Ninja Foodi cooking pot. Close the Ninja Foodi with Crisping Lid and select "Bake/Roast". 3. Bake for about 20 minutes at 400°F and open the lid. 4. Take out and serve hot.

Nutritional Information Per Serving: Calories: 95; Fat: 6.9g; Carbs: 1.7g; Protein: 6.8g

Ninja Foodi Pancakes

Prep Time: 10 minutes | Cook Time: 25 minutes | Serves: 2

Ingredients:

¼ cup fat-free milk
½ tbsp canola oil
¼ tsp ground nutmeg
¼ cup all-purpose flour
1 egg
2 tbsp sugar

Directions:

1. Add milk, ground nutmeg, all-purpose flour, egg and sugar in a large bowl. Whisk properly. 2. Pour egg mixture in the Ninja Foodi cooking pot and close the unit with Crisping Lid. 3. Select the unit on Bake/Roast function. 4. Bake for 20 minutes at 400°F and open the Crisping Lid. 5. Take out, serve and enjoy!

Nutritional Information Per Serving: Calories: 177; Fat: 5.9g; Carbs: 25.7g; Protein: 5.4g

Egg Bites

Prep Time: 8 minutes | Cook Time: 12-15 minutes | Serves: 2

Ingredients:

3 egg whites
½ cup whipping cream
¼ tsp salt
½ cup chopped mushrooms
½ cup tomatoes
¼ cup green onions
1 tbsp cheddar cheese
Water per requirement

Directions:

1. Take a container and whisk eggs, cream (heavy), salt, and pepper together well. 2. Add up the remaining ingredients and again mix well. 3. Prepare the mold and spray with olive oil or use any greased baking tray. 4. Fill half of the mold with the mixture. Place its cover. 5. Place the Ninja Foodi deluxe reversible rack in the Low position. Put the covered mold onto the rack. In the Ninja Foodi cooking pot, add 2 cups of water. Place covered mold on the rack. 6. Set the timer of the Steam option to 12 minutes. 7. Once ready, pop-out the egg bites of the mold!

Nutritional Information Per Serving: Calories: 140; Fat: 9.3g; Carbs: 2.5g; Protein: 3.8g

Breakfast Oats Bowl

Prep Time: 3 minutes | Cook Time: 8 minutes | Serves: 2

Ingredients:

1 cup oats
1.5 cup milk
Optional Toppings:
Flax seeds
Honey

1.5 tsp ground cinnamon powder
Water as required

Granola mix

Directions:

1. Add all the ingredients in the Ninja Foodi cooking pot. 2. Oats should be fully submerged in water. Secure the pressure lid and turn the valve to Seal. Set the Ninja Foodi to High Pressure for 5 minutes. 3. After 5 minutes turn the valve off and let the oats sit for about 5 minutes after being fully cooked and all pressure to release. 4. Serve with your favorite toppings!

Nutritional Information Per Serving: Calories: 162; Fat: 4.8g; Carbs: 12g; Protein: 9.3g

Chapter 2 Snack and Appetizer Recipes

24	Breadsticks	30	Air Crisped Chicken Nuggets
24	Avocado Deviled Eggs	30	Garlic Pretzels with Ranch Dressing
24	Zucchini Muffins	30	Ninja Foodi Herb Crackers
25	Japanese Eggs	31	Chicken Wings
25	Dried Tomatoes	31	Coated Onion Rings
25	Zucchini Egg Tots	31	Buttery Potatoes
26	Parmesan Breadsticks	32	Cheese Stuffed Dates
26	Ninja Foodi Cheddar Biscuits	32	Garlicky Tomato
26	Ninja Foodi Cod Sticks	32	Cashew Cream
27	Ninja Foodi Spicy Popcorns	33	Pork Shank
27	Ninja Foodi Popcorn	33	Roasted Chickpeas
27	Ninja Foodi Spinach Chips	33	Instant Cheesy Broccoli
28	Ninja Foodi Spiced Almonds	34	Tortilla Crackers
28	Ninja Foodi Spicy Cashews	34	Herbed Cauliflower Fritters
28	Ninja Foodi Chickpea Crackers	34	Nutmeg Peanuts
29	Ninja Foodi Lemon Scones	35	Ninja Foodi Spicy Peanuts
29	Loaded Zucchini Chips	35	Ninja Foodi Banana Cookies
29	Buffalo Cauliflower Platter		

Breadsticks

Prep Time: 25 minutes | Cook Time: 10 minutes | Serves: 8

Ingredients:

1 tsp baking powder
½ tsp erythritol
½ tsp salt
1 cup warm water
2 cups almond flour

5 oz parmesan, grated
1 tbsp olive oil
1 tsp onion powder
1 tsp basil

Directions:

1. Combine the baking powder, erythritol, and warm water in a mixing bowl. 2. Stir the mixture well. Add the almond flour, onion powder, salt, and basil. 3. Knead the dough until smooth. 4. Separate the dough into 10 pieces to make long logs. Twist the logs into braids. 5. Preheat the Ninja Foodi on Bake/Roast mode for 10 minutes at 325°F. 6. Place the twisted logs into the cooking pot of the Ninja Foodi. 7. Sprinkle the logs with the grated parmesan cheese and the olive oil, and close the lid. 8. Bake the breadsticks on Bake/Roast mode for 15 minutes at 325°F. 9. Leave the breadsticks for 10 minutes to rest.

Nutritional Information Per Serving: Calories: 242; Fat: 18.9g; Carbs: 2.7g; Protein: 11.7g

Avocado Deviled Eggs

Prep Time: 10 minutes | Cook Time: 5 minutes | Serves: 6

Ingredients:

6 eggs
1 avocado, peeled
1 tbsp cream

½ tsp minced garlic
1 cup water for cooking

Directions:

1. Place the eggs in the Ninja Foodi cooking pot and add water. Close and seal with Pressure Lid. Turn the pressure release valve to SEAL position. Select the unit on Pressure Cook function. 2. Cook the eggs on High-pressure mode for 5 minutes. 3. Then use natural pressure release for 5 minutes more. 4. After this, blend together avocado, minced garlic, and cream. 5. Once the mixture is smooth, transfer to the mixing bowl. 6. Peel the cooked eggs and cut them into halves. 7. Remove the eggs yolks and transfer them to the avocado mixture. 8. Fill the boiled egg whites with the avocado mixture. 9. Serve.

Nutritional Information Per Serving: Calories: 133; Fat: 11g; Carbs: 3.4g; Protein: 6.2g

Zucchini Muffins

Prep Time: 15 minutes | Cook Time: 15 minutes | Serves: 6

Ingredients:

1 cup coconut flour
1 medium zucchini, finely chopped
1 tsp baking soda
1 tbsp lemon juice
½ tsp salt

½ tsp black pepper
1 tbsp butter
⅓ cup of coconut milk
1 tsp poppy seeds
2 tbsp flax meal

Directions:

1. Place the chopped zucchini in a blender and mix until smooth. 2. Combine the salt, baking soda, lemon juice, poppy seeds, coconut flour, butter, black pepper, and flax meal together. 3. Add the milk and blended zucchini. 4. Knead the dough until smooth. It can be a little bit sticky. 5. Place the muffins in the muffin's tins and transfer the zucchini muffins in the Ninja Foodi cooking pot. 6. Cook the muffins on the" Steam" mode for 15 minutes. 7. Once done, check if the dish is done using a toothpick. 8. If the muffins are cooked, remove them from the Ninja Foodi cooking pot and serve.

Nutritional Information Per Serving: Calories: 146; Fat: 8.9g; Carbs: 13.5g; Protein: 4g

Japanese Eggs

Prep Time: 30 minutes | Cook Time: 20 minutes | Serves: 4

Ingredients:

1 cup Chinese master stock
4 eggs
1 tsp salt

Directions:

1. Pour the Chinese master stock in the Ninja Foodi cooking pot and close the Ninja Foodi with Pressure Lid. 2. Cook the liquid on the "Pressure Cook" mode for 10 minutes at LO. 3. Remove the Chinese master stock from the Ninja Foodi cooking pot and chill it. 4. Meanwhile, place the eggs in the Ninja Foodi cooking pot. 5 Add water and boil the eggs on the "Pressure Cook" mode for 10 minutes. 6. Once eggs are done, remove from the Ninja Foodi's insert and chill well. 7. Peel the eggs and place them in the Chinese master stock. 8. Leave the eggs in the liquid for 20 minutes. 9. Remove the eggs from the liquid. Cut the eggs into halves.

Nutritional Information Per Serving: Calories: 134; Fat: 9.7g; Carbs: 2.01g; Protein: 9g

Dried Tomatoes

Prep Time: 5 minutes | Cook Time: 8 hours | Serves: 8

Ingredients:

5 medium tomatoes
1 tbsp basil
1 tsp cilantro, chopped
1 tbsp onion powder
5 tbsp olive oil
1 tsp paprika

Directions:

1. Wash the tomatoes and slice them. 2. Combine the cilantro, basil, and paprika together and stir well. 3. Place the sliced tomatoes in the Ninja Foodi cooking pot and sprinkle them with the spice mixture. 4. Add olive oil and close the unit with Pressure Lid. Turn the pressure release valve to SEAL position. Cook the dish on the "Slow Cook" mode for 8 hours at LO. 5. Once done, the tomatoes should be semi-dry. 6. Remove them from the Ninja Foodi. 7. Serve the dish warm or keep it in the refrigerator.

Nutritional Information Per Serving: Calories: 92; Fat: 8.6g; Carbs: 3.84g; Protein: 1g

Zucchini Egg Tots

Prep Time: 15 minutes | Cook Time: 9 minutes | Serves: 8

Ingredients:

2 medium zucchinis
1 egg
1 tsp salt
½ tsp baking soda
1 tsp lemon juice
1 tsp basil
1 tbsp oregano
⅓ cup oatmeal flour
1 tbsp olive oil
1 tsp minced garlic
1 tbsp butter

Directions:

1. Wash the zucchini and grate it. Beat the egg in a suitable mixing bowl and blend it using a whisk. 2. Add the baking soda, lemon juice, basil, oregano, and flour to the egg mixture. 3. Stir it carefully until smooth. Combine the grated zucchini and egg mixture together. 4. Knead the dough until smooth. Mix olive oil with minced garlic together. 5. Set the Ninja Foodi's insert to "Sear/Sauté" mode. 6. Add butter and transfer the mixture to the Ninja Foodi cooking pot. Melt the mixture. 7. Make the small tots from the zucchini dough and place them in the melted butter mixture. 8. Sauté the dish at MD for 3 minutes on each side. 9. Once the zucchini tots are cooked, remove them from the Ninja Foodi cooking pot and serve.

Nutritional Information Per Serving: Calories: 64; Fat: 4.4g; Carbs: 4.35g; Protein: 2g

Parmesan Breadsticks

Prep Time: 25 minutes | Cook Time: 10 minutes | Serves: 8

Ingredients:

1 tsp baking powder
½ tsp erythritol
½ tsp salt
1 cup warm water
2 cups almond flour
5 ounces Parmesan
1 tbsp olive oil
1 tsp onion powder
1 tsp basil

Directions:

1. Combine the baking powder, erythritol, and warm water in a mixing bowl. 2. Stir the mixture well. Add the almond flour, onion powder, salt, and basil. 3. Knead the dough until smooth. Separate dough into 10 pieces and make the long logs. 4. Twist the logs in braids. Grate the Parmesan cheese. 5. Place the twisted logs in the Ninja Foodi. 6. Sprinkle the grated Parmesan cheese and olive oil, and close the Ninja Foodi with Pressure Lid. Turn the pressure release valve to SEAL position. 7. Cook the breadsticks at the "Pressure Cook" mode for 10 minutes at LO. 8. Release the pressure and remove the lid. 9. Leave the breadsticks for 10 minutes to rest. 10. Serve the breadsticks immediately or keep them in a sealed container.

Nutritional Information Per Serving: Calories: 242; Fat: 18.9g; Carbs: 2.7g; Protein: 11.7g

Ninja Foodi Cheddar Biscuits

Prep Time: 10 minutes | Cook Time: 15 minutes | Serves: 8

Ingredients:

¼ tsp baking powder
¼ cup butter
¼ tsp ginger powder
¼ tsp garlic powder
4 eggs
¼ cup coconut flour, sifted
1 cup cheddar cheese
Salt, to taste

Directions:

1. Add flour, baking powder, garlic powder, and salt in a large bowl. Mix well. 2. Now, add butter and eggs in another bowl. Whisk well. 3. Combine the two mixtures and mix properly. Set aside. 4. Place the batter in Ninja Foodi. Close the unit with Crisping Lid and select the "Bake/Roast" function. 5. Bake for 15-minutes at 400°F and open the lid. 6. Take out, serve and enjoy!

Nutritional Information Per Serving: Calories: 155; Fat: 13g; Carbs: 3g; Protein: 6.9g

Ninja Foodi Cod Sticks

Prep Time: 10 minutes | Cook Time: 15 minutes | Serves: 8

Ingredients:

1 cup almond flour
2 eggs
1 cod fillet, thinly sliced
2 tsp dried parsley, crushed
½ tsp cayenne pepper
Salt and black pepper, to taste

Directions:

1. Add eggs in one bowl and all the other ingredients except cod slices in another bowl. Mix well. 2. Dip cod slices first in egg mixture and then in the other mixture. Set aside. 3. Arrange cod slices in Ninja Foodi cooking pot and close the unit with Crisping Lid. Select the unit on "Bake/Roast" function. 4. Bake for 6 minutes on each side at 350°F and open the lid. 5. Take out, serve and enjoy!

Nutritional Information Per Serving: Calories: 111; Fat: 7.9g; Carbs: 3.2g; Protein: 6.9g

Ninja Foodi Spicy Popcorns

Prep Time: 10 minutes | Cook Time: 5 minutes | Serves: 6

Ingredients:

1 cup popping corns
2 tsp ground turmeric
½ tsp garlic powder
6 tbsp olive oil
Salt, to taste

Directions:

1. Heat 4 tbsp of olive oil in the Ninja Foodi cooking pot and add popping corns in it. 2. Close the unit with Pressure Lid and turn the pressure release valve to SEAL position. Select the unit on Pressure Cook function. 3. Pressure cook for about 5 minutes at HI. 4. Take out and set aside. 5. Meanwhile, add remaining olive oil, turmeric, garlic powder, and salt in a bowl. Mix well. 6. Pour the mixture on popcorns and toss to coat well. 7. Serve and enjoy!
Nutritional Information Per Serving: Calories: 143; Fat: 14.1g; Carbs: 5.3g; Protein: 0.3g

Ninja Foodi Popcorn

Prep Time: 5 minutes | Cook Time: 10 minutes | Serves: 14

Ingredients:

3 tbsp oil, whatever kind you like
½ cup popcorn kernels
½ tsp salt
4 tbsp butter, salted and room temp

Directions:

1. Measure out a piece of foil that is 4" larger than the diameter of the Ninja Foodi cooking pot and wide enough to be able to fold into a pouch. Tuck the ends under the lip of the cooking pot and make multiple holes with a thin sharp object. I used the pointy end of my cake tester. You don't want the holes too big or the butter will just pour out in places. 2. Add 3 tbsp of oil to the cooking pot and half cup of popped corn kernel. Turn the Ninja Foodi on High Sear/Sauté and cover with Pressure Lid and turn Vent. 3. While you are waiting for the kernel to pop, cut or spread your butter on the foil. 4. When you hear the kernel pop, add in the remaining unpopped kernels and the salt. Stir to combine. 5. Close the foil packet and secure by tucking under the lid of the cooking pot. Cover with Pressure Lid. Leave the Sear/Sauté on HI until to begin to hear the kernels rapidly popping (less than one second between pops), turn the heat down to Medium/Low. Insert a spatula or wooden spoon and stir the bottom to move the kernels around. 6. Once the popping has slowed down to about one pop every few seconds, turn the Ninja Foodi off and stir again. If there is any butter left in the foil, shake it over the popcorn and stir. 7. Serve and enjoy!
Nutritional Information Per Serving: Calories: 78; Fat: 7g; Carbs: 4g; Protein: 1g

Ninja Foodi Spinach Chips

Prep Time: 12 minutes | Cook Time: 10 minutes | Serves: 4

Ingredients:

½ tsp paprika
¼ tsp ground cumin
¼ tsp olive oil
2 cups fresh spinach leaves
Salt, to taste

Directions:

1. Add everything in a large bowl and mix well. Set aside. 2. Place spinach leaves in Ninja Foodi cooking pot. Close the unit with Crisping Lid and select the unit on Bake/Roast function. 3. Bake for about 10 minutes at 325°F and open the lid. 4. Take out, serve and enjoy!
Nutritional Information Per Serving: Calories: 7; Fat: 0.4g; Carbs: 0.7g; Protein: 0.5g

Ninja Foodi Spiced Almonds

Prep Time: 10 minutes | Cook Time: 14 minutes | Serves: 6

Ingredients:

2 tbsp unsweetened applesauce
1 cup almonds
¼ tsp cayenne pepper
¼ tsp ground cumin
½ tsp olive oil
½ tbsp water
¼ tsp ground cinnamon
¼ tsp red chili powder
Salt, to taste

Directions:

1. Arrange almonds in Ninja Foodi cooking pot. Close the unit with Crisping Lid and select the unit on "Bake/Roast". 2. Bake for about 10 minutes at 350°F and open the lid. 3. Take out and set aside. 4. Meanwhile, add oil, water, and applesauce in a bowl. Mix well. 5. Add in almonds and toss to coat well. 6. Add cinnamon, ground cumin, red chili powder, cayenne pepper, and salt in another bowl. Mix well. 7. Arrange almonds again in the Ninja Foodi cooking pot and top them with cinnamon mixture. 8. Bake them for about 4 minutes at 350°F and open the lid. 9. Take out, serve and enjoy!

Nutritional Information Per Serving: Calories: 98; Fat: 8.4g; Carbs: 4.2g; Protein: 3.4g

Ninja Foodi Spicy Cashews

Prep Time: 10 minutes | Cook Time: 2 hours 45 minutes | Serves: 12

Ingredients:

2½ cups cashews
3 tbsp chili seasoning mix
1½ tbsp butter

Directions:

1. Add everything in the Ninja Foodi cooking pot and mix well. 2. Close the unit with Pressure Lid and turn the pressure release valve to VENT position. Select "Slow Cook". 3. Pressure cook for about 2 hours and 30 minutes on LO. 4. Open the lid and cook for 15 more minutes. 5. Take out, serve and enjoy!
Serving Suggestions: Top with red chili powder before serving.
Variation Tip: You can add cayenne pepper for a stronger taste.
Nutritional Information Per Serving: Calories: 741; Fat: 61.2g; Carbs: 40.2g; Protein: 18.6g

Ninja Foodi Chickpea Crackers

Prep Time: 15 minutes | Cook Time: 20 minutes | Serves: 5

Ingredients:

½ cup chickpea flour
1 tbsp yeast
¼ cup water
¼ tsp sesame oil
¼ tsp baking powder
1 tsp toasted sesame seeds
¼ tsp turmeric
Salt, to taste

Directions:

1. Add baking powder, chickpea flour, sesame seeds, yeast, salt and turmeric in a bowl. Mix well. 2. Add water and oil gradually in the mixture and mix until proper dough is formed. 3. Cover the dough and set aside till the dough rises. 4. Make square shapes out of the dough and place them in Ninja Foodi cooking pot. 5. Close the unit with Crisping Lid and select the unit on Bake/Roast function. 6. Bake for about 20 minutes at 350°F. 7. Open the Crisping Lid and take out. 8. Serve and enjoy!
Nutritional Information Per Serving: Calories: 86; Fat: 1.9g; Carbs: 13.4g; Protein: 4.9g

Ninja Foodi Lemon Scones

Prep Time: 10 minutes | Cook Time: 25 minutes | Serves: 3

Ingredients:

- ¾ cup all-purpose flour
- ¼ cup unsweetened soymilk
- 2 tbsp sugar
- ½ tsp lemon extract
- ½ tbsp sunflower oil
- ½ tbsp baking powder
- Salt, to taste

Directions:

1. Add wet ingredients in one bowl and dry ingredients in another. Mix well. 2. Combine the two mixtures and mix until dough is formed. 3. Make spheres out of the mixture and press them with tortilla press. 4. Make triangular shapes out of the dough and place them in Ninja Foodi cooking pot. 5. Close the unit with Crisping Lid and select the unit on Bake/Roast function. 6. Bake for 15 minutes at 400°F. 7. Open the Crisping Lid and take out. 8. Serve and enjoy!

Nutritional Information Per Serving: Calories: 175; Fat: 3g; Carbs: 33.4g; Protein: 3.8g

Loaded Zucchini Chips

Prep Time: 9 minutes | Cook Time: 23-25 minutes | Serves: 6

Ingredients:

- 2 medium-sized zucchinis
- 1 cup toasted bread crumbs
- 1.2 cup grated parmesan
- ½ tsp kosher salt
- Chili powder ¼ tsp
- Black pepper to taste
- 1 beaten egg
- Oil spray

Directions:

1. Start by cutting the ends of the zucchini and then cut it into a round shape. Place a clean towel on a plate. Then place zucchini chips and sprinkle a little salt. Now place another towel on top and then a heavy pan on top. 2. Let it sit for about 12 to 15 minutes for the extra moisture to be drawn out. 3. On the other hand, mix crumbs, salt, pepper, and parmesan at the end. In a separate bowl beat the egg. Place the bowl with egg, crumb mix, and place side by side. 4. Dip the cut zucchini in the egg bowl with one of your hands, now with the other hand, coat it in the crumbs, and place it on a clean plate. At this step spray the zucchini rounds with a good amount of olive oil and let them sit for about 2 minutes. 5. Now you can either spray or brush the Ninja Foodi Cook & Crisp Basket with olive oil. 6. Make sure you place the chips in a single layer. 7. Lastly, bake the zucchini chips for 6 minutes at 375°F.

Nutritional Information Per Serving: Calories: 153; Fat: 6 g; Carbs: 11 g; Protein: 11.5 g

Buffalo Cauliflower Platter

Prep Time: 12 minutes | Cook Time: 12-17 minutes | Serves: 4

Ingredients:

- 1 medium-sized cauliflower head
- 1 cup buffalo sauce
- 1 tbsp melted butter

For Sides
- Carrot sticks
- Celery sticks
- 1 cup bread crumbs
- Salt to taste

- 2 tbsp orange dressing

Directions:

1. Cut the cauliflower into florets and place them in a mixing bowl. 2. Mix the buffalo sauce and butter in a separate bowl. 3. Now on top of the cauliflower pieces, pour the buffalo sauce. 4. Let it marinate for 15 minutes, making sure you keep stirring it from time to time. Now in another shallow dish put the bread crumbs and season it with a bit of salt. 5. Now to coat the cauliflower, dip it in the crumb mixture. 6. Place the cauliflower pieces on the Cook & Crisp Basket and make sure to not overlap them. 7. It is recommended to cook this recipe in two batches so that the cauliflower does not get overcrowded. 8. Set the Air Crisp at 390°F and let it cook for about 12 to 15 minutes. 9. Serve these cauliflower buffalo bites with optional orange dressing, carrot, and celery sticks!

Nutritional Information Per Serving: Calories: 201; Fat: 10.1g; Carbs: 18.5g; Protein: 5.8g

Air Crisped Chicken Nuggets

Prep Time: 10 minutes | Cook Time: 8-10 minutes | Serves: 6

Ingredients:

1 pound minced chicken
Salt and pepper to taste
1 tbsp olive oil
5 tbsp season bread crumbs
1 tbsp panko mix
1 tbsp parmesan cheese (grated)

Directions:

1. At 320°F, preheat the Ninja Foodi cooking pot at Air Crisp mode for 8 minutes. 2. In a bowl, add bread crumbs, panko mix, parmesan cheese, and olive oil. 3. For the seasoning, dump in salt and pepper on the chicken. 4. To ensure the olive oil is evenly coated on all the chicken, put the olive oil well if needed. 5. Shape up the small pieces of chicken that pop out of the batter. 6. Don't add too many chicken chunks at a time into the breadcrumb mixture for the coating purpose. Then place it on the Cook & Crisp Basket and give a slight olive oil spray on the top. 7. Let it Air Crisp at 320°F for 8 minutes, make sure to turn it halfway until the color is golden!

Nutrition Information per Serving: Calories: 112; Fat: 3.9g; Carbs: 5.5g; Protein: 10.4g

Garlic Pretzels with Ranch Dressing

Prep Time: 6 minutes | Cook Time: 10 minutes | Serves: 1

Ingredients:

4 oz. regular pretzels
1 packet Ranch seasoning
⅓ tsp garlic powder
1 tbsp olive oil
⅛ tsp cayenne pepper

Directions:

1. Align the Ninja Foodi Cook & Crisp Basket with aluminum foil and give it an olive oil spray. 2. In the Ninja Foodi Cook & Crisp Basket, place the pretzels and top up with the dry seasonings. 3. Now use an olive oil spray and spray a few coats of it. Then mix it up until they are fully coated at 390°F. 4. Cook in the Air Crisp mode for 3 minutes at 390°F, then open the lid and remove the pretzels carefully. Spray a little bit of olive oil and mix up very well. 5. For another 3 minutes cook again then remove the pretzels carefully or open the lid, spray a bit of olive oil and mix well. 6. Cook it for two more minutes or you can wait until the pretzels are crispy enough!

Nutrition Information per Serving: Calories: 159; Fat: 4.7g; Carbs: 17.3 g; Protein: 3.4g

Ninja Foodi Herb Crackers

Prep Time: 10 minutes | Cook Time: 20 minutes | Serves: 4

Ingredients:

½ cup almond flour
½ tbsp water
½ tbsp herbes de Provence
¼ tbsp olive oil
Salt, to taste

Directions:

1. Add herbes de Provence, salt, and almond flour in a large bowl. Mix well. 2. Add in olive oil and water. Mix until a soft dough is formed. 3. Make small spheres out of the dough and press them with a tortilla press. 4. Arrange them in the Ninja Foodi. Close the unit with Crisping Lid and select the unit on Bake/Roast function. 5. Bake for about 20 minutes at 350°F and open the Crisping Lid. 6. Take out, serve and enjoy!

Nutritional Information Per Serving: Calories: 154; Fat: 12.6g; Carbs: 3.5g; Protein: 6.8g

Chicken Wings

Prep Time: 6 minutes | Cook Time: 22 minutes | Serves: 2

Ingredients:

8 chicken medium-sized wings
2 tbsp flour
1 tbsp brown sugar
1 tbsp salt
½ tbsp garlic paste

1 tsp pepper
½ tbsp chili powder
½ tbsp paprika
1 tbsp olive oil

Directions:

1. Use paper towels to pat dry the wings. Add olive oil and spread it on all sides to coat them well. 2. Mix all dry ingredients and put them in the polythene bag. Then add the wings coated with olive oil into the bag and shake well. Now carefully place the wings inside the Ninja Foodi Cook & Crisp Basket, making sure they don't overlap each other. 3. Air Crisp them for 8 minutes in Ninja Foodi at Air Crisp mode at 390°F and then flip to the other side and continue cooking for another 8 minutes until you get the desired crispiness.
Nutritional Information Per Serving: Calories: 200; Fat: 13g; Carbs: 6g; Protein: 10.9g

Coated Onion Rings

Prep Time: 8 minutes | Cook Time: 9 minutes | Serves: 2

Ingredients:

1 large onion
2 tbsp all-purpose flour
½ tsp baking powder
¼ tsp salt

1 egg
½ cup milk
1 tsp chili powder
4 tbsp bread crumbs

Directions:

1. Start by slicing the onions into ¼ inch circular rings. The center of the onion needs to be removed. 2. Then divide the slices. Now take a large bowl and place the onion slices on it. 3. Add the flour and toss the slices making sure each piece of onion is coated well. 4. Take another bowl and whisk together the egg, milk, and baking powder. 5. Then add salt, bread crumbs, and chili powder into another bowl. 6. Now dip the coated rings into the egg mixture and then into the bread crumbs until coated well. 7. Spray the Ninja Foodi Cook & Crisp Basket with a bit of olive oil or Air Crisp parchment paper can also be used. Place the coated rings into Cook & Crisp Basket until it's full. 8. At 390°F, Air Crisp it for 7 to 8 minutes or wait until the coating is crispy!
Nutritional Information Per Serving: Calories: 142; Fat: 4.6g; Carbs: 17g; Protein: 7.9g

Buttery Potatoes

Prep Time: 5 minutes | Cook Time: 19 minutes | Serves: 2

Ingredients:

2 large potatoes
1 cup water
Salt to taste

1 tbsp butter
½ tsp oregano

Directions:

1. Start by washing the potatoes well and add with the help of a fork, brick it 5 to 6 times. 2. Pour 1 cup of water, or enough water into the Ninja Foodi cooking pot so that potatoes should not be sitting in the water, they should be raised enough. Place those potatoes onto the Ninja Foodi Cook & Crisp Basket. And place that Cook & Crisp Basket into Ninja Foodi. 3. Now close the unit with Pressure Lid. Set Ninja Foodi on Pressure Cook, cook it on HI for about 15 to 20 minutes keeping in mind the size of the potatoes. 4. Lastly, remove the lid and peel the potatoes. Mash the potatoes and add the melted butter, oregano, and salt and give it a good mix to get the butter flavor in every bite!
Nutritional Information Per Serving: Calories: 80; Fat: 6.3g; Carbs: 5.2g; Protein: 0.6g

Cheese Stuffed Dates

Prep Time: 5 minutes | Cook Time: 7 minutes | Serves: 7

Ingredients:

6 oz parmesan cheese, grated
8 oz ripe dates
1 tsp garlic, minced
1 tbsp sour cream
1 tsp butter
½ tsp ground white pepper
1 tsp oregano

Directions:

1. Remove the stones from the dates. 2. Combine the garlic, sour cream, ground white pepper, and oregano, and stir the mixture. Add in the parmesan. Blend the mixture until smooth. 3. Stuff the dates with the cheese mixture and place them in the Ninja Foodi's cooking pot. Add the butter. 4. Close the unit with Pressure Lid and turn the pressure release valve to the VENT position. Select the unit on Steam function. 5. Cook for 7 minutes. 6. When the cooking time ends, remove the dates from the Ninja Foodi, let them rest briefly, and serve.

Nutritional Information Per Serving: Calories: 203; Fat: 7.6g; Carbs: 28.3g; Protein: 8g

Garlicky Tomato

Prep Time: 10 minutes | Cook Time: 5 minutes | Serves: 5

Ingredients:

5 tomatoes
¼ cup chives, chopped
⅓ cup garlic clove, minced
½ tsp salt
½ tsp black pepper
1 tbsp olive oil
7 ounces Parmesan cheese

Directions:

1. Wash the tomatoes and slice them into thick slices. 2. Place the sliced tomatoes in the Ninja Foodi cooking pot. 3. Combine the grated cheese and minced garlic and stir the mixture. 4. Sprinkle the tomato slices with chives, black pepper, and salt. 5. Then sprinkle the sliced tomatoes with the cheese mixture. 6. Close the Ninja Foodi with Pressure Lid and cook the dish in the "Pressure Cook" mode for 5 minutes at LO. 7. Once done, remove the tomatoes carefully and serve.

Nutritional Values Per Serving: Calories: 224; Fat: 14g; Carbs: 12.55g; Protein: 13g

Cashew Cream

Prep Time: 8 minutes | Cook Time: 10 minutes | Serves: 10

Ingredients:

3 cups cashew
2 cups chicken stock
1 tsp salt
1 tbsp butter
2 tbsp ricotta cheese

Directions:

1. Combine the cashews with the chicken stock in the Ninja Foodi's insert. 2. Add salt and close the Ninja Foodi with Pressure Lid. Turn the pressure release valve to SEAL position. 3. Cook the dish in the "Pressure Cook" mode for 10 minutes at HI. 4. Remove the cashews from the Ninja Foodi's insert and drain the nuts from the water. 5. Transfer the cashews to a blender, and add the ricotta cheese and butter. 6. Blend the mixture until it is smooth. When you get the texture you want, remove it from a blender. 7. Serve it immediately, or keep the cashew butter in the refrigerator.

Nutritional Values Per Serving: Calories: 252; Fat: 20.6g; Carbs: 13.8g; Protein: 6.8 g

Pork Shank

Prep Time: 15 minutes | Cook Time: 45 minutes | Serves: 6

Ingredients:

- 1-pound pork shank
- ½ cup parsley, chopped
- 4 garlic cloves
- 1 tsp salt
- ½ tsp paprika
- 2 tbsp olive oil
- 1 tsp cilantro, chopped
- 1 tbsp celery
- 1 carrot, grated
- 1 cup of water
- 1 red onion, chopped
- ⅓ cup wine
- 2 tbsp lemon juice

Directions:

1. Chop the parsley and slice the garlic cloves. 2. Combine the vegetables together and add salt, paprika, cilantro, wine, and lemon juice and stir the mixture. 3. Combine the pork shank and marinade together and leave the mixture. 4. Combine the sliced onion and grated carrot together. 5. Add celery and blend well. Add the vegetables to the pork shank mixture and stir using your hands. 6. Place the meat in the Ninja Foodi cooking pot and add water. 7. Close the Ninja Foodi's lid, and set the Ninja Foodi to "Pressure Cook" function. 8. Cook for 45 minutes at HI. Once done, remove the meat from the Ninja Foodi's insert and chill the dish well. 9. Slice the pork shank and serve.

Nutritional Values Per Serving: Calories: 242; Fat: 19.8g; Carbs: 5.38g; Protein: 11g

Roasted Chickpeas

Prep Time: 5 minutes | Cook Time: 15 minutes | Serves: 1

Ingredients:

- 2 oz. chickpeas
- 1 tsp olive oil
- 1 packet salad dressing
- 1 tbsp seasoning mix
- 1 tbsp parmesan cheese

Directions:

1. Rinse the chickpeas, and dry them. 2. Toss in with 1 tbsp of extra virgin olive oil. 3. Now again toss with the parmesan cheese and the seasoning mix, make sure you get a nice coating. 4. Now put the chickpeas in the Ninja Foodi Cook & Crisp Basket. Close the unit with Crisping Lid. Air Crisp the chickpeas at 390°F for about 15 minutes. Make sure you toss it a couple of times. 5. Remove them from the Cook & Crisp Basket and grab them for snacking. Store in an air-tight container!

Nutritional Values Per Serving: Calories: 205; Fat: 12.7g; Carbs: 12.2g; Protein: 6.2g

Instant Cheesy Broccoli

Prep Time: 6 minutes | Cook Time: 2-3 minutes | Serves: 4

Ingredients:

- 1 broccoli head (florets)
- ½ cup chicken chunks
- 2 tbsp melted butter
- 4 tbsp parmesan cheese

Directions:

1. Pour in 1.5 cups of water in the Ninja Foodi cooking pot and then place your vegetable in Cook & Crisp Basket inside it 2. Next, wash off your broccoli well then cut it into florets. Close the lid after putting it into the Ninja Foodi Cook & Crisp Basket. Close the unit with Pressure Lid and turn the pressure release valve to VENT position. Select the unit on Steam function. Steam it for about 1 minute. 3. When cooked, dump those florets into a platter. Top up with chicken chunks. 4. Now put the melted butter and sprinkle the parmesan cheese on top and serve!

Nutritional Values Per Serving: Calories: 122; Fat: 8.7g; Carbs: 5.7g; Protein: 5.7g

Tortilla Crackers

Prep Time: 6 minutes | Cook Time: 6 minutes | Serves: 4

Ingredients:

4 small tortillas
Cooking spray
Salt per taste
1 tsp Mexican Seasoning

Directions:

1. Start by preheating your Ninja Foodi at Air Crisp mode at 390°F for 5 minutes. 2. Give the tortillas a cooking oil spray, and season them with salt to taste. Sprinkle the Mexican seasoning slightly. 3. Stack the tortillas and cut them in half. Then cut pieces once again into small triangles. Once the Air Crisp is ready, take out the Cook & Crisp Basket now and scatter the tortilla pieces. 4. Now put the basket back. 5. After 2 to 3 minutes take the basket out and gently flip the chips. 6. Put the Cook & Crisp Basket back into the Ninja Foodi and Air Crisp at 390°F for 2 more minutes, until you get the golden brown and crispy texture. 7. Cool them before serving, the reason being they will become crispier as they cool down!

Nutritional Values Per Serving: Calories: 65; Fat: 10.5g; Carbs: 10.3g; Protein: 1g

Herbed Cauliflower Fritters

Prep Time: 15 minutes | Cook Time: 13 minutes | Serves: 7

Ingredients:

1-pound cauliflower
1 medium white onion
1 tsp salt
½ tsp ground white pepper
1 tbsp sour cream
1 tsp turmeric
½ cup dill, chopped
1 tsp thyme
3 tbsp almond flour
1 egg
2 tbsp butter

Directions:

1. Wash the cauliflower and separate it into the florets. 2. Chop the florets and place them in a blender. 3. Peel the onion and dice it. Add the diced onion to a blender and blend the mixture. 4. When you get the smooth texture, add salt, ground white pepper, sour cream, turmeric, dill, thyme, and almond flour. 5. Add egg blend the mixture well until a smooth dough form. 6. Remove the cauliflower dough from a blender and form the medium balls. 7. Flatten the balls a little. Set the Ninja Foodi to "Sear/Sauté" mode. 8. Add the butter to the Ninja Foodi cooking pot and melt it. 9. Add the cauliflower fritters in the Ninja Foodi cooking pot, and sauté them for 6 minutes. 10. Flip them once. Cook the dish in "Sear/Sauté" mode for 7 minutes. 11. Once done, remove the fritters from the Ninja Foodi's insert. 12. Serve immediately.

Nutritional Values Per Serving: Calories: 143; Fat: 10.6g; Carbs: 9.9g; Protein: 5.6g

Nutmeg Peanuts

Prep Time: 5 minutes | Cook Time: 1.5 hour | Serves: 8

Ingredients:

3 cups peanuts in shells
1 tbsp salt
4 cups water
½ tsp nutmeg

Directions:

1. Combine the water, nutmeg, and salt together. 2. Stir the mixture well until salt is dissolved. 3. Transfer the water in the Ninja Foodi cooking pot. 4. Add peanuts in shells and close the Ninja Foodi cooking pot. 5. Cook the dish on the "Pressure Cook" mode for 90 minutes at Lo. 6. Once done, remove the peanuts from the Ninja Foodi cooking pot. 7. Let the peanuts cool before serving.

Nutritional Values Per Serving: Calories: 562; Fat: 36.8g; Carbs: 8.57g; Protein: 28g

Ninja Foodi Spicy Peanuts

Prep Time: 5 minutes | Cook Time: 2 hours 45 minutes | Serves: 6

Ingredients:

¾ cups peanuts
1½ tbsp chili seasoning mix
½ tbsp butter

Directions:

1. Add peanuts, chili seasoning mix, and butter in the Ninja Foodi cooking pot. Mix well. Close the unit with Pressure Lid and turn the pressure release valve to the VENT position. 2. Select "Slow Cook". 3. Slow cook for about 2 hours and 30 minutes at Lo. Stir after every 30 minutes. 4. Open the lid and cook for 15 minutes. 5. Take out, serve and enjoy!

Nutritional Values Per Serving: Calories: 134; Fat: 11.1g; Carbs: 6.7g; Protein: 5.6g

Ninja Foodi Banana Cookies

Prep Time: 15 minutes | Cook Time: 20 minutes | Serves: 7

Ingredients:

1 banana, mashed
¼ cup soymilk
½ tbsp canola oil
¼ tbsp baking powder
1 cup white flour

Directions:

1. Add mashed bananas, oil, and soymilk in a bowl. Mix well. 2. Add in flour and baking powder. Stir properly. 3. Knead the dough and roll it with the help of a rolling pin. 4. Cut the dough into circles and place them in Ninja Foodi cooking pot. 5. Close the Crisping Lid and choose the "Bake/Roast" function. 6. Bake for about 20 minutes at 400°F. 7. Open the lid and take out. 8. Serve and enjoy!

Nutritional Values Per Serving: Calories: 94; Fat: 1.4g; Carbs: 18.3g; Protein: 2.3g

Chapter 3 Chicken and Poultry Recipes

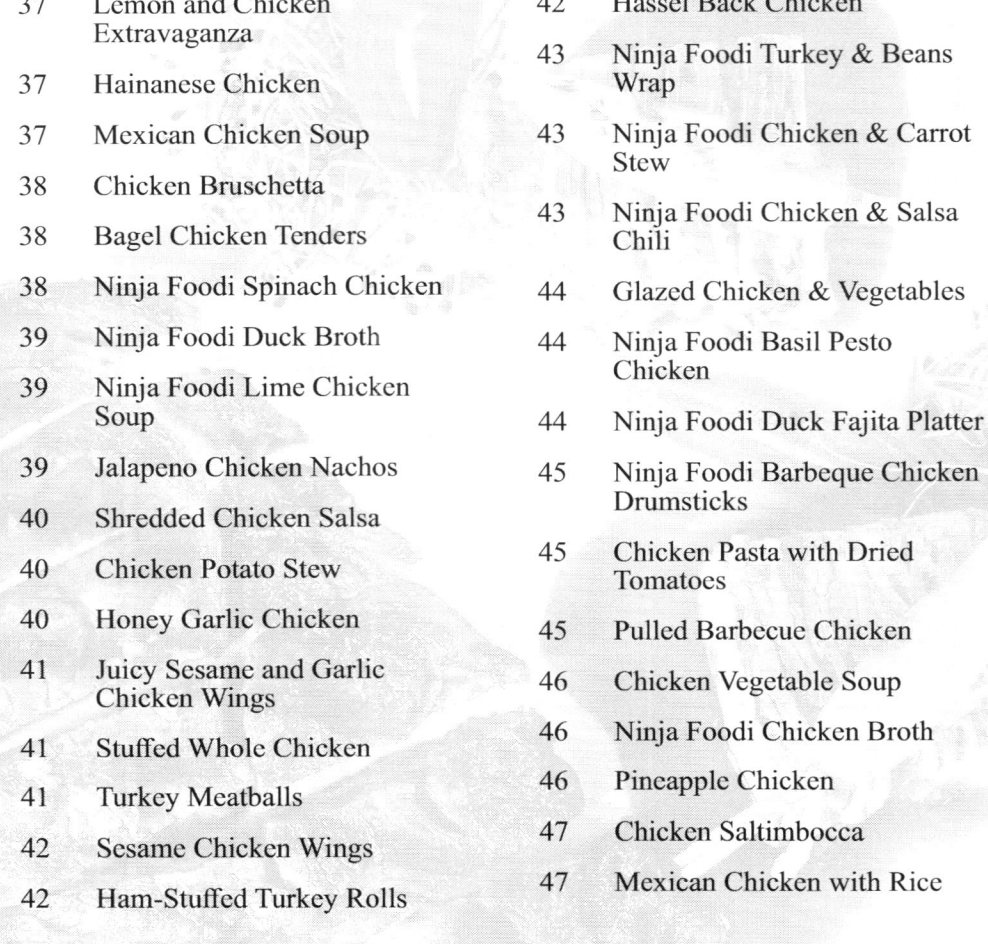

37	Lemon and Chicken Extravaganza	42	Hassel Back Chicken
37	Hainanese Chicken	43	Ninja Foodi Turkey & Beans Wrap
37	Mexican Chicken Soup	43	Ninja Foodi Chicken & Carrot Stew
38	Chicken Bruschetta	43	Ninja Foodi Chicken & Salsa Chili
38	Bagel Chicken Tenders	44	Glazed Chicken & Vegetables
38	Ninja Foodi Spinach Chicken	44	Ninja Foodi Basil Pesto Chicken
39	Ninja Foodi Duck Broth	44	Ninja Foodi Duck Fajita Platter
39	Ninja Foodi Lime Chicken Soup	45	Ninja Foodi Barbeque Chicken Drumsticks
39	Jalapeno Chicken Nachos	45	Chicken Pasta with Dried Tomatoes
40	Shredded Chicken Salsa	45	Pulled Barbecue Chicken
40	Chicken Potato Stew	46	Chicken Vegetable Soup
40	Honey Garlic Chicken	46	Ninja Foodi Chicken Broth
41	Juicy Sesame and Garlic Chicken Wings	46	Pineapple Chicken
41	Stuffed Whole Chicken	47	Chicken Saltimbocca
41	Turkey Meatballs	47	Mexican Chicken with Rice
42	Sesame Chicken Wings		
42	Ham-Stuffed Turkey Rolls		

Lemon and Chicken Extravaganza

Prep Time: 5 minutes | Cook Time: 18 minutes | Serves: 4

Ingredients:

4 bone-in, skin-on chicken thighs
Salt and pepper, to taste
2 tbsp butter, divided
2 tsp garlic, minced

½ cup herbed chicken stock
½ cup heavy whip cream
½ lemon, juiced

Directions:

1. Season the chicken thighs generously with salt and pepper. 2. Set the Ninja Foodi to Sear/Sauté mode on MD: HI temperature setting, add the oil to the cooking pot, and let it heat up. 3. Add the thighs. Sauté both sides for 6 minutes. 4. Remove the thighs, place them on a platter and keep it to one side. 5. Add the garlic to the cooking pot and sauté for 2 minutes. 6. Whisk in the chicken stock, heavy cream, and lemon juice, and gently stir. 7. Bring the mix to a simmer and reintroduce the chicken thighs. 8. Put on the Pressure Lid, turn the pressure release valve to the SEAL position, select PRESSURE mode, and cook for 10 minutes on HI. 9. Release the pressure over 10 minutes. 10. Serve and enjoy!
Nutritional Information Per Serving: Calories: 294; Fat: 26g; Carbs: 4g; Protein: 12g

Hainanese Chicken

Prep Time: 20 minutes | Cook Time: 4 hours | Serves: 4

Ingredients:

1 oz ginger, peeled
6 garlic cloves, crushed
6 bundles cilantro/basil leaves
For Dip
2 tbsp ginger, minced
1 tsp garlic, minced
1 tbsp chicken stock

1 tsp salt
1 tbsp sesame oil
3 (1½ lb. each) chicken meat, ready to cook

1 tsp sesame oil
½ tsp erythritol
Salt to taste

Directions:

1. Add chicken, garlic, ginger, leaves, and salt to your Ninja Food. 2. Add enough water to fully submerge chicken; Lock and secure the Ninja Foodi's lid cooks on SLOW COOK mode on LO for 4 hours. 3. Release pressure naturally. 4. Take chicken out of the pot and chill for 10 minutes. 5. Take a suitable bowl and add all the dipping ingredients and blend well in a food processor. 6. Take chicken out of ice bath and drain, chop into serving pieces. 7. Set onto a serving platter. 8. Brush chicken with sesame oil. 9. Serve with ginger dip. 10. Enjoy.
Nutrition Values Per Serving: Calories: 535; Fat: 45g; Carbs: 5g; Protein: 28g

Mexican Chicken Soup

Prep Time: 5 minutes | Cook Time: 20 minutes | Serves: 4

Ingredients:

2 cups chicken, shredded
4 tbsp olive oil
½ cup cilantro, chopped
8 cups chicken broth
⅓ cup salsa
1 tsp onion powder
½ cup scallions, chopped

4 ounces green chilies, chopped
½ tsp habanero, minced
1 cup celery root, chopped
1 tsp cumin
1 tsp garlic powder
Black pepper and salt to taste

Directions:

1. Add all ingredients to Ninja Foodi. 2. Stir, close the unit with Pressure Lid, turn the pressure release valve to SEAL position, and cook on Pressure Cook mode at HI for 10 minutes. 3. Release pressure naturally over 10 minutes. 4. Serve and enjoy.
Nutrition Values Per Serving: Calories: 204; Fat: 14g; Carbs: 4g; Protein: 14g

Chicken Bruschetta

Prep Time: 5 minutes | Cook Time: 9 minutes | Serves: 4

Ingredients:

- 2 tbsp balsamic vinegar
- ⅓ cup olive oil
- 2 tsp garlic cloves, minced
- 1 tsp black pepper
- ½ tsp salt
- ½ cup sun-dried tomatoes, in olive oil
- 2 pounds chicken breasts, quartered, boneless
- 2 tbsp fresh basil, chopped

Directions:

1. Take a suitable bowl and whisk in vinegar, oil, garlic, pepper, and salt. 2. Fold in tomatoes, basil, and breast; mix well. 3. Transfer to fridge and let it sit for 30 minutes. 4. Add everything to Ninja Foodi. Close the unit with Pressure Lid, turn the pressure release valve to SEAL position. 5. Pressure cook at HI for 9 minutes. 6. Quick-release pressure. 7. Serve and enjoy.

Nutrition Values Per Serving: Calories: 480; Fat: 26g; Carbs: 4g; Protein: 52g

Bagel Chicken Tenders

Prep Time: 8 minutes | Cook Time: 15-20 minutes | Serves: 2

Ingredients:

- 6-8 chicken tenders
- ½ cup bread crumbs/ pork rind crumbs
- 2 tbsp bagel seasoning
- 1 egg

Directions:

1. Start by washing the chicken breasts and cut them into tenders. You can also buy chicken tenderloins. 2. Now take two bowls and add eggs to one and bread crumb mixture to the other. Add bagel seasoning to the bread crumbs and mix it well. 3. Prepare one tender at a time by first coating it with an egg then rolling it in the crumb mixture. 4. Air Crisp it in the Ninja Foodi by selecting Air Crisp Mode at 390°F for 20 minutes in a single layer.

Nutritional Values Per Serving: Calories: 433; Fat: 6.3g; Carbs: 15.9g; Protein: 44.3g

Ninja Foodi Spinach Chicken

Prep Time: 10 minutes | Cook Time: 10 minutes | Serves: 4

Ingredients:

- 1 pound chicken tenders
- 2 tbsp sour cream
- 2 garlic cloves, minced
- 1¼ cups chopped spinach
- 2 tbsp olive oil
- ¼ cup parmesan cheese, shredded
- Salt and black pepper, to taste

Directions:

1. Heat half of the olive oil in the Ninja Foodi D and add chicken, salt, and pepper in it. 2. Close the unit with Pressure Lid and turn the pressure release valve to SEAL position. Select the unit on Pressure Cook mode. 3. Cook for about 2-minutes per side at HI and take out the chicken. Set aside. 4. Add remaining oil in the Ninja Foodi cooking pot and sauté garlic in it for about 1 minute. 5. Add spinach, cream, and cheese in the skillet and cook for about 2 minutes. 6. Place chicken in the Ninja Foodi cooking pot and simmer for about 5 minutes. 7. Take out and serve hot.

Serving Suggestions: Serve with onion rings on the top.

Variation Tip: Mozzarella cheese can also be used.

Nutritional Values Per Serving: Calories: 301; Fat: 17.1g; Carbs: 1.6g; Protein: 34.3g

Ninja Foodi Duck Broth

Prep Time: 10 minutes | Cook Time: 8 hours | Serves: 16

Ingredients:

1 roasted duck, meat removed
2 tsp apple cider vinegar
8 cups water
2 carrots, chopped
2 onions, chopped
Salt, to taste

Directions:

1. Add duck bones in a Ninja Foodi and sprinkle some salt on it. 2. Add in remaining ingredients. Close the unit with Pressure Lid and turn the pressure release valve to VENT position. Select "Slow Cook". 3. Slow cook for 8 hours at LO and open the lid. 4. Take out the broth and serve.
Nutritional Values Per Serving: Calories: 21; Fat: 0.7g; Carbs: 2g; Protein: 1.8g

Ninja Foodi Lime Chicken Soup

Prep Time: 10 minutes | Cook Time: 8 hours | Serves: 5

Ingredients:

¼ cup fresh lime juice
4 garlic cloves, minced
½ tsp oregano
1 onion, chopped
4 cups chicken broth
2 cups boneless chicken, cubed
1 tomato, chopped
½ tsp red chili powder
¾ cup chopped mushrooms
½ tsp ground cumin
Salt and black pepper, to taste

Directions:

1. Add everything in Ninja Foodi cooking pot. 2. Close the unit with Pressure Lid, turn the pressure release valve to SEAL position. Then select "Slow Cook". 3. Slow cook the chicken soup at LO for about 8 hours. When cooked, open the lid. 4. Take out the chicken cubes and shred them properly. 5. Stir the shredded chicken in the cooking pot and take out. 6. Serve and enjoy!
Nutritional Values Per Serving: Calories: 157; Fat: 5.4g; Carbs: 4.9g; Protein: 21g

Jalapeno Chicken Nachos

Prep Time: 8-9 minutes | Cook Time: 8-9 minutes | Serves: 2

Ingredients:

1 cup tortillas chips
1 pound minced chicken
¼ cup BBQ sauce
Salt to taste
½ cup chicken broth
½ cup cheddar cheese
½ corn
2 tbsp chopped olives
½ cup sliced jalapeno
1 coarsely cut onion
Coriander to garnish

Directions:

1. Add the chicken, broth, and salt to the Ninja Foodi cooking pot. For 8 minutes, Pressure Cook it on HI and releases the pressure when finished quickly. 2. Stir in BBQ sauce after draining the liquid. 3. At 390°F, preheat the Ninja Foodi on Air Crisp Mode. Take Cook & Crisp Basket and align the parchment paper. 4. Place tortilla chips on the base. Now give a layer of shredder BBQ chicken and corn and top it off with cheddar cheese evenly. 5. For about 5 to 10 minutes place it in the Ninja Foodi and wait until cheese is melted. Then add olives, onions, and jalapenos slice to the desired amount. Follow it by adding fresh coriander!
Nutritional Values Per Serving: Calories: 550; Fat: 25.5g; Carbs: 29.7g; Protein: 55g

Shredded Chicken Salsa

Prep Time: 5 minutes | Cook Time: 20 minutes | Serves: 4

Ingredients:

- 1-pound chicken breast, boneless
- ¾ tsp cumin
- ½ tsp salt
- Pinch of oregano
- Pepper to taste
- 1 cup chunky salsa

Directions:

1. Season chicken with spices and add to Ninja Foodi. 2. Cover with salsa. Close the unit with Pressure Lid and select unit on Pressure Cook mode. 3. Pressure cook at HI for 20 minutes. 4. Quick-release pressure. 5. Add chicken to a platter and shred the chicken. 6. Serve and enjoy.

Nutrition Values Per Serving: Calories: 125; Fat: 3g; Carbs: 2g; Protein: 22g

Chicken Potato Stew

Prep Time: 10-15 minutes | Cook Time: 8-10 minutes | Serves: 4-6

Ingredients:

- 2 pounds boneless chicken thighs
- 4 potatoes (coarsely sliced)
- Salt and pepper to taste
- 2-3 peppercorns
- 2 tbsp olive oil
- 1 tbsp thyme
- ½ tbsp onion powder
- 1 tsp paprika powder
- 1 tbsp chopped garlic
- 4 tbsp chopped onion
- ½ cup chicken broth

Directions:

1. Start by combining thyme, paprika, salt, pepper, and onion powder. Now take chicken thighs and season both sides with this spice mix. 2. Put olive oil in the cooking pot. Close the unit with Crisping Lid and select the unit on Air Crisp Mode at 390°F. 3. Air Crisp chicken thigh cuts in Ninja Foodi cooking pot. Cook each side for about 2 to 3 minutes. Now take out the chicken and set it aside. 4. Add onions and chopped garlic to the Ninja Foodi cooking pot. Add the peppercorns and steam for about 2 minutes. Now add chicken broth to it and continue to cook. 5. Now add potatoes and chicken. Close the unit with Pressure Lid and turn the pressure release valve to SEAL position. Select Pressure Cook mode at HI for 8 minutes. Then allow it to naturally release for about four to 5 minutes then quick release!

Nutritional Information Per Serving: Calories: 385; Fat: 16.3g; Carbs: 7.7g; Protein: 35.5g

Honey Garlic Chicken

Prep Time: 12 minutes | Cook Time: 15-20 minutes | Serves: 2

Ingredients:

- 1 pound bone-in chicken pieces
- 1 tbsp sesame oil
- ¼ cup broth
- 2 tbsp honey
- 2 tbsp soy sauce
- ½ tbsp apple cider vinegar
- 1 tsp chopped garlic
- Salt to taste
- Pepper to taste
- 1 tbsp cornstarch
- ¼ cup water

Directions:

1. Combine honey, broth, soy sauce, and apple cider vinegar in a bowl and whisk it well. 2. Meanwhile, add chicken and garlic to the Ninja Foodi. Steam for 2 to 3 minutes and pour the chicken broth mixture. 3. Now Seal the pressure lid and secure the valve and set Ninja Foodi on Pressure Cook mode at HI and cook for 8 minutes. 4. Whisk cornstarch and water together in a small bowl and prepare a slurry while the chicken is being cooked. 5. After 8 minutes, allow natural release of pressure for about 10 minutes and then turn it to quick release manually. Carefully open the lid and take it out then set Ninja Foodi on Pressure Cook mode at LO and mix the slurry into the sauce and keep stirring. Allow it to thicken for about 2 to 3 minutes. Coat all the chicken well. 6. Garnish it with some fresh green onion and a few sesame seeds!

Nutritional Information Per Serving: Calories: 219; Fat: 13.4g; Carbs: 11.7g; Protein: 22.8g

Juicy Sesame and Garlic Chicken Wings

Prep Time: 10 minutes | Cook Time: 25 minutes | Serves: 4

Ingredients:

- 24 chicken wing segments
- 2 tbsp toasted sesame oil
- 2 tbsp Asian chili-garlic sauce
- 2 tbsp stevia
- 2 garlic cloves, minced
- 1 tbsp toasted sesame seeds

Directions:

1. Add 1 cup of water to Ninja Foodi cooking pot. Put the reversible rack in the pot in the lower position, and place the chicken wings on the rack. 2. Put on the Pressure Lid and seal the valve. 3. Select Pressure Cook mode on HI and cook for 10 minutes. 4. Meanwhile, make the glaze by taking a large bowl and whisking in the sesame oil, chili-garlic sauce, honey, and garlic. 5. Once the chicken is cooked, quick release the pressure and remove the lid. 6. Remove the rack from the pot and empty out the remaining water from the pot. 7. Return the cooking pot to the Ninja Foodi Cooker base. 8. Cover the Ninja Foodi with the Crisping Lid and select Air Crisp mode. Adjust the temperature to 375°F and allow it to preheat for 3 minutes. 9. While the Ninja Foodi is preheating, add the wings to the glaze and toss well to coat. 10. Transfer the wings to the Cook & Crisp Basket, leaving any excess sauce in the bowl. 11. Place the basket in the Ninja Foodi and close with the Crisping Lid. Select Air Crisp mode and let the chicken cook at 375°F for 8 minutes. Gently toss the wings and then let them cook for 8 minutes more. 12. Serve and enjoy!

Nutritional Information Per Serving: Calories: 440; Fat: 32g; Carbs: 12g; Protein: 28g

Stuffed Whole Chicken

Prep Time: 10 minutes | Cook Time: 8 hours | Serves: 6

Ingredients:

- 1 cup mozzarella cheese
- 4 whole garlic cloves, peeled
- 1 (2 lb.)whole chicken, cleaned and pat dried
- Black pepper and salt, to taste
- 2 tbsp fresh lemon juice

Directions:

1. Stuff the chicken cavity with garlic cloves and mozzarella cheese. 2. Season chicken generously with black pepper and salt. 3. Transfer chicken to your Ninja Foodi and drizzle lemon juice. 4. Lock and secure the Ninja Foodi's lid and set to "Slow Cook" mode, let it cook on LO for 8 hours. 5. Once done, serve and enjoy.

Nutrition Values Per Serving: Calories: 309; Fat: 12g; Carbs: 1.6g; Protein: 45g

Turkey Meatballs

Prep Time: 15 minutes | Cook Time: 4 minutes | Serves: 4

Ingredients:

- 1-pound ground turkey
- 1 cup onion, shredded
- ¼ cup heavy whip cream
- 2 tsp salt
- 1 cup carrots, shredded
- ½ tsp ground caraway seeds
- 1½ tsp black pepper
- ¼ tsp ground allspice
- 1 cup almond meal
- ½ cup almond milk
- 2 tbsp unsalted butter

Directions:

1. Transfer meat to a suitable bowl. 2. Add cream, almond meal, onion, carrot, 1 tsp of salt, caraway, ½ tsp of pepper, allspice, and mix well. 3. Refrigerate the mixture for 30 minutes. 4. Once the mixture is cooled, use your hands to scoop the mixture into meatballs. 5. Place the turkey balls in your Ninja Foodi cooking pot. 6. Add milk, pats of butter and sprinkle 1 tsp salt and 1 tsp black pepper. 7. Lock and secure the Ninja Foodi with Pressure Lid, turn the pressure release valve to SEAL position, and then cook on "HIGH" pressure for 4 minutes. 8. Quick-release pressure. 9. Unlock the Ninja Foodi's lid and serve. 10. Enjoy.

Nutrition Values Per Serving: Calories: 338; Fat: 23g; Carbs: 7g; Protein: 23g

Sesame Chicken Wings

Prep Time: 10 minutes | Cook Time: 25 minutes | Serves: 4

Ingredients:

- 24 chicken wing segments
- 2 tbsp toasted sesame oil
- 2 tbsp Asian-Chile-Garlic sauce
- 2 tbsp stevia
- 2 garlic cloves, minced
- 1 tbsp toasted sesame seeds

Directions:

1. Add 1 cup of water to Ninja Foodi cooking pot, place reversible rack in the pot in lower portions, place chicken wings in the rack. 2. Close the unit with Pressure Lid and then turn the pressure release valve to SEAL position. 3. Select Pressure Cook mode to HI and cook for 10 minutes. 4. Make the glaze by taking a large bowl and whisking in sesame oil, Chile-Garlic sauce, choc zero maple syrup, and garlic. 5. Once the chicken is done, quick release the pressure and remove the pressure lid. 6. Remove rack from the pot and empty it. 7. Return the cooking pot to the base. 8. Cover with crisping lid and select Air Crisp mode, adjust the temperature to 375°F, pre-heat for 3 minutes. 9. While the Foodi pre-heats, add wings to the sauce and toss well to coat it. 10. Transfer wings to the basket, leaving any excess sauce in the bowl. 11. Place the basket in Ninja Foodi and close with Crisping mode, select Air Crisp mode and let it cook for 8 minutes, gently toss the wings and let it cook for 8 minutes more. 12. Once done, drizzle any sauce and sprinkle sesame seeds. 13. Enjoy.

Nutrition Values Per Serving: Calories: 440; Fat: 32g; Carbs: 12g; Protein: 28g

Ham-Stuffed Turkey Rolls

Prep Time: 10 minutes | Cook Time: 20 minutes | Serves: 8

Ingredients:

- 4 tbsp fresh sage leaves
- 8 ham slices
- 8 (6 ounces each) turkey cutlets
- Black pepper and salt to taste
- 2 tbsp butter, melted

Directions:

1. Season turkey cutlets with black pepper and salt. 2. Roll turkey cutlets and wrap each of them with ham slices tightly. 3. Coat each roll with butter and gently place sage leaves evenly over each cutlet. 4. Transfer them to your Ninja Foodi. 5. Lock and secure the Ninja Foodi's lid and select the "Bake/Roast" mode, bake for 10 minutes at 360°F. 6. Open the Ninja Foodi's lid and gently give it a flip. Lock and secure the Ninja Foodi's lid again and bake for 10 minutes more. 7. Once done, serve and enjoy.

Nutrition Values Per Serving: Calories: 467; Fat: 24g; Carbs: 1.7g; Protein: 56g

Hassel Back Chicken

Prep Time: 5 minutes | Cook Time: 60 minutes | Serves: 4

Ingredients:

- 4 tbsp butter
- Black pepper and salt to taste
- 2 cups fresh mozzarella cheese, sliced
- 8 large chicken breasts
- 4 large Roma tomatoes, sliced

Directions:

1. Make few deep slits in chicken breasts, season with black pepper and salt. 2. Stuff mozzarella cheese slices and tomatoes in chicken slits. 3. Grease Ninja Foodi pot with butter and set stuffed chicken breasts. 4. Lock and secure the Ninja Foodi's lid and "Bake/Roast" for 1 hour at 365°F. 5. Serve and enjoy.

Nutrition Values Per Serving: Calories: 278; Fat: 15g; Carbs: 3.8g; Protein: 15g

Ninja Foodi Turkey & Beans Wrap

Prep Time: 10 minutes | Cook Time: 13 minutes | Serves: 3

Ingredients:

- ¼ pound lean ground turkey
- ¼ tsp ground cumin
- 3 butternut lettuce leaves
- ¼ tsp garlic powder
- 1½ tbsp tomato sauce
- ¼ cup cooked black beans
- ¼ cup chopped onion
- 1½ tbsp extra-virgin olive oil
- Salt and black pepper, to taste

Directions:

1. Add turkey, onion, tomato sauce, garlic powder, cumin, salt, and pepper in a large bowl. Mix well. 2. Meanwhile, heat oil in Ninja Foodi and add turkey mixture in it. 3. Close the unit with Pressure Cook and turn the pressure release valve to SEAL position. 4. Pressure cook at LO for 10 minutes and stir in tomato sauce and beans. 5. Cook for about 3 minutes and take out. 6. Divide the mixture evenly on lettuce leaves and serve.

Nutritional Information Per Serving: Calories: 356; Fat: 28.7g; Carbs: 14.8g; Protein: 12.5g

Ninja Foodi Chicken & Carrot Stew

Prep Time: 10 minutes | Cook Time: 6 hours | Serves: 3

Ingredients:

- 2 (¼ pound) boneless chicken breasts, cubed
- ½ cup chopped onions
- ½ tsp dried thyme
- 1 garlic clove, minced
- 1½ cup cubed carrots
- ½ cup chopped tomatoes
- 1 cup chicken broth
- Salt and black pepper, to taste

Directions:

1. Add everything in the Ninja Foodi cooking pot. Close the Ninja Foodi with Pressure Lid and then turn the pressure release valve to VENT position. 2. Then select the Ninja Foodi on "Slow Cook" function. 3. Slow cook the stew at HI for 6 hours and take out. 4. Serve and enjoy!

Nutritional Information Per Serving: Calories: 226; Fat: 6.4g; Carbs: 16.6g; Protein: 25g

Ninja Foodi Chicken & Salsa Chili

Prep Time: 10 minutes | Cook Time: 8 hours 5 minutes | Serves: 4

Ingredients:

- 1 cup salsa
- ¾ cup water
- ½ jalapeno pepper, minced
- ½ tsp ground cumin
- 1 tsp chili powder
- ½ pound boneless chicken breast
- 1 garlic clove, minced
- ½ onion, chopped
- ½ avocado, chopped
- 1½ green bell peppers, chopped
- Salt and black pepper, to taste

Directions:

1. Add chicken, garlic, cumin, salsa, and water in a Ninja Foodi. Close the unit with Pressure Lid and turn the pressure release valve to VENT position. Select "Slow Cook". 2. Cook for about 6 hours at HI and open the lid. 3. Meanwhile, heat the non-stick skillet and cook onions, jalapeno pepper, and bell pepper in it for about 5 minutes. 4. Now, take the chicken out of the Ninja Foodi and shred it properly. 5. Place it back in the Slow Cook along with onion mixture, chili powder, avocado, salt and pepper. Mix well. 6. Cook for about 2 hours and take out. 7. Serve and enjoy!

Nutritional Information Per Serving: Calories: 239; Fat: 9.8g; Carbs: 20.7g; Protein: 19.9g

Glazed Chicken & Vegetables

Prep Time: 8-10 minutes | Cook Time: 20-25 minutes | Serves: 2

Ingredients:

½ pound chicken thighs boneless
2 tbsp soya sauce
2 tsp Worcestershire sauce
2 tbsp brown sugar
4 crushed garlic cloves

1 pound bag of frozen mixed vegetables
1 tbsp vinegar optional
1 tbsp olive oil
Black pepper to taste

Directions:

1. Start by adding soya sauce, Worcestershire sauce, brown sugar, and garlic in a closable container or zip lock bag. Now add chicken in it and seal to coat it well with the marinade. Let it rest in the fridge for 2 to 3 hours. 2. Oil spray the Ninja Foodi Cook & Crisp Basket. Now put vegetables and chicken in the Cook & Crisp Basket. 3. Give a spray of olive oil again and sprinkle just a pinch of salt if preferred. 4. Air Crisp it for about 25 minutes at 390°F. 5. When the chicken reaches 165°F internally, serve it!

Nutritional Information Per Serving: Calories: 397; Fat: 11.3g; Carbs: 25.5g; Protein: 27.4g

Ninja Foodi Basil Pesto Chicken

Prep Time: 20 minutes | Cook Time: 30 minutes | Serves: 4

Ingredients:

4 boneless chicken breasts
3 garlic cloves, minced
½ cup pine nuts
2 cups fresh basil leaves

½ tsp red pepper flakes
½ cup olive oil
Salt and black pepper, to taste

Directions:

1. Add olive oil, garlic, pine nuts, basil, and red pepper flakes in a food processor. Pulse well. 2. Now, arrange chicken breasts in the Ninja Foodi cooking pot and pour basil mixture on it. 3. Close the unit with Crisping Lid and select the unit on Bake/Roast mode. 4. Bake for about 30 minutes at 375°F. 5. Open the Crisping Lid and take out. 6. Serve and enjoy!

Nutritional Information Per Serving: Calories: 603; Fat: 47.3g; Carbs: 3.4g; Protein: 43.4g

Ninja Foodi Duck Fajita Platter

Prep Time: 10 minutes | Cook Time: 25 minutes | Serves: 4

Ingredients:

1 pound duck breasts, sliced
½ green bell pepper, chopped
½ red bell pepper, chopped
1 onion, sliced
2 tbsp olive oil

1 tsp garlic powder
1 tsp ground cumin
2 tsp chili powder
½ tsp dried oregano
Salt, to taste

Directions:

1. Add duck breasts, green bell pepper, red bell pepper, and garlic powder in a large bowl. Mix well. 2. Add in chili powder, cumin, onion, olive oil, oregano and salt in the bowl. Toss to coat well. 3. Place the duck breasts in Ninja Foodi cooking pot. Close the unit with Crisping Lid and select the unit on Bake/Roast mode. 4. Bake for about 25 minutes at 400°F and open the lid. 5. Take out and serve hot.

Nutritional Information Per Serving: Calories: 237; Fat: 12g; Carbs: 6.7g; Protein: 26.1g

Ninja Foodi Barbeque Chicken Drumsticks

Prep Time: 10 minutes | Cook Time: 8 hours | Serves: 4

Ingredients:

- 12 chicken drumsticks
- 2 tbsp red chili powder
- 1 tsp onion powder
- 1 tsp garlic powder
- 4 tbsp honey
- 2 tbsp apple cider vinegar
- 1 cup barbeque sauce
- 1 tbsp paprika
- ½ tbsp ground cumin
- Salt and black pepper, to taste

Directions:

1. Add everything except honey in a Ninja Foodi. Close the unit with Pressure Lid, turn the pressure release valve to VENT position, and select the unit on "Slow Cook" mode. 2. Slow cook for about 8 hours at HI and open the lid. 3. Take out the drumsticks and pour honey on them. 4. Serve and enjoy!

Nutritional Information Per Serving: Calories: 416; Fat: 9.1g; Carbs: 44.4g; Protein: 39g

Chicken Pasta with Dried Tomatoes

Prep Time: 6 minutes | Cook Time: 15-20 minutes | Serves: 4

Ingredients:

- 1 pound chicken thigh
- 1 pound penne pasta
- 1 tbsp butter
- 1 diced onion
- 1 tsp chopped garlic
- ½ cup dried tomatoes
- 1 tbsp tomato paste
- 1 tbsp Italian Seasoning
- Salt to taste
- 2 tbsp parmesan cheese
- ¼ cup heavy cream
- 2 tbsp cream cheese
- ¼ cup chicken broth
- 1 tbsp extra-virgin olive oil

Directions:

1. When water comes to a boil, boil the pasta, don't forget to add salt to the pasta water. You can simply boil according to the given instructions on the package. 2. On the other hand, cut the chicken into strips. Preheat the Ninja Foodi on Low Pressure setting. 3. Add half the oil and butter into a large skillet. Let it melt. 4. Add chicken and let it cook for 3 to 4 minutes. 5. Flip and cook it for another 2 minutes. Now take out the chicken from the skillet. 6. Keep Ninja Foodi to Pressure Cook mode at LO. Now add the remaining olive oil and onion into the pan and cook the onions until they become translucent. 7. Add garlic and cook it for about 1 minute. Then add tomato paste and dried tomatoes. 8. Season it with salt and Italian seasoning and mix it well. 9. Now add chicken broth and let it simmer for 2 minutes. 10. Add parmesan cheese, heavy cream, and cream cheese, and stir it well. After the cheese melts, add chicken into it, then pour it over the pasta and serve it hot!

Nutritional Information Per Serving: Calories: 470; Fat: 14.5g; Carbs: 59g; Protein: 24.8g

Pulled Barbecue Chicken

Prep Time: 6 minutes | Cook Time: 9-10 minutes | Serves: 2

Ingredients:

- 1 pound chicken breast
- 1 cup broth
- 4 tbsp BBQ sauce
- ½ tsp liquid smoke
- Salt and pepper to taste

Directions:

1. Now inside the Ninja Foodi cooking pot, place the chicken breast and sprinkle a little salt and pepper on both sides. 2. Then, add in broth over the chicken breasts, and install the Pressure Lid and switch the vent knob to Seal properly. Select the Ninja Foodi on Pressure Cook mode at HI for about 8 minutes and then press the Star/Stop button. 3. Quickly release the pressure after the timer goes off and then remove the lid carefully. 4. Make sure that broth is reduced to half. Then add the barbecue sauce and let it cook on Air Crisp Mode at 390°F for 5 to 10 minutes. Make sure to shred it a bit with a spatula or fork. 5. Add the liquid smoke and it's good to go!

Nutritional Information Per Serving: Calories: 311; Fat: 4g; Carbs: 6.1g; Protein: 34.7g

Chicken Vegetable Soup

Prep Time: 8 minutes | Cook Time: 3 minutes | Serves: 2

Ingredients:

- ½ pound boneless chicken thigh (bite-size cuts)
- 1 diced carrot
- 1 chopped onion
- 1 tsp garlic
- ½ cup boiled pasta
- 4 cups broth
- 1 tsp salt
- ¾ tsp white pepper
- 1 tbsp soy sauce
- 1 tsp oregano
- ¼ tsp red chili powder
- 2 bay leaves
- ¼ cup corn flour slurry

Directions:

1. In the Ninja Foodi cooking pot, add carrots, onion, garlic, bay leaves then add the bite-size chicken cuts. 2. Now season it with salt, white pepper, oregano, red chili powder, and soy sauce and pour in the chicken broth. 3. Give it a good stir. Close the unit with Pressure Lid and turn the pressure release valve to SEAL position. 4. Select the Pressure Cook mode and set it to HI. Cook for 2 minutes. Usually, the pressure takes about 10 minutes to start building up. 5. Once it beeps, allow the pressure to naturally release for about 10 minutes after the completion of pressure cooking. And quickly release any remaining pressure by setting the valve to venting. 6. Now take out the bay leaves and discard them. Turn the pressure release valve to VENT position, select the unit on Steam mode, and let the soup simmer for another 3 to 5 minutes. 7. Pour in slurry and stir it well. Give it a boil until it's completely thickened. Serve instantly!

Nutritional Information Per Serving: Calories: 389; Fat: 10.3g; Carbs: 16g; Protein: 31.9g

Ninja Foodi Chicken Broth

Prep Time: 10 minutes | Cook Time: 3 hours | Serves: 3

Ingredients:

- 1½ pounds chicken
- 1 bay leaf
- 1 celery stalk, chopped
- ¼ tsp dried rosemary, crushed
- 1 carrot, chopped
- ¼ tsp dried thyme
- 4 peppercorns
- 1 onion, quartered
- 4 cups cold water

Directions:

1. Add everything in the Ninja Foodi cooking pot. Close the unit with Pressure Lid and turn the pressure release valve to VENT position. Select "Slow Cook". 2. Slow cook at HI for about 3 hours and open the lid. 3. Take out and set aside. 4. Strain the broth and serve hot.

Nutritional Information Per Serving: Calories: 1281; Fat: 25.3g; Carbs: 5.9g; Protein: 241.6g

Pineapple Chicken

Prep Time: 2 hours | Cook Time: 9-10 minutes | Serves: 2

Ingredients:

- 2 chicken steaks
- 1 tbsp onion paste
- 4 tbsp teriyaki sauce
- 2 tbsp pineapple juice
- 1 tbsp ginger garlic paste
- Salt and pepper to taste
- Coriander and cilantro to garnish

Directions:

1. Take a large bowl and combine all ingredients. Refrigerate it overnight. 2. Now remove it from the refrigerator and place the leftover marination in the bowl. 3. Place the chicken steak directly in the Ninja Foodi cooking pot. 4. Now cook the chicken in the Ninja Foodi on Pressure Cook mode at HI for 3 minutes and use the reserved marinade to baste when meat is cooked halfway. 5. Now turn over the meat for 5 to 7 minutes to cook and do this until the meat is cooked properly. 6. Turn off and plate the chicken, and garnish it with fresh coriander or cilantro!

Nutritional Information Per Serving: Calories: 391; Fat: 18.1g; Carbs: 36.4g; Protein: 20.4g

Chicken Saltimbocca

Prep Time: 6 minutes | Cook Time: 10-15 minutes | Serves: 2

Ingredients:

2 chicken cutlets
2 tbsp all-purpose flour
2-3 slices of dry ham/prosciutto
2-3 sage leaves large
Pepper as required
1 tbsp extra-virgin olive oil
1 tbsp butter

Directions:

1. Put the flour in a shallow dish. Fold each chicken cutlet in the flour and coat evenly. Make sure to shake off the excess flour. Now arrange the cutlets on a plate, place a slice of prosciutto on it and add a sage leaf over it and then secure it with a toothpick. 2. Grease the cooking pot with extra-virgin olive oil. 3. Align chicken cutlets in a single layer in the pot and make sure the prosciutto side is down. Close the unit with Crisping Lid and select the unit on Broil mode. 4. Sear the chicken from one side for about 5 minutes until it's golden and crispy then flip the cutlets and season it with pepper. Until the chicken is cooked, continue to sear. 5. Take out the chicken from the pan, arrange it on the platter and cover it with foil to keep it warm. Now add the butter to the pan and cook it until it starts foaming. 6. Pour wine to it and gently stir it to combine. Now pour the sauce onto the chicken cutlets and it's ready to be served immediately!

Nutritional Information Per Serving: Calories: 319; Fat: 18.1g; Carbs: 12g; Protein: 28g

Mexican Chicken with Rice

Prep Time: 12-15 minutes | Cook Time: 10 minutes | Serves: 4

Ingredients:

1 pound chicken breasts boneless
1 cup uncooked rice
Salt to taste
½ tsp chili flakes
2-3 minced garlic cloves
1 can black beans
¼ cup corn
½ cup chicken broth
¼ cup cheese
2 diced onions
1 tbsp olive oil

Directions:

1. Turn on the Ninja Foodi on Pressure Cook mode at 390°F and then add olive oil. 2. Add onions, garlic powder, chicken cubes, chili flakes, and salt once oil is hot and cook it until the protein changes its color. 3. Dump in black beans and corn alongside chicken broth after turning off the Ninja Foodi cooking pot. Stir well together. 4. Now on top of that, sprinkle uncooked rice and by using the back of the spoon, submerge it into the liquid but don't stir it. 5. Put the lid back on and close the steam valve for 9 minutes. After that let it naturally release pressure. 6. Lift the lid, fluff up the rice mixture and add cheese on top, mix it gently and set the top back again for about 3 minutes for the cheese to melt!

Nutritional Information Per Serving: Calories: 31.5; Fat: 14.4g; Carbs: 31.5g; Protein: 61g

Chapter 4 Beef, Pork and Lamb Recipes

49	Garlicky Pork Chops
49	Beef Jerky
49	Adobo Steak
50	Lamb Curry
50	Ninja Foodi Carrot & Pork Stew
50	Ninja Foodi Lamb & Kale Stew
51	Ninja Foodi Beef Chili
51	Roasted Beef
51	Ninja Foodi Spinach Beef Soup
52	Ninja Foodi Mushroom & Beef Stew
52	Pork Chili Verde
52	Char Siu Pork
53	Mongolian Beef
53	Crusted Pork Chops
53	Pork Meatballs
54	Maple Glazed Pork Chops
54	Taco Meatballs
54	Eastern Lamb Stew
55	Bacon Strips
55	Corned Cabbage Beef
55	Corned Beef
56	Beef Bourguignon
56	Veggies & Beef Stew
56	Braised Lamb Shanks
57	Beef Enchiladas
57	Instant Lamb Steaks
57	Ninja Foodi Pork Shoulder Roast
58	Ninja Foodi Beef Casserole
58	Ninja Foodi Minced Beef with Tomatoes
58	Beef Stew
59	Ninja Foodi Steak Fajitas
59	Ninja Foodi Lamb & Carrot Stew
59	Lamb Shanks
60	Ninja Foodi Lamb Chops with Tomatoes
60	Ninja Foodi Plum & Beef Salad
60	Sweet and Sour Pork
61	Ninja Foodi Ground Beef Soup
61	Tomahawk Rib-Eye Steak
61	Beef Onion Pattie Burgers
62	Roasted Lamb
62	Maple Lamb Chops
62	Pork Tenderloin
63	Lamb Balls

Garlicky Pork Chops

Prep Time: 1 hour and 30 minutes | Cook Time: 10 minutes | Serves: 2

Ingredients:

- 1 tbsp coconut butter
- 1 tbsp coconut oil
- 2 tsp cloves garlic, grated
- 2 tsp parsley, chopped
- Black pepper and salt to taste
- 4 pork chops, sliced into strips

Directions:

1. Combine all the ingredients except the pork strips. Mix well. 2. Marinate the pork in the mixture for 1 hour. Put the pork on the Ninja Foodi Cook & Crisp Basket. 3. Set it inside the cooking pot. Seal with the crisping lid. Choose Air Crisp function. 4. Cook at 400°F for 10 minutes.

Nutritional Values Per Serving: Calories: 388; Fat: 23.3g; Carbs: 0.5g; Protein: 18.1g

Beef Jerky

Prep Time: 10 minutes | Cook Time: 20 minutes | Serves: 4

Ingredients:

- ½-pound beef, sliced into ⅛-inch-thick strips
- ½ cup soy sauce
- 2 tbsp Worcestershire sauce
- 2 tsp black pepper
- 1 tsp onion powder
- ½ tsp garlic powder
- 1 tsp salt

Directions:

1. Add listed ingredient to a large-sized Ziploc bag, seal it shut. 2. Shake well, seal and leave it in the fridge overnight. 3. Lay strips on the deluxe reversible rack in the cooking pot in the lower position, making sure not to overlap them. Set thee unit on Dehydrate mode. 4. Lock Crisping Lid and set its cooking temperature to 135°F, cook for 7 hours.

Nutritional Values Per Serving: Calories: 62; Fat: 7g; Carbs: 2g; Protein: 9g

Adobo Steak

Prep Time: 5 minutes | Cook Time: 25 minutes | Serves: 4

Ingredients:

- 2 cups water
- 8 steaks, cubed, 28 ounces pack
- Pepper to taste
- 1 ¾ tsp adobo seasoning
- 1 can (8-ounce) tomato sauce
- ⅓ cup green pitted olives
- 2 tbsp brine
- 1 small red pepper
- ½ medium onion, sliced

Directions:

1. Chop peppers, onions into ¼-inch strips. 2. Prepare beef by seasoning with adobo and pepper. 3. Add into Ninja Foodi cooking pot. 4. Stir in remaining ingredients and close the unit with Pressure Lid. Turn the pressure release valve to SEAL position. Set the unit on Pressure Cook mode and then cook on "HIGH" pressure for 25 minutes. 5. Release pressure naturally. 6. Serve and enjoy.

Nutritional Values Per Serving: Calories: 154; Fat: 5g; Carbs: 3g; Protein: 23g

Lamb Curry

Prep Time: 1 hour and 30 minutes | Cook Time: 20 minutes | Serves: 6

Ingredients:

- 1-½ lb. lamb stew meat, cubed
- 1 tbsp lime juice
- 4 cloves garlic, minced
- ½ cup coconut milk
- 1-inch piece fresh ginger, grated
- Black pepper and salt to taste
- 1 tbsp coconut oil
- 14 oz. diced tomatoes
- ¾ tsp turmeric
- 1 tbsp curry powder
- 1 onion, diced
- 3 carrots, sliced

Directions:

1. In a suitable bowl, toss the lamb meat in lime juice, garlic, coconut milk, ginger, black pepper and salt. Marinate for 30 minutes. 2. Put the meat with its marinade and the rest of the ingredients in the Ninja Foodi. 3. Mix well. Close the unit with Pressure Lid and turn the pressure release valve to SEAL position. Set the unit on Pressure Cook. 4. Cook at "HI" pressure for 20 minutes. 5. Release the pressure naturally. 6. Garnish with chopped cilantro. 7. Use freshly squeezed lime juice.

Nutritional Values Per Serving: Calories: 631; Fat: 31.4g; Carbs: 19.7g; Protein: 67.2g

Ninja Foodi Carrot & Pork Stew

Prep Time: 10 minutes | Cook Time: 8 hours | Serves: 4

Ingredients:

- 1 pound pork meat, trimmed
- 1½ onions, sliced thinly
- 3 carrots, sliced thinly
- ¾ cup vegetable broth
- Salt and black pepper, to taste

Directions:

1. Add everything in the Ninja Foodi and mix well. 2. Close the unit with Pressure Lid and turn the pressure release valve to VENT position. Select the unit on "Slow Cook" mode. 3. Cook at LO for about 8 hours. 4. Open the lid and take out. 5. Serve and enjoy!

Nutritional Values Per Serving: Calories: 465; Fat: 34.8g; Carbs: 21.2g; Protein: 17.1g

Ninja Foodi Lamb & Kale Stew

Prep Time: 10 minutes | Cook Time: 6 hours 5 minutes | Serves: 10

Ingredients:

- 3 pounds lamb meat, cubed
- 1 tsp dried thyme
- 1 celery stalk, chopped
- 2 tbsp olive oil
- 1 tsp dried basil
- 1 cup chopped tomatoes
- 2 onions, chopped
- ½ cup chopped carrots
- 2 cups water
- 2 garlic cloves, minced
- 10 cups fresh kale, chopped
- Salt and black pepper, to taste

Directions:

1. Heat oil in the Ninja Foodi cooking pot and add lamb, salt and pepper in it. 2. Close the unit with Pressure Lid and turn the pressure release valve to VENT position. Set the unit on "Slow Cook". 3. Slow cook at HI for about 5 minutes and take out. Set aside. 4. Now, add lamb with all the other ingredients in a Ninja Foodi and close the pressure Lid. 5. Cook for about 6 hours at HI and open the lid. 6. Take out, serve and enjoy!

Nutritional Values Per Serving: Calories: 350; Fat: 20.9g; Carbs: 10.6g; Protein: 27.8g

Ninja Foodi Beef Chili

Prep Time: 10 minutes | Cook Time: 6 hours | Serves: 3

Ingredients:

- ¾ pound lean ground beef
- ¼ tbsp garlic, minced
- ½ tbsp dried basil
- ¼ onion, chopped
- 1 tbsp tomato paste
- ½ tbsp chili powder
- ¼ cup chicken broth
- ½ tbsp balsamic vinegar
- 2 tbsp water
- ¾ tbsp capers
- ½ tbsp dried thyme
- ¼ tbsp cayenne pepper
- Salt, to taste

Directions:

1. Add everything in a Ninja Foodi. Close the unit with Pressure Lid and turn the pressure release valve to VENT position. Set the unit on "Slow Cook" mode. 2. Cook at LO for about 6 hours and open the lid. 3. Take out and serve hot.

Nutritional Values Per Serving: Calories: 231; Fat: 7.6g; Carbs: 3.5g; Protein: 35.5g

Roasted Beef

Prep Time: 9-10 minutes | Cook Time: 25-30 minutes | Serves: 2

Ingredients:

- 1 pound beef round steaks
- Salt to taste
- Pepper to taste
- 2 tbsp onion powder
- 1 tbsp garlic powder
- ½ tsp red pepper
- ½ tsp paprika
- 1 tsp cumin powder
- 1 tbsp coriander powder
- 1 tbsp butter

Directions:

1. Combine the dry ingredients with butter and apply them generously to the meat. 2. Select the option Broil and let the beef be broiled for 25 minutes on the reversable rack in a lower position. Turn off the Ninja Foodi and keep the lid closed for about 20 to 25 minutes.
Remove it and let it rest for 10 minutes, slice it finely and serve!

Nutritional Values Per Serving: Calories: 327; Fat: 15.4g; Carbs: 16.5g; Protein: 27.7g

Ninja Foodi Spinach Beef Soup

Prep Time: 10 minutes | Cook Time: 30 minutes | Serves: 4

Ingredients:

- 1 tbsp olive oil
- 4 cups spinach, chopped
- 1 onion, chopped
- 4 cups chicken broth
- 1 pound ground beef
- 1 tsp ground ginger
- 1 cup chopped carrots
- Salt and black pepper, to taste

Directions:

1. Add oil and beef in the Ninja Foodi. Close the unit with Pressure Lid and turn the pressure release valve to SEAL position. Set the unit on Pressure Cook mode. 2. Pressure cook at HI for about 5 minutes. 3. Add in broth, spinach, carrots, onions, ginger, salt, and pepper. Mix well. 4. Cook for about 25 minutes at LO and take out. 5. Serve and enjoy!

Nutritional Values Per Serving: Calories: 310; Fat: 12.1g; Carbs: 7.6g; Protein: 40.7g

Ninja Foodi Mushroom & Beef Stew

Prep Time: 10 minutes | Cook Time: 8 hours | Serves: 5

Ingredients:

1 pound beef, chopped
1½ onions, chopped
1 cup mushrooms, sliced
½ cup vegetable broth
Salt and black pepper, to taste

Directions:

1. Add everything in the Ninja Foodi. Close the unit with Pressure Lid and turn the pressure release valve to VENT position. Set the unit on "Slow Cook" mode. 2. Cook at LO for about 8 hours and open the lid. 3. Take out, serve and enjoy!

Nutritional Values Per Serving: Calories: 224; Fat: 6g; Carbs: 11.9g; Protein: 29.8g

Pork Chili Verde

Prep Time: 25 minutes | Cook Time: 30-35 minutes | Serves: 6

Ingredients:

2 pounds pork sirloin (1-inch cuts)
4 tbsp Enchilada sauce
1 tsp garlic paste
2 tbsp canola oil
½ cup sliced carrot
1 diced onion
½ cup cold water
2-3 sliced jalapenos
¼ cup fresh cilantro

Directions:

1. Pour in oil and pork and cook the pork in it on Pressure Cook mode at HI for 5 minutes or more until it changes its color. 2. Then add carrots, onion, and garlic in it until garlic becomes fragrant and onion becomes translucent. 3. Now add enchilada sauce, water, cilantro, and jalapenos to the Ninja Foodi cooking pot on Pressure Cook mode at HI. Stir it and seal the pressure lid and close the valve. Cook for 30 minutes then allow the pressure to release naturally for 10 minutes. 4. Dish it out and serve it with tortillas!

Nutritional Information Per Serving: Calories: 464; Fat: 20.7g; Carbs: 13g; Protein: 49.6g

Char Siu Pork

Prep Time: 25 minutes | Cook Time: 1.5 hours | Serves: 2

Ingredients:

1 pound pork fillet
½ cup chicken broth
2 tbsp soy sauce
¼ cup ketchup
2 tbsp honey
3 tbsp bean paste
1 tsp garlic paste
1 tsp ginger paste
1 tsp five-spice powder
¼ cup fresh coriander leaves

Directions:

1. Start by combining honey, bean paste, soy sauce, ketchup, ginger, garlic, and the five-spice powder into a large shallow dish. Now add pork to the dish and turn to coat evenly in the dry mix. 2. Transfer pork in the Ninja Foodi cooking pot. Pour chicken broth into it. Seal the pressure lid and close the valve, adjust your Ninja Foodi on Pressure Cook at HI. Cook for 75 minutes and then after time allow for 10 minutes to pressure to release naturally. Then quickly release the remaining pressure manually. 3. When pork is done, cut the pork coarsely. 4. Then turn on Sauté setting and let it cook for 2 to 3 minutes at LO. Top up with fresh coriander!

Nutritional Information Per Serving: Calories: 521; Fat: 15g; Carbs: 34.6g; Protein: 59.7g

Mongolian Beef

Prep Time: 30 minutes | Cook Time: 20 minutes | Serves: 2

Ingredients:

1 lb. flank steak, sliced
¼ cup corn starch
Sauce:
2 tsp vegetable oil
½ tsp ginger, minced
1 tbsp garlic, minced
½ cup soy sauce
½ cup water
¾ cup brown erythritol

Directions:

1. Coat the beef with corn starch. Put in the Ninja Foodi Cook & Crisp Basket. 2. Seal the crisping lid. Set it to Air Crisp. 3. Cook at 390°F for about 10 minutes per side. 4. Remove and set aside. Set the Ninja Foodi to Sear/Sauté at MD. Stir in the vegetable oil. 5. Sauté the ginger and garlic for 1 minute. Stir in the soy sauce, water and brown erythritol. 6. Pour the prepared sauce on top of the beef.

Nutritional Information Per Serving: Calories: 399; Fat: 11.7g; Carbs: 39g; Protein: 33.7g

Crusted Pork Chops

Prep Time: 30 minutes | Cook Time: 12 minutes | Serves: 6

Ingredients:

Cooking spray
6 pork chops
Black pepper and salt to taste
½ cup bread crumbs
2 tbsp Parmesan cheese, grated
¼ cup cornflakes, crushed
1¼ tsps sweet paprika
½ tsp onion powder
½ tsp garlic powder
¼ tsp chili powder
1 egg, beaten

Directions:

1. Season the pork chops liberally with black pepper and salt. 2. In a suitable bowl, mix the rest of the ingredients except the egg. 3. Beat the egg in a suitable bowl. Dip the pork chops in the egg. 4. Coat the pork with the breading. Place the pork on the Ninja Foodi Cook & Crisp Basket. 5. Close the unit with Crisping Lid and set the unit on Air Crisp mode. 6. Cook at 400°F for about 12 minutes, flipping halfway through.

Nutritional Information Per Serving: Calories: 310; Fat: 21.3g; Carbs: 8.2g; Protein: 20.3g

Pork Meatballs

Prep Time: 30 minutes | Cook Time: 6 minutes | Serves: 4

Ingredients:

1-pound ground pork
¼ cup heavy whip cream
2 tsp salt
½ tsp ground caraway seeds
1 and ½ tsp black pepper
¼ tsp ground allspice
2 zucchinis, shredded
½ cup almond milk
2 tbsp unsalted butter

Directions:

1. Transfer meat to a suitable bowl and add cream, 1 tsp salt, caraway seeds, ½ tsp pepper, allspice, and mix it well. 2. Let the mixture chill for 30 minutes. 3. Once the mixture is ready, use your hands to scoop the mixture into meatballs. 4. Add half of your balls to the Ninja Foodi cooking pot and cover with half of the cabbage. 5. Add remaining balls and cover with rest of the cabbage. 6. Add milk, pats of butter, season with black pepper and salt. 7. Close the Ninja Foodi with Pressure Lid and turn the pressure release valve to SEAL position. Set 8. the unit on Pressure Cook mode at "HIGH" pressure for 4 minutes. 9. Quick-release pressure. 10. Unlock and secure the Ninja Foodi's lid and serve. 11. Enjoy.

Nutrition Values Per Serving: Calories: 294; Fat: 26g; Carbs: 4g; Protein: 12g

Maple Glazed Pork Chops

Prep Time: 45 minutes | Cook Time: 12 minutes | Serves: 4

Ingredients:

2 tbsp choc zero maple syrup
4 tbsp mustard
2 tbsp garlic, minced
Black pepper and salt to taste
4 pork chops
Cooking spray

Directions:

1. Mix the choc zero maple syrup, mustard, garlic, black pepper, and salt in a suitable bowl. 2. Marinate the choc zero maple syruped pork chops in the mixture for 20 minutes. 3. Place the pork chops on the Ninja Foodi basket. 4. Put the basket inside the pot. Seal with the crisping lid. 5. Set it to air crisp. Cook at 350°F for about 12 minutes, flipping halfway through.
Nutritional Information Per Serving: Calories: 348; Fat: 23.3g; Carbs: 14g; Protein: 21.1g

Taco Meatballs

Prep Time: 8 minutes | Cook Time: 11 minutes | Serves: 4

Ingredients:

2 cups ground beef
1 egg, beaten
1 tsp taco seasoning
1 tbsp sugar-free marinara sauce
1 tsp garlic, minced
½ tsp salt

Directions:

1. Take a suitable mixing bowl and place all the ingredients into the bowl. 2. Stir in all the ingredients into the bowl. Mix together all the ingredients by using a spoon or fingertips. Then make the small size meatballs and put them in a layer in the deluxe reversible rack. 3. Lower the crisping lid. 4. Air Crisp the meatballs for 11 minutes at 350°F. 5. Serve immediately and enjoy.
Nutritional Information Per Serving: Calories: 205; Fat: 12.2g; Carbs: 2.2g; Protein: 19.4g

Eastern Lamb Stew

Prep Time: 1 hour and 30 minutes | Cook Time: 60 minutes | Serves: 4

Ingredients:

2 tbsp olive oil
1½ lbs. lamb stew meat, sliced into cubes
1 onion, diced
6 garlic cloves, chopped
1 tsp cumin
1 tsp coriander
1 tsp turmeric
1 tsp cinnamon
Black pepper and salt to taste
2 tbsp tomato paste
¼ cup red wine vinegar
2 tbsp choc zero maple syrup
1¼ cups chicken broth
15 oz. chickpeas, rinsed and drained

Directions:

1. Choose Sear/Sauté function in the Ninja Foodi. Stir in the oil. Sauté onion at MD for 3 minutes. 2. Add the lamb and seasonings. Cook for 5 minutes, stirring frequently. 3. Stir in the rest of the ingredients. Cover the pot. Set it to Pressure Cook mode. 4. Cook at "HI" pressure for 50 minutes. Release the pressure naturally. 5. Serve with quinoa. 6. Freeze and serve the next day for a more intense flavor.
Nutritional Information Per Serving: Calories: 867; Fat: 26.6g; Carbs: 87.4g; Protein: 71.2g

Bacon Strips

Prep Time: 5 minutes | Cook Time: 7 minutes | Serves: 2

Ingredients:

10 bacon strips
¼ tsp chili flakes
⅓ tsp salt
¼ tsp basil, dried

Directions:

1. Rub the bacon strips with chili flakes, dried basil, and salt. 2. Turn on your Ninja Foodi and place the bacon on the rack. 3. Lower the crisping lid. Set the unit on Bake/Roast mode. Cook the bacon at 400°F for 5 minutes. 4. Cook for 3 minutes more if the bacon is not fully cooked. Serve and enjoy.

Nutritional Information Per Serving: Calories: 500; Fat: 46g; Carbs: 0g; Protein: 21g

Corned Cabbage Beef

Prep Time: 10 minutes | Cook Time: 100 minutes | Serves: 4

Ingredients:

1 corned beef brisket
4 cups water
1 small onion, peeled and quartered
3 garlic cloves, smashed and peeled
2 bay leaves
3 whole black peppercorns
½ tsp allspice berries
1 tsp dried thyme
5 medium carrots
1 cabbage, cut into wedges

Directions:

1. Stir in corned beef, onion, garlic cloves, water, allspice, peppercorn, thymes to the Ninja Foodi. 2. Close the Ninja Foodi with Pressure Lid and turn the pressure release valve to SEAL position. 3. Pressure cook for about 90 minutes at "HI" pressure. 4. Allow the pressure to release naturally once done. 5. Open up and transfer the meat to your serving plate. 6. Cover it with tin foil and allow it to cool for 15 minutes. 7. Stir in carrots and cabbage to the lid and let them cook for 10 minutes at "HIGH" pressure. 8. Once done, do a quick release. Take out the prepped veggies and serve with your corned beef.

Nutritional Information Per Serving: Calories: 297; Fats: 17g; Carbs:1g; Protein: 14g

Corned Beef

Prep Time: 10 minutes | Cook Time: 60 minutes | Serves: 4

Ingredients:

4 pounds beef brisket
2 garlic cloves, peeled and minced
2 yellow onions, peeled and sliced
11 ounces celery, sliced
1 tbsp dried dill
3 bay leaves
4 cinnamon sticks, cut into halves
Black pepper and salt to taste
2 cups water

Directions:

1. Take a suitable bowl and stir in beef, add water and cover, let it soak for 2-3 hours. 2. Drain and transfer to the Ninja Foodi. 3. Stir in celery, onions, garlic, bay leaves, dill, cinnamon, dill, salt, pepper and the rest of the water to the Ninja Foodi. 4. Stir and combine it well. 5. Close the unit with Pressure Lid and turn the pressure release valve to SEAL position. Set the unit on Pressure Cook and then cook on "HIGH" pressure for 50 minutes. 6. Release pressure naturally over 10 minutes. 7. Transfer meat to cutting board and slice, divide amongst plates and pour the cooking liquid alongside veggies over the servings. 8. Enjoy.

Nutritional Information Per Serving: Calories: 289; Fat: 21g; Carbs: 14g; Protein: 9g

Beef Bourguignon

Prep Time: 10 minutes | Cook Time: 30 minutes | Serves: 4

Ingredients:

- 1-pound stewing steak
- ½-pound bacon
- 5 medium carrots, diced
- 1 large red onion, peeled and sliced
- 2 garlic cloves, minced
- 2 tsp salt
- 2 tbsp fresh thyme
- 2 tbsp fresh parsley, chopped
- 2 tsp ground pepper
- ½ cup beef broth
- 1 tbsp olive oil
- 1 tbsp sugar-free maple syrup

Directions:

1. Select "Sear/Sauté" mode at MD on your Ninja Foodi and stir in 1 tbsp of oil, allow the oil to heat up. 2. Pat your beef dry and season it well. 3. Stir in beef into the Ninja Foodi in batches and sauté them until nicely browned up. 4. Slice up the cooked bacon into strips and add the strips to the pot. 5. Add onions as well and brown them. 6. Stir in the rest of the listed ingredients. Close the unit with Pressure Lid and turn the pressure release valve to SEAL position. Set the unit on Pressure Cook. 7. Cook for 30 minutes on "HI" pressure. 8. Allow the pressure to release naturally over 10 minutes. Enjoy.

Nutritional Information Per Serving: Calories: 416; Fats: 18g; Carbs: 12g; Protein:27g

Veggies & Beef Stew

Prep Time: 10 minutes | Cook Time: 10 minutes | Serves: 4

Ingredients:

- 1-pound beef roast
- 4 cups beef broth
- 3 garlic cloves, chopped
- 1 carrot, chopped
- 2 celery stalks, chopped
- 2 tomatoes, chopped
- ½ white onion, chopped
- ¼ tsp salt
- ⅛ tsp black pepper

Directions:

1. Stir in listed ingredients to your Ninja Foodi and lock lid, cook on "HI" pressure for 10 minutes. 2. Quick-release pressure. 3. Open the Ninja Foodi's lid and shred the bee using forks. 4. Serve and enjoy.

Nutritional Information Per Serving: Calories: 211; Fat: 7g; Carbs: 2g; Protein: 10g

Braised Lamb Shanks

Prep Time: 20 minutes | Cook Time: 46 minutes | Serves: 4

Ingredients:

- 2 tbsp olive oil
- 4 lamb shanks
- Black pepper and salt to taste
- 4 cloves garlic, minced
- ¾ cup dry red wine
- 1 tsp dried basil
- ¾ tsp dried oregano
- 28 oz. crushed tomatoes

Directions:

1. Turn the Ninja Foodi to Sear/Sauté. Stir in the oil. Season the lamb with black pepper and salt. 2. Cook until brown. Remove and set aside. Add the garlic and cook for 15 seconds. 3. Pour in the wine. Simmer for 2 minutes. Stir in the basil, oregano and tomatoes. 4. Put the lamb back to the pot. Seal the pot. Set it to Pressure Cook. 5. Cook at "HI" pressure for 45 minutes. Release the pressure naturally. 6. Serve over polenta.

Nutritional Information Per Serving: Calories: 790; Fat: 31g; Carbs: 18.3g; Protein: 96.8g

Beef Enchiladas

Prep Time: 15 minutes | Cook Time: 10-12 minutes | Serves: 4

Ingredients:

1 pound ground beef
1 packet taco seasoning
4 tortillas
2 diced tomatoes
For Sauce:
1 tbsp red chili sauce
1 cup Mexican cheese

2 sliced green chilies
1 can of black beans
1 tbsp olive oil

½ cup fresh coriander
¼ cup sour cream

Directions:

1. In a medium-size skillet, take a start by browning the ground beef in olive oil. 2. Then add the taco seasoning to it. Give it a good mix. 3. Once mixed well, put in tomatoes, beans, and chilies. Give it a good mix and set aside. 4. Stir in all the sauce ingredients in a pan and heat the sauce until the cheese melts. Keep stirring until well-thickened. Stuff in the beef batter in the tortillas and wrap them. 5. Place the tortilla wraps in a foil-lined Ninja Foodi Cook & Crisp Basket. Pour the prepared sauce on it. 6. Top up with cheese evenly. Air Crisp it for 5 to 8 minutes at 390°F, until the cheese melts. Enchiladas are ready to be served.
Nutritional Information Per Serving: Calories: 255; Fat: 14.8g; Carbs: 23.1g; Protein: 9.2g

Instant Lamb Steaks

Prep Time: 3 minutes | Cook Time: 7-8 minutes | Serves: 1

Ingredients:

1 pound lamb steaks
Dry Ingredients:
Salt to taste
Black pepper to taste
1 tsp paprika powder
1 tbsp garlic powder

Olive oil

1 tbsp ginger powder
¼ tsp red chili flakes
1 tsp five-spice powder
1 tsp oregano

Directions:

1. Take out the steaks from the refrigerator and allow them to defrost. 2. Preheat the Ninja Foodi at Air Crisp Mode at 390°F. Pat dry the lamb steaks and rub them with olive oil. 3. Combine all dry ingredients in a bowl. Press each side of the steaks into the dry mixture then place it in the Ninja Foodi Cook & Crisp Basket. 4. Air Crisp the lamb sticks at Medium-rare for 7 to 8 minutes. Instant bread meat treatment can be used to check the internal temperature at 145°F. Dish out the steaks and serve!
Nutritional Information Per Serving: Calories: 647; Fat: 43.4g; Carbs: 8.2g; Protein: 1.9g

Ninja Foodi Pork Shoulder Roast

Prep Time: 10 minutes | Cook Time: 10 hours | Serves: 14

Ingredients:

4 pounds pork shoulder roast
4 carrots, peeled and sliced
4 onions, sliced

4 tbsp Italian seasonings
Salt and black pepper, to taste

Directions:

1. Add pork shoulder, Italian seasonings, salt, and pepper in a large bowl. Mix well and set aside for about 4 hours. 2. Now, place carrots and onions in the bottom of Ninja Foodi and add marinated pork shoulder in it. Close the unit with Pressure Lid and turn the pressure release valve to VENT position. 3. Set the unit on "Slow Cook" function. 4. Slow cook at LO for 10 hours. 5. Open the Pressure Lid and take out. 6. Serve and enjoy!
Nutritional Information Per Serving: Calories: 365; Fat: 27.6g; Carbs: 5.1g; Protein: 22.3g

Ninja Foodi Beef Casserole

Prep Time: 10 minutes | Cook Time: 8 hours | Serves: 3

Ingredients:

- ½ pound beef steak, chopped
- ½ cup chopped tomatoes
- ½ onion, chopped
- ¼ cup beef broth
- Salt and black pepper, to taste

Directions:

1. Add everything in the Ninja Foodi. Close the unit with Pressure Lid and turn the pressure release valve to VENT position. Set the unit on "Slow Cook" mode. 2. Cook at LO for about 8 hours and open the lid. 3. Take out, serve and enjoy!

Nutritional Information Per Serving: Calories: 156; Fat: 4.9g; Carbs: 3g; Protein: 23.8g

Ninja Foodi Minced Beef with Tomatoes

Prep Time: 10 minutes | Cook Time: 10 hours | Serves: 4

Ingredients:

- ¾ cup chopped tomatoes
- ½ cup water
- ½ pound minced beef
- 1½ tbsp mixed herbs
- Salt and black pepper, to taste

Directions:

1. Mix all the ingredients in the Ninja Foodi. Close the unit with Pressure Lid and turn the pressure release valve to VENT position. Set the unit on "Slow Cook" mode. 2. Pressure cook at LO for about 8 hours and open the lid. 3. Take out, serve and enjoy!

Nutritional Information Per Serving: Calories: 116; Fat: 3.7g; Carbs: 2.3g; Protein: 17.7g

Beef Stew

Prep Time: 9-10 hours | Cook Time: 25-30 minutes | Serves: 2-3

Ingredients:

- 1 pound beef cuts
- 2 carrots (coarsely sliced)
- 2 potatoes (coarsely sliced)
- 4 tbsp gram flour
- 1 tsp salt
- 1 tsp dried thyme
- 1 tsp pepper
- 1 diced onion
- 1 cup red wine
- 2 tbsp Worcestershire sauce
- 4-5 minced garlic cloves
- 1 cup sliced mushrooms
- 1 tbsp olive oil

Directions:

1. Add flour, thyme, pepper, and salt into a container. Take the beef cuts and add them into the flour mixture to coat them well. 2. Add olive oil in the Ninja Foodi cooking pot. Add floured beef when the oil is very hot. Close the unit with Pressure Lid and turn the pressure release valve to SEAL position. Set the unit on Pressure Cook mode at High. Sear it from all sides for about 10 minutes. 3. Then add chopped garlic and onion into the Ninja Foodi cooking pot. 4. Now with the help of wine, deglaze the Ninja Foodi cooking pot and remove the brown bits from the bottom with a non-stick spatula. 5. Once the wine thickens, add beef broth and Worcestershire sauce to Ninja Foodi cooking pot. Put on the pressure lid and turn the valve to Seal and cook in Ninja Foodi on Pressure Cook mode at HI for 20 minutes. Release the pressure naturally when time is up. 6. Cut carrots, mushrooms, potatoes, and onions into slices while beef is being Pressure Cooked. After the pressure has been released, add in vegetables, put on the Pressure Lid and Seal the valve. 7. Pressure Cook it for 2 minutes and serve. Enjoy!

Nutritional Information Per Serving: Calories: 390; Fat: 7.8g; Carbs: 25.2g; Protein: 38.4g

Ninja Foodi Steak Fajitas

Prep Time: 10 minutes | Cook Time: 8 hours | Serves: 3

Ingredients:

- 1 pound beef, trimmed and sliced
- 1¼ cups salsa
- 1 tbsp fajita seasoning
- ½ bell pepper, sliced
- ½ onion, sliced
- Salt and black pepper, to taste

Directions:

1. Place salsa in the bottom of Ninja Foodi cooking pot and top it with fajita seasoning, onion, beef, bell pepper, salt, and pepper. 2. Stir well. Close the unit with Pressure Lid and turn the pressure release valve to VENT position. Set the unit on "Slow Cook" mode. 3. Slow cook at LO for about 8 hours. 4. Open the lid and take out. 5. Serve and enjoy!

Nutritional Information Per Serving: Calories: 369; Fat: 9.9g; Carbs: 20.3g; Protein: 49.9g

Ninja Foodi Lamb & Carrot Stew

Prep Time: 10 minutes | Cook Time: 9 hours | Serves: 3

Ingredients:

- ¾ pound lamb chops, trimmed
- ½ cup vegetable broth
- 2½ carrots, chopped
- 1 onion, chopped
- Salt and black pepper, to taste

Directions:

1. Add all the ingredients in Ninja Foodi and mix well. Close the unit with Pressure Lid and turn the pressure release valve to VENT position. Select "Slow Cook". 2. Cook at LO for about 9 hours and open the lid. 3. Serve and enjoy!

Nutritional Information Per Serving: Calories: 320; Fat: 8.6g; Carbs: 24.6g; Protein: 34.8g

Lamb Shanks

Prep Time: 35-40 minutes | Cook Time: 1 hour and 20 minutes | Serves: 1

Ingredients:

- 2 skinless lamb shanks
- 1 tsp ginger garlic paste
- 1 tsp oregano
- ¾ tsp paprika
- ¾ tsp salt
- ½ tsp black pepper
- ½ tsp ground cumin powder
- 1 tbsp brown sugar
- 1 onion
- 2 small carrots
- 2 bay leaves
- ½ cup red wine
- 2 cups beef stock
- 2 tbsp cornstarch
- ¼ cup water
- ¼ cup olive oil
- 1 tbsp olive oil (for cooking)

Directions:

1. Combine lamb, salt, pepper, oregano, ginger garlic paste, paprika, cumin powder, brown sugar, and in a large bowl, and then add oil to it. Coat it well and let it marinate for 30 minutes, or over a night. 2. Now pour in olive oil and place shanks side by side. Close the unit with Pressure Lid and turn the pressure release valve to SEAL position. Set the unit on Pressure Cook on LO. Cook for 15 minutes and then remove lamb shanks once they are brown and put them aside. 3. Now add bay leaves, carrots, onions, and the remaining leftover marinade to the Ninja Foodi cooking pot and cook it until onions become translucent. Cook for about 5 minutes. 4. To deglaze the pot, add red wine and make sure to scrape out all the bits that are stuck on the bottom. Now return the shanks to the pot for 10 minutes, simmer it to reduce by half. 5. Pour in the stock, close the unit with Pressure Lid, and turn the pressure release valve to SEAL position. Set the unit on Pressure Cook. Cook for 30 minutes at HI . 6. And then naturally release the pressure once it's cooked. Now remove shanks and put them aside. 7. Make a slurry of cornstarch with water in a bowl and add it to the pot. 8. Switchback the Ninja Foodi on Pressure Cook at LO until sauce reaches the desired thickness. Now return lamb to the cooking pot and let it sit in the sauce until it's ready to be served!

Nutritional Information Per Serving: Calories: 995; Fat: 69.3g; Carbs: 56g; Protein: 12.2g

Ninja Foodi Lamb Chops with Tomatoes

Prep Time: 10 minutes | Cook Time: 8 hours | Serves: 4

Ingredients:

- 1 pound lamb chops
- 3 tbsp mixed herbs
- 1 cup water
- 1½ cups chopped tomatoes
- Salt and black pepper, to taste

Directions:

1. Mix everything in Ninja Foodi and cover the unit with Pressure Lid. Turn the pressure release valve to VENT position. 2. Select the unit on "Slow Cook" mode. 3. Slow cook at LO for about 8 hours and open the lid. 4. Take out, serve and enjoy!

Nutritional Information Per Serving: Calories: 258; Fat: 8.9g; Carbs: 10.2g; Protein: 34.2g

Ninja Foodi Plum & Beef Salad

Prep Time: 20 minutes | Cook Time: 10 minutes | Serves: 6

Ingredients:

- 2 pounds beef, trimmed
- 2 tsp unsweetened applesauce
- 8 plums, thinly sliced
- 4 tbsp olive oil
- Salt and black pepper, to taste

Directions:

1. Add 1 tbsp salt, olive oil, and pepper in a large bowl. Mix well. 2. Add in beef and toss to coat well. 3. Place beef in Ninja Foodi. Close the unit with Pressure Lid and turn the pressure release valve to SEAL position. Select the unit on Pressure Cook mode. 4. Pressure cook at LO for about 5 minutes per side and open the lid. 5. Take out the beef in a bowl and add in remaining ingredients. Mix properly. 6. Serve and enjoy!

Nutritional Information Per Serving: Calories: 402; Fat: 19g; Carbs: 10.9g; Protein: 46.5g

Sweet and Sour Pork

Prep Time: 15-20 minutes | Cook Time: 15 minutes | Serves: 4

Ingredients:

- 2 pound boneless pork
- 3 tsp paprika powder
- 1 can pineapple chunks
- 1 chopped onion
- 1 tsp chopped green chili
- 2 tbsp apple cider vinegar
- 2 tbsp brown sugar
- 2 tbsp Worcestershire sauce
- Salt to taste
- 2 tbsp of cornstarch
- ½ cup sliced green onion

Directions:

1. Add pork to a large shallow dish, and sprinkle paprika all over it. Turn on the Sear/Sauté setting and adjust the temperature at MD. Pour in oil and sear the pork cuts. 2. Now invert the pork to the Ninja Foodi and set it on Pressure Cook at HI. Now add onion, green pepper, Worcestershire sauce, vinegar, salt, brown sugar, and pineapple juice to the Ninja Foodi. Close the unit with Pressure Lid and turn the pressure release valve to SEAL position. Select the unit on Pressure Cook mode. 3. Cook in your Ninja Foodi at HI For 10 minutes. Then release the pressure quickly. Turn the pressure release valve to VENT position and set the unit on Slow Cook setting and adjust on HI and let it simmer. Now take a small bowl and make a slurry with cornstarch and water. 4. Stir it slowly into the pork gravy, then add pineapple and cook until the sauce thickens up for about one to 2 minutes and sprinkle refreshing green onion on it!

Nutritional Information Per Serving: Calories: 403; Fat: 12.7g; Carbs: 31.8g; Protein: 42.8g

Ninja Foodi Ground Beef Soup

Prep Time: 20 minutes | Cook Time: 21 minutes | Serves: 6

Ingredients:

- 1 pound lean ground beef
- 1 ginger, minced
- ½ pound fresh mushrooms, sliced
- 1 onion, chopped
- 2 tbsp soy sauce
- 1 garlic clove, minced
- 4 cups chicken broth
- Salt and black pepper, to taste

Directions:

1. Add beef in the Ninja Foodi deluxe reversible rack. Close the Crisping Lid. Select the unit on Broil mode. 2. Cook for 2 minutes. Stir in mushrooms, garlic, and onion and cook for about 4 minutes. 3. Add in remaining ingredients and cook for 15 minutes. 4. Take out, serve and enjoy!

Nutritional Information Per Serving: Calories: 186; Fat: 5.8g; Carbs: 4.4g; Protein: 27.9g

Tomahawk Rib-Eye Steak

Prep Time: 10 minutes | Cook Time: 52 minutes | Serves: 1-2

Ingredients:

- 1 tomahawk rib-eye steak, about 1 ¾ inches thick
- Kosher salt, to taste
- Freshly ground pepper, to taste
- 1 small head garlic
- 2 tbsp oil, plus more for drizzling (canola or grapeseed)
- 4 tbsp (½ stick) unsalted butter
- 4 large sprigs fresh thyme

Directions:

1. Pat dry the tomahawk steak with paper towels. 2. Season steak very liberally with kosher salt and freshly ground pepper. Let the steak come to room temperature. 3. Meanwhile, prepare the garlic. Trim off the top ¼ inch of the garlic bulb. Drizzle with the oil and add a pinch of salt, then wrap in a foil tent, and cook the garlic in Ninja Foodi on Pressure Cook at LO for 30 minutes, until the cloves are soft. Remove from the Ninja Foodi and allow to cool. 4. Moisten a paper towel and wrap it around the steak's rib bone, then wrap aluminum foil around the paper towel. 5. In the Ninja Foodi, lay the tomahawk steak into the Ninja Foodi and Sear for 3 minutes in 2 tbsp oil without touching it, on Sear/Sauté mode at MD. 6. Using tongs and the bone as a handle, turn the steak over and cook for another 3 minutes without touching it on Sear/Sauté setting on MD. Using tongs and the bone as a handle, sear the short side of the steak opposite the bone, about 3 minutes. 7. Sear tomahawk rib-eye steak on both sides. 8. Transfer the steak to a rimmed baking sheet and place again in the Ninja Foodi, and set it at Bake/Roast Setting at 400°F and roast for 10 minutes, or until the desired doneness is reached. 9. Use an instant-read thermometer to measure the steak's internal temperature—125°F for rare, 135°F for Medium-rare, or 145°F for Medium. 10. Make paste of butter and garlic. 11. When the steak is ready, take it out of the Ninja Foodi, and use a spoon to paste the butter and garlic over the steak. Turn the steak, and paste again, about 1 minute total. Transfer the steak to a cutting board, tent it with foil, and let it rest 10 minutes. 12. Then add this cutted steaks into Ninja Foodi and cook tomahawk rib-eye steak again in Ninja Foodi on Pressure Cook mode at HI for 5 minutes. 13. Then take out steaks and top with butter and garlic. You can, simply spoon the butter and garlic over the steak. Serve and enjoy.

Nutritional Information Per Serving: Calories: 1990; Fat: 145g; Carbs: 7g; Protein: 160g

Beef Onion Pattie Burgers

Prep Time: 6 minutes | Cook Time: 12-15 minutes | Serves: 4

Ingredients:

- 1 pound ground beef
- **For Assembling:**
- Cheese slices
- Onion rings
- Lettuce leaves
- 8 tbsp onion soup mix
- Ketchup
- 4 burger buns

Directions:

1. Combine the ground beef and onion soup mix in a large bowl to make 4 patties. 2. Oil spray the parchment paper-lined Ninja Foodi Cook & Crisp Basket evenly. 3. Place the patties in Ninja Foodi cooking pot. Close the unit with Crisping Lid and turn on the Air Crisp function at 390°F for 5 minutes. Once done, assemble the burgers as per your likings. 4. Again, place the burgers in the Ninja Foodi. Turn the burgers carefully and for an additional 6 to 7 minutes. Air Crisp it, until the internal temperature reaches 165°F.

Nutritional Information Per Serving: Calories: 329; Fat: 13.7g; Carbs: 23.9g; Protein: 27.3g

Roasted Lamb

Prep Time: 7 minutes | Cook Time: 25 minutes | Serves: 4

Ingredients:

10 oz. Lamb leg
1 tbsp ginger garlic paste
1 tsp black pepper
1 tbsp rosemary
1 tbsp olive oil
1 tbsp dried thyme

Directions:

1. Preheat the Ninja Foodi at Air Crisp Mode at 390°F for 5 minutes. 2. Mix olive oil with rosemary, black pepper, ginger garlic paste, and thyme in a bowl. Pat dry the lamb roast leg and then rub the herb oil mixture until it is well-coated. Let it rest to infuse the flavors. 3. Place it carefully in the Ninja Foodi Cook & Crisp Basket and Air Crisp it at 390°F for 15 minutes. 4. It's recommended to check the temperature with a meat thermometer to ensure that it's cooked according to your preference. 5. Cook it for another 8 to 10 minutes and then wrap it with kitchen foil for 5 minutes and leave it to rest before serving!

Nutritional Information Per Serving: Calories: 321; Fat: 11.2g; Carbs: 49.3g; Protein: 21.8g

Maple Lamb Chops

Prep Time: 6-8 minutes | Cook Time: 12-15 minutes | Serves: 2

Ingredients:

4 lamb chops
2 tbsp maple syrup
1 tbsp rosemary
2 tbsp extra-virgin olive oil
1 tsp garlic paste
Salt and pepper to taste
8-10 fresh mint leaves

Directions:

1. Add oil, maple syrup, rosemary, and garlic to a bowl to mix the ingredients well. Now add pepper and salt to it. Dump in lamb chops and coat it well, leave it to marinate in the refrigerator for 2 to 4 hours. 2. Preheat Ninja Foodi on Bake/Roast function at 375°F for 10 minutes. 3. Place the marinated lamb and close the unit with Crisping Lid. Let the chops cook for 6 minutes on the Bake/Roast function. Then flip the chops by opening the top lid and then cook them for 6 more minutes with a closed lid. 4. Once cooked, its internal temperature should reach 145°F. Now plate it out and add chopped mint and maple syrup on top of it!

Nutritional Information Per Serving: Calories: 508; Fat: 24.9g; Carbs: 19.6g; Protein: 29.4g

Pork Tenderloin

Prep Time: 5 minutes | Cook Time: 15-20 minutes | Serves: 1

Ingredients:

1 pound pork tenderloin
Salt to taste
1 tsp Schezwan pepper
1 tbsp soy sauce
1 tbsp vinegar
1 tsp hot sauce
1 tbsp oyster sauce
¼ tsp chili flakes

Directions:

1. Preheat the Ninja Foodi on Air Crisp Mode at 390°F for 5 minutes. 2. Combine all the sauces, chili flakes, salt, and pepper in a bowl. Put in the tenderloin and let it rest for 15-20 minutes. 3. Place the tenderloin in the Ninja Foodi Cook & Crisp Basket. Give it an olive oil spray. Close the unit with Crisping Lid and let it cook at 390°F for 20 minutes. Once the internal temperature reaches 145°F, it's done. 4. Serve pork with cooked brown gravy!

Nutritional Information Per Serving: Calories: 367; Fat: 9.1g; Carbs: 5.1g ; Protein: 59.9g

Lamb Balls

Prep Time: 10 minutes | Cook Time: 10-12 minutes | Serves: 2

Ingredients:

- 11 oz. lamb mince
- 1 tsp ginger garlic paste
- 1 small onion

Spice Mix Ingredients:
- 1 tsp cumin powder
- 1 tsp coriander powder
- ½ tsp turmeric powder
- 1 tbsp soy sauce
- ½ cup bread crumbs
- Salt to taste
- Black pepper to taste

Directions:

1. Grate the onion and put it in a bowl. Now add the remaining ingredients and with the help of your hand mix all the ingredients. Mix it until the batter is well-combined. 2. Shape the balls in a round shape and set them aside on a plate. 3. Now at 390°F, preheat the Ninja Foodi at Air Crisp Mode for 5 minutes. Then align balls in the Cook & Crisp Basket in Ninja Foodi for 10 to 12 minutes.

Nutritional Information Per Serving: Calories: 506; Fat: 31.5g; Carbs: 19g; Protein: 36.6g

Chapter 5 Fish and Seafood Recipes

Page	Recipe
65	Low-Carb Crab Soup
65	Awesome Shrimp Roast
65	Roasted BBQ Shrimp
66	Ninja Foodi Parsley Baked Salmon
66	Ninja Foodi Salmon with Sweet Potatoes
66	Butter Lime Salmon
67	Bay Crab Legs
67	White Fish with Garlic Lemon Pepper Seasoning
67	Spicy Indian Shrimp Curry
68	Glazed Coho Salmon
68	Spicy Crispy Shrimp
68	Coconut Curry Salmon with Zucchini Noodles
69	Fish Stew
69	Sweet and Sour Fish
69	Mahi-Mahi with Citrus Sauce
70	Lobster with Fried Rice
70	Fish Broccoli Stew
70	Buttered Fish
71	Air Fried Scallops
71	Cajun Shrimp
71	Shrimp Scampi Linguini
72	Lobster Tail
72	Panko Crusted Cod
72	Buttery Scallops
73	Shrimp Zoodles
73	Beer Battered Fish
73	Ninja Foodi Stir-Fried Shrimp
74	Ninja Foodi Broiled Mahi-Mahi
74	Ninja Foodi Ginger Cod
74	Gluten-free fish tacos
75	Ninja Foodi Salmon
75	Ninja Foodi Asparagus Scallops
75	Spicy Shrimps
76	Ninja Foodi Ginger Salmon
76	Ninja Foodi Air Crisp Herbed Salmon
76	Mixed Seafood Platter
77	Fish Skewers
77	Crumbed Tilapia
77	Lemon Garlic Scallops

Low-Carb Crab Soup

Prep Time: 5 minutes | Cook Time: 15 minutes | Serves: 6

Ingredients:

Soup

- 12 oz lump crab meat
- 24 oz marinara sauce
- 4 cups chicken broth
- 3 ribs celery, chopped
- 2 bell peppers, chopped
- 2 tbsp Old Bay Seasoning
- ½ cup butter
- Salt and pepper, to taste
- 1 cup heavy cream

Onion and cream cheese topping

- 8 oz cream cheese, softened for 30 seconds in the microwave
- 3 green onions, chopped
- ½ tsp Old Bay Seasoning

Directions:

1. Place all the soup ingredients except the heavy cream into the Ninja Foodi cooking pot and stir well. Close the unit with Pressure Lid and turn the pressure release lid to SEAL position. Set the unit on Pressure Cook mode. 2. Pressure cook at HI for 15 minutes. 3. When done, naturally release the pressure for 15 minutes before venting the rest of the steam. 4. Meanwhile, combine the cream cheese topping ingredients. Put the mixture in an air-tight container and refrigerate. 5. Once the soup is done cooking, stir in the heavy cream.

Nutritional Information Per Serving: Calories: 391; Fat: 36.6g; Carbs: 8.3g; Protein: 9.32g

Awesome Shrimp Roast

Prep Time: 5-10 minutes | Cook Time: 7 minutes | Serves: 2

Ingredients:

- 3 tbsp chipotle in adobo sauce, minced
- ¼ tsp salt
- ¼ cup BBQ sauce
- ½ orange, juiced
- ½ pound large shrimps

Directions:

1. Add all the ingredients in a mixing bowl and toss well to combine. 2. Set shrimps over rack and close the Crisping Lid. Set the Ninja Foodi on Bake/Roast mode at 400°F for 7 minutes, cook until the timer runs out. 3. Serve and enjoy.

Nutritional Values Per Serving: Calories: 173; Fat: 2g; Carbs: 21g; Protein: 17g

Roasted BBQ Shrimp

Prep Time: 5-10 minutes | Cook Time: 7 minutes | Serves: 2

Ingredients:

- 3 tbsp chipotle in adobo sauce, minced
- ¼ tsp salt
- ¼ cup BBQ sauce
- ½ orange, juiced
- ½-pound large shrimps

Directions:

1. Toss shrimp with chipotles and rest of the ingredients in a suitable bowl. 2. Set the shrimps over the cooking pot. Close the Crisping Lid. 3. Set the Ninja Foodi by pressing the "Bake/Roast" mode and setting it to "400°F" and timer to 7 minutes. 4. Cook until the timer runs out. 5. Serve and enjoy.

Nutritional Values Per Serving: Calories: 173; Fat: 2g; Carbs: 21g; Protein: 17g

Ninja Foodi Parsley Baked Salmon

Prep Time: 10 minutes | Cook Time: 20 minutes | Serves: 3

Ingredients:

1 pound salmon fillets

¾ tbsp olive oil

1½ tbsp fresh parsley, minced

¼ tsp ginger powder

Salt and black pepper, to taste

Directions:

1. Place salmon fillets in Ninja Foodi and top them with olive oil, parsley, ginger powder, salt, and pepper. 2. Close the Crisping Lid. Set the unit on Bake/Roast mode. 3. Bake for 20 minutes at 400°F. 4. Open the lid and take out. 5. Serve and enjoy!

Nutritional Values Per Serving: Calories: 233; Fat: 12.9g; Carbs: 0.6g; Protein: 29.6g

Ninja Foodi Salmon with Sweet Potatoes

Prep Time: 10 minutes | Cook Time: 9 hours | Serves: 3

Ingredients:

½ pound salmon fillets, cubed

¾ cup chicken broth

¼ tsp ground nutmeg

2 sweet potatoes, sliced thinly

½ onion, chopped

Salt and black pepper, to taste

Directions:

1. Place half of the sweet potatoes in the bottom of the Ninja Foodi and season them with salt and pepper. 2. Place salmon fillets and onion on the top and sprinkle ground nutmeg on it. 3. Then, top with remaining sweet potato slices and close the pressure Lid. 4. Turn the pressure release valve to SEAL position. Set the unit on Pressure Cook mode. 5. Cook for about 9 hours at LO and open the lid. 6. Take out, serve and enjoy!

Nutritional Values Per Serving: Calories: 236; Fat: 5.3g; Carbs: 29.9g; Protein: 17.6g

Butter Lime Salmon

Prep Time: 5-6 minutes | Cook Time: 4-5 minutes | Serves: 1

Ingredients

2 salmon fillets

4 tbsp lemon juice

½ tsp lemon zest

1 tsp rosemary

2 fresh dill stalks

Salt and pepper to taste

Directions:

1. Pour water and lemon juice in the Ninja Foodi cooking pot. 2. Then add lemon zest and dill into it. 3. Add a wire rack at the lowest position in the cooking pot. 4. Now place salmon fillets on the rack, it is suggested to cut them if they don't fit well in it. 5. Season it by sprinkling salt and pepper on it. Sprinkle rosemary on both sides. 6. Secure the Pressure Lid. 7. Make sure to set the valve on the Seal. Cook on Pressure Cook mode at HI for 4 minutes. For the frozen fillet add another minute to the cook time. Release the valve on the Vent and then open its lid once done fully. And it's ready to be served instantly or it can also be stored in the freezer!

Nutritional Values Per Serving: Calories: 405; Fat: 15.1g; Carbs: 26g; Protein: 41.7g

Bay Crab Legs

Prep Time: 6 minutes | Cook Time: 5-6 minutes | Serves: 1

Ingredients:

1 pound crab legs
1-2 cups water
2 tbsp bay seasoning
1 tsp lime juice
1 tbsp garlic infused butter

Directions:

1. Marinate the crab legs with bay seasoning and lime juice. Let it marinate for 30-40 minutes. 2. Pour in water inside the Ninja Foodi cooking pot. Any other seasonings can also be used here. Place the rack in Ninja Foodi and place the crab legs on top. 3. Close the Pressure Lid and turn the pressure release valve to SEAL position. Set the unit on Pressure Cook mode. 4. Pressure cook at HI for 5 minutes. 5. When cooked, move the nozzle to Vent quickly release the steam, and serve it with garlic-infused butter on top!
Nutritional Values Per Serving: Calories: 272; Fat: 4g; Carbs: 1.1g; Protein: 43.4g

White Fish with Garlic Lemon Pepper Seasoning

Prep Time: 5 minutes | Cook Time: 10-12 minutes | Serves: 2

Ingredients:

2 whitefish fillets
1 tsp garlic powder
1 tbsp olive oil
2 tbsp lemon pepper seasoning
Salt to taste
2 tbsp fresh chopped coriander
1 lemon (rings)

Directions:

1. Preheat the Ninja Foodi at Air Crisp Mode to 390°F for 5 minutes. 2. Drizzle olive oil on the fillets and season it with garlic powder, lemon pepper seasoning, and salt. Now repeat the step for both the sides. 3. Inside the base of the Ninja Foodi Cook & Crisp Basket, lay the perforated bay paper. Spray the paper lightly with olive oil. 4. Place fish fillets on the paper and add lemon veggies to it. Close the Crisping Lid. 5. Air Crisp it for about 10 to 12 minutes at 390°F or until fish can be flaked with the help of a fork. Keep in mind the timings depend on how thick the fillet is. 6. Sprinkle chopped parsley and serve it warm with the toasted lemon wedges!
Nutritional Values Per Serving: Calories: 146; Fat: 7.4g; Carbs: 3.7g; Protein: 17.2g

Spicy Indian Shrimp Curry

Prep Time: 10 minutes | Cook Time: 20 minutes | Serves: 4

Ingredients:

1 tbsp olive oil
1 onion, chopped
1 tbsp garlic, minced
2 lbs. shrimp, peeled and cleaned
1 (48 oz) can crushed tomatoes
1 tsp cayenne pepper
1 tsp curry powder
1 tsp ground ginger
2 tsp parsley flakes
1 tsp garlic powder
2 tsp salt
1 tbsp sugar
½–1 cup sour cream
3 tbsp corn starch and ½ cup cold water, combined

Directions:

1. Turn the Ninja Foodi to Sear/Sauté mode on HI. 2. Add the olive oil and sauté the onion and garlic. Add the shrimp. Try to leave the shrimp a little undercooked. Remove from the pot. 3. Add the crushed tomatoes, cayenne pepper, curry, ginger, parsley flakes, garlic powder, salt, and sugar. Cook until bubbling hot. 4. Return the shrimp to the pot and stir in your preferred amount of sour cream, depending on how creamy you want it. 5. Turn to Bake/Roast mode at 400°F for about 10 minutes. Adjust any seasonings you prefer. 6. Take the corn starch slurry and add it to the curry. Stir well. Cook for another 3 minutes until thickened to the desired consistency.
Nutritional Information Per Serving: Calories: 197.3; Fat: 11.6g; Carbs: 21.5g ; Protein: 2.5g

Glazed Coho Salmon

Prep Time: 10 minutes | Cook Time: 25 minutes | Serves: 4

Ingredients:

- 1–2 coho salmon fillets
- 1 cup water
- ¼ cup soy sauce
- ¼ cup brown sugar
- 1 tbsp honey
- 1½ tbsp ginger root, minced
- ½ tsp white pepper
- 2 tbsp corn starch
- ¼ cup cold water

Directions:

1. Preheat the Ninja Foodi on Air Crisp mode at 350°F for 5 minutes. 2. Put a medium saucepan over medium heat. Add in all the ingredients (except the salmon, corn starch, and cold water) and bring to a gentle boil. 3. Combine the corn starch and water in another bowl. Then, slowly whisk the corn starch mixture into the sauce in the saucepan until it thickens. 4. Brush the sauce over the salmon fillets (reserving some of the sauce for serving). 5. Place the salmon in the Cook & Crisp Basket and close the Crisping Lid. 6. Cook on Air Crisp for 15 minutes at 350°F. 7. When done, brush the salmon with another coat of sauce and serve.

Nutritional Information Per Serving: Calories: 163; Fat: 2g; Carbs: 15g; Protein: 18g

Spicy Crispy Shrimp

Prep Time: 5–10 minutes (plus 60 minutes for marinating) | Cook Time: 6 minutes | Serves: 4

Ingredients:

- 1 tsp garlic salt
- ½ tsp black pepper
- 1 tbsp paprika
- 1 tbsp garlic powder
- 2 tbsp olive oil
- 1 lb. jumbo shrimps, peeled and deveined
- 2 tbsp brown sugar

Directions:

1. Mix together all the ingredients in a large mixing bowl until well combined. 2. Let the mixture chill and marinate for 30–60 minutes. 3. Preheat the Ninja Foodi on Bake/Roast mode at 360°F for 6 minutes. 4. Arrange the prepared shrimp over the reversible rack in the Ninja Foodi. Lock the unit with Crisping Lid and cook for 3 minutes. Open the lid, flip the shrimp, close the lid, and cook for 3 minutes more. 5. Serve and enjoy!

Nutritional Information Per Serving: Calories: 370; Fat: 27.9g; Carbs: 23g; Protein: 6g

Coconut Curry Salmon with Zucchini Noodles

Prep Time: 10 minutes | Cook Time: 15 minutes | Serves: 2

Ingredients:

- 2 tbsp yellow curry paste
- 1 small sweet onion, halved and sliced
- 1 red bell pepper seeded, halved, and sliced
- 2 garlic cloves, pressed
- 1 (14½ oz) can coconut milk
- 1 dash fish sauce
- ¾-lb salmon, skinned, deboned, and cut into 2 fillets
- 1 zucchini, spiralized

Directions:

1. Set the Ninja Foodi to Sear/Sauté mode at HI. Allow it to preheat for 3 minutes. 2. When the Ninja Foodi has preheated, add the yellow curry paste and onions. Stir the onions around with a wooden spoon to coat them with the curry. Allow them to cook for 5 minutes. 3. Add the bell pepper and garlic once the onions are tender, cooking for an additional 2 minutes. 4. Pour in the coconut milk and add a dash of fish sauce. Stir to combine. 5. Place the salmon fillets on top of the curry mixture. 6. Place the Pressure Lid on and turn the pressure release valve to SEAL position. Set the unit on Pressure Cook and cook for 3 minutes on HI. 7. After the cooking time is up, open the Foodi and place the zucchini delicately on top of the fish. Replace the lid and steam for an additional minute. 8. Turn off the Foodi, and remove the lid. Use tongs to transfer the zucchini noodles to wide bowls. Place a salmon fillet on top of each mound of zucchini, then ladle on the sauce with the onions and bell peppers.

Nutritional Information Per Serving: Calories: 251.8; Fat: 12.3g ; Carbs: 33.7g ; Protein: 2.6g

Fish Stew

Prep Time: 5 minutes | Cook Time: 20 minutes | Serves: 4

Ingredients:

- 1 lb. white fish fillets, chopped
- 1 cup broccoli, chopped
- 3 cups fish stock
- 1 onion, diced
- 2 cups celery stalks, chopped
- 1 cup heavy cream
- 1 bay leaf
- 1½ cups cauliflower, diced
- 1 carrot, sliced
- 2 tbsp butter
- ¼ tsp garlic powder
- ½ tsp salt
- ¼ tsp pepper

Directions:

1. Set your Ninja Foodi to Sear/Sauté mode on HI temperature setting. 2. Add the butter, and let it melt. 3. Add the onion and carrots, cook for 3 minutes. 4. Stir in the remaining ingredients. 5. Close the Pressure Lid. Turn the pressure release valve to SEAL position. 6. Cook for 4 minutes on HI on Pressure Cook mode. 7. Release the pressure naturally over 10 minutes. 8. Remove the bay leaf once cooked.

Nutritional Information Per Serving: Calories: 298; Fat: 18g; Carbs: 6g; Protein: 24g

Sweet and Sour Fish

Prep Time: 10 minutes | Cook Time: 6 minutes | Serves: 4

Ingredients:

- 1 lb. fish chunks
- 1 tbsp vinegar
- 2 drops liquid stevia
- ¼ cup butter
- Salt and pepper, to taste

Directions:

1. Set your Ninja Foodi to Sear/Sauté mode on MD: HI temperature setting. 2. Add the butter to the Ninja Foodi cooking pot and melt it. 3. Add the fish chunks, sauté for 3 minutes. 4. Add the stevia, salt, and pepper, and stir. 5. Close the Ninja Foodi with Crisping Lid. Select Air Crisp mode. 6. Cook for 3 minutes at 360°F. 7. Serve and enjoy!

Nutritional Information Per Serving: Calories: 274; Fat: 15g; Carbs: 2g; Protein: 33g

Mahi-Mahi with Citrus Sauce

Prep Time: 5 minutes | Cook Time: 10 minutes | Serves: 4

Ingredients:

- 1 cup water
- 1 tbsp olive oil
- 1 cup white wine
- ½ cup orange juice
- 2 tbsp soy sauce
- 1 tbsp lime juice
- 4 (4 oz each) mahi-mahi fillets
- Salt and pepper, to taste
- 4 tsp Chinese five-spice powder
- 1 tsp sesame seeds
- 2 tsp butter

Directions:

1. Add the water, olive oil, white wine, orange juice, soy sauce, and lime juice to the Ninja Foodi cooking pot. Close the unit with Pressure Lid and turn the pressure release valve to VENT position. Set to Steam mode and set the timer to 10 minutes. 2. Meanwhile, season each fillet with salt and pepper, five-spice, and sesame seeds. 3. When the beep sounds, carefully place the reversible rack into the pot topped with the fish fillets. Cover and steam for 8–10 minutes for the desired doneness. 4. Remove the rack with the fish. Whisk butter into the sauce at the bottom of the pot.

Nutritional Information Per Serving: Calories: 215.3; Fat: 14.7g; Carbs: 19.4g ; Protein: 3.7g

Lobster with Fried Rice

Prep Time: 5 minutes | Cook Time: 15 minutes | Serves: 3

Ingredients:

- 1 cup cooked lobster flesh
- 2–3 cups cooked rice
- 2 tbsp sesame oil
- 1 small white onion, chopped
- 1 cup peas
- 7 mini carrots, chopped
- 2-3 tbsp soy sauce
- 2 eggs, lightly beaten
- 2 tbsp green onions, chopped

Directions:

1. Preheat the Ninja Foodi on Sear/Sauté mode on HI for 5 minutes. 2. When the Ninja Foodi has preheated, pour the sesame oil into the Ninja Foodi cooking pot. Add the white onion and carrots and fry until tender. Add the peas and cook for 5 minutes. 3. Place the onion, peas, and carrots to one side of the pot, and pour the beaten eggs onto the other side. 4. Using a spatula, scramble the eggs. Once cooked, mix the eggs with the vegetable mix. 5. Add the rice to the veggie and egg mixture. Pour the soy sauce on top. Stir and fry the rice and veggie mixture until heated through and combined. 6. Add the lobster meat and stir. Switch the Ninja Foodi to KEEP WARM mode for about 2 minutes. 7. Add the chopped green onions on top.

Nutritional Information Per Serving: Calories: 190; Fat: 9g; Carbs: 26g ; Protein: 4g

Fish Broccoli Stew

Prep Time: 5 minutes | Cook Time: 20 minutes | Serves: 4

Ingredients:

- 1-pound white fish fillets, chopped
- 1 cup broccoli, chopped
- 3 cups fish stock
- 1 onion, diced
- 2 cups celery stalks, chopped
- 1 cup heavy cream
- 1 bay leaf
- 1½ cups cauliflower, diced
- 1 carrot, sliced
- 2 tbsp butter
- ¼ tsp garlic powder
- ½ tsp salt
- ¼ tsp black pepper

Directions:

1. Select "Sear/Sauté" mode on your Ninja Foodi. 2. Add butter, and let it melt 3. Stir in onion and carrots, cook for 3 minutes. 4. Stir in remaining ingredients 5. Close the Ninja Foodi with Pressure Lid and turn the pressure release valve to SEAL position. Set the unit on Pressure Cook mode. 6. Pressure Cook at HI for 4 minutes. . 7. Release the pressure naturally over 10 minutes. 8. Remove the bay leave once cooked. 9. Serve and enjoy.

Nutritional Information Per Serving: Calories: 298g; Fat: 18g; Carbs: 6g; Protein: 24g

Buttered Fish

Prep Time: 10 minutes | Cook Time: 6 minutes | Serves: 4

Ingredients:

- 1-pound fish chunks
- 1 tbsp vinegar
- 2 drops liquid stevia
- ¼ cup butter
- Black pepper and salt to taste

Directions:

1. Select "Sear/Sauté" mode at MD on your Ninja Foodi. 2. Stir in butter and melt it. 3. Add fish chunks, sauté for 3 minutes. 4. Stir in stevia, salt, and pepper. 5. Close the unit with Crisping Lid. 6. Cook on "Air Crisp" mode for 3 minutes to 360°F 7. Serve and enjoy.

Nutritional Information Per Serving: Calories: 274g; Fat: 15g; Carbs: 2g; Protein: 33g

Air Fried Scallops

Prep Time: 5 minutes | Cook Time: 5 minutes | Serves: 4

Ingredients:

12 scallops
3 tbsp olive oil

Black pepper and salt, to taste

Directions:

1. Rub the scallops with salt, pepper and olive oil. 2. Transfer it to Ninja Foodi. 3. Place the insert in your Ninja Foodi. 4. Close the Crisping Lid. 5. Air crisp for 4 minutes to 390°F. 6. Flip them after 2 minutes. 7. Serve and enjoy.

Nutritional Information Per Serving: Calories: 372g; Fat: 11g; Carbs: 0.9g; Protein: 63g

Cajun Shrimp

Prep Time: 10 minutes | Cook Time: 7 minutes | Serves: 4

Ingredients:

1¼ pound shrimp
¼ tsp cayenne pepper
½ tsp old bay seasoning
¼ tsp smoked paprika
1 pinch of salt
1 tbsp olive oil

Directions:

1. Preheat Ninja Foodi by pressing the "Air Crisp" option and setting it to 390°F and timer to 10 minutes. 2. Dip the shrimp into a spice mixture and oil. 3. Transfer the prepared shrimp to your Ninja Foodi Cook & Crisp Basket and cook for 5 minutes. 4. Serve and enjoy.

Nutritional Information Per Serving: Calories: 170; Fat: 2g; Carbs: 5g; Protein: 23g

Shrimp Scampi Linguini

Prep Time: 5 minutes | Cook Time: 3 minutes | Serves: 8

Ingredients:

1¼ pound linguini
1 pound (31 to 40) shrimp
Salt and pepper (to taste)
3 tbsp olive oil
3 tbsp butter (salted)
2 tbsp garlic (minced)
1 cup dry white wine
1 cup chicken broth
¼ tsp red pepper flakes
1 lemon (juice of the lemon)
¼ cup parmesan cheese (shredded)

Directions:

1. Turn Ninja Foodi on Sear/Sauté on HI. 2. Pour in olive oil. 3. Add butter and stir. 4. Add shrimp, season with salt and pepper and then stir. 5. Add garlic and juice of one lemon. Be careful not to get the lemon seeds in the pot. 6. Pour in white wine and chicken broth. 7. Add red pepper flakes and stir. 8. Break linguine in half and add in layers, crossing each layer so the pasta does not stick to itself. 9. Once all pasta has been added to the Ninja Foodi cooking pot, press pasta into liquid as much as possible, without stirring. Do not stir once you have added the pasta. If you do, your pasta may burn to the bottom of the pan. 10. Put Pressure Lid on Ninja Foodi and move valve to Seal position. 11. Change Ninja Foodi to Pressure Cook setting on High for 3 minutes. 12. Quick release pressure by moving valve to Vent position. Turn Ninja Foodi off. 13. Open the Pressure Lid and stir shrimp and pasta until its well-combined. Don't panic if your pasta is not 100% cooked. It will continue to cook after you add in the parmesan cheese. 14. Add parmesan cheese and stir. 15. Close the Pressure Lid (do not turn on) and let the pasta and sauce continue to combine for about 5 minutes. Stir and enjoy!!!

Nutritional Information Per Serving: Calories: 396; Fat: 12g; Carbs: 45g; Protein: 21g

Lobster Tail

Prep Time: 4 minutes | Cook Time: 6 minutes | Serves: 2

Ingredients:

4 lobster tails
4 tbsp butter (unsalted)
2 crushed garlic cloves

1 tbsp mixed dried herbs
1 tsp Slash parsley
Salt and pepper to taste

Directions:

1. Preheat the Ninja Foodi at 375°F for the Bake/Roast function by setting the cook time for 5 minutes. 2. Meanwhile, cut the lobster using kitchen scissors then cut the center of the tail until you reach the fins. Do not cut them. Use your fingers to bring the meat up to the top by pulling apart the tail and closing the shell. 3. It should create a butterfly with the meat when you're cutting it so that it can easily be moved to the top of the shell. 4. Melt the butter, add garlic and parsley and mix well in a small bowl. Now drench the lobster tails in a butter mixture. 5. Now place the lobster tail in the Cook & Crisp Basket very carefully, and spray olive oil generously. 6. For 5 minutes cook the lobsters, or until the internal temperature of the meat reaches at least 145°F. Lift the lid once it's done. 7. Take out the golden lobsters and serve!

Nutritional Information Per Serving: Calories: 565; Fat: 36g; Carbs: 0.2g; Protein: 46.3g

Panko Crusted Cod

Prep Time: 10 minutes | Cook Time: 15 minutes | Serves: 4

Ingredients:

2 uncooked cod fillets
3 tsp kosher salt
¾ cup panko bread crumbs

2 tbsp butter, melted
¼ cup fresh parsley, minced
1 lemon. Zested and juiced

Directions:

1. Place the Cook & Crisp Basket inside. Preheat the Ninja Foodi by setting on Air Crisp mode and setting the temperature to 390°F and the time to 5 minutes. 2. Season cod and salt. 3. Take a suitable bowl and stir in bread crumbs, parsley, lemon juice, zest, and butter, and mix well. 4. Coat fillets with the bread crumbs mixture and place fillets in your basket. 5. Lock Crisping Lid and cook on Air Crisp mode for 15 minutes at 360°F. 6. Serve and enjoy.

Nutritional Information Per Serving: Calories: 554; Fat: 24g; Carbs: 5g; Protein: 37g

Buttery Scallops

Prep Time: 18 minutes | Cook Time: 6 minutes | Serves: 4

Ingredients:

2 pounds sea scallops
12 cup butter
4 garlic cloves, minced

4 tbsp rosemary, chopped

Black pepper and salt to taste

Directions:

1. Select "Sear/Sauté" mode on your Ninja Foodi on MD: HI. 2. Add rosemary, garlic and butter, sauté for 1 minute. 3. Stir in scallops, black pepper, and salt, Sauté for 2 minutes. 4. Cook for 3 minutes. 5. Serve and enjoy.

Nutritional Information Per Serving: Calories: 278g; Fat: 15g; Carbs: 5g; Protein: 25g

Shrimp Zoodles

Prep Time: 10 minutes | Cook Time: 3 minutes | Serves: 4

Ingredients:

4 cups zoodles
1 tbsp basil, chopped
2 tbsp Ghee
1 cup vegetable stock
2 garlic cloves, minced
2 tbsp olive oil
½ lemon
½ tsp paprika

Directions:

1. Select "Sear/Sauté" mode at MD on your Ninja Foodi and add ghee, let it heat up. 2. Stir in olive oil as well. 3. Add garlic and cook for 1 minute. 4. Stir in lemon juice and shrimp, and cook for 1 minute approximately. 5. Stir in the rest of the ingredients then lock lid, cook on LO pressure for 5 minutes. 6. Quick-release pressure and serve. 7. Enjoy.
Nutritional Information Per Serving: Calories: 277; Fat: 6g; Carbs: 5g; Protein: 27g

Beer Battered Fish

Prep Time: 8-10 minutes | Cook Time: 12-15 minutes | Serves: 4

Ingredients:

1 pound codfish cuts
1 cup flour
½ tsp baking soda
2 tbsp Cornstarch
4 ounces beer
For Flour Mix
¾ cup of flour
1 tsp paprika powder
1 beaten egg
Salt as required
¼ tsp Cayenne pepper
1 tbsp olive oil

½ tsp black pepper

Directions:

1. Combine flour, cornstarch, salt, cayenne pepper, and baking soda in a large bowl. Then add egg and beer, and stir it until it becomes a smooth batter. Let it refrigerate for 20 minutes. 2. Take ¾ cup of flour, paprika, and black pepper in a shallow pan. 3. The fish should be at least one half-inch thick so that it does not dry out in the Ninja Foodi Cook & Crisp Basket. Take a paper towel and pat dry the codfish cuts. 4. Now coat all sides while dipping the fish into the batter. 5. Allow the eggs batter to dip off and again coat it with seasoned flour mix. Any leftover flour can be sprinkled on the fish fillet. 6. Now preheat the Ninja Foodi at Air Crisp Mode at 390°F for 5 minutes. Spray both sides of the coated fish fillet with vegetable oil and then place them in the Ninja Foodi Cook & Crisp Basket for 12 minutes. 7. During the cooking process, add a little more oil if there is any dryness in the coating!
Nutritional Information Per Serving: Calories: 407; Fat: 6g; Carbs: 26.6g; Protein: 7.3g

Ninja Foodi Stir-Fried Shrimp

Prep Time: 5 minutes | Cook Time: 6 minutes | Serves: 6

Ingredients:

2 pounds shrimp, peeled and deveined
8 tbsp tamari
8 garlic cloves, minced
2 tbsp olive oil
Salt and black pepper, to taste

Directions:

1. Add oil in Ninja Foodi and sauté garlic in it at MD for about 1 minute. 2. Stir in shrimp, salt, tamari, and black pepper and close the Pressure Lid. Turn the pressure release valve to SEAL position. 3. Select "Pressure Cook". 4. Cook for about 5 minutes at HI pressure and open the lid. 5. Take out, serve and enjoy!
Nutritional Information Per Serving: Calories: 240; Fat: 7.3g; Carbs: 5g; Protein: 37.2g

Ninja Foodi Broiled Mahi-Mahi

Prep Time: 10 minutes | Cook Time: 10 minutes | Serves: 2

Ingredients:

- ½ pound mahi-mahi fillets
- ½ tbsp olive oil
- 2 tbsp fresh orange juice
- ½ tsp dried thyme
- ½ tsp cayenne pepper
- Salt and black pepper, to taste

Directions:

1. Add everything except mahi-mahi fillets in a large bowl and mix well. 2. Stir in mahi-mahi and toss to coat well. 3. Set aside the mixture for about half an hour and remove the fillets from the bowl. 4. Place them in Ninja Foodi. Close the Crisping Lid and set the Ninja Foodi on Broil mode. 5. Broil for about 10 minutes and open the lid. 6. Dish out and serve hot.

Nutritional Information Per Serving: Calories: 130; Fat: 3.6g; Carbs: 2.1g; Protein: 21.3g

Ninja Foodi Ginger Cod

Prep Time: 10 minutes | Cook Time: 20 minutes | Serves: 2

Ingredients:

- ½ pound cod fillets
- 1 tbsp fresh lime juice
- ½ tbsp fresh ginger, minced
- 1 tbsp coconut aminos
- Salt and black pepper, to taste

Directions:

1. Add lime juice, fresh ginger, coconut aminos, salt, and pepper in a bowl. Mix well. 2. Add cod fillets in the mixture and toss to coat well. 3. Place them in the Ninja Foodi cooking pot. Close the Crisping Lid. Set the unit on Bake/Roast mode. 4. Bake for about 20-minutes at 325°F and open the lid. 5. Take out, serve and enjoy!

Nutritional Information Per Serving: Calories: 109; Fat: 1.1g; Carbs: 4.3g; Protein: 20.5g

Gluten-free fish tacos

Prep Time: 8 minutes | Cook Time: 15-17 minutes | Serves: 6

Ingredients:

- 4 fish fillets
- 1 tsp paprika powder
- ½ tsp salt and pepper
- **For Corn Salsa:**
- 1 cup soft-cooked corn
- 1 cup tomatoes
- ½ cup onion
- 1 tsp mixed herbs
- 6-8 tortillas wrap

- ½ cup chopped coriander
- 1 tbsp lemon juice

Directions:

1. Take the thawed fish and place it into the Cook & Crisp Basket, then add paprika, salt, and pepper. 2. Spray the Cook & Crisp Basket with olive oil and put it in the Ninja Foodi. 3. Preheat Ninja Foodi at Air Crisp Mode at 390°F for 12 minutes. 4. Meanwhile, combine the ingredients in a bowl for corn salsa. Squeeze a lemon juice on top of corn salsa then remove and flake it apart with a fork once the fish is cooked fully. 5. Now place each tortilla on a plate and add fish and then top it with the corn salsa. Now place each tortilla next to each other in the Ninja Foodi Cook & Crisp Basket. 6. Give it a cooking spray, for 5 minutes Air Crisp it at 390°F with tongs, remove it carefully, and serve it.

Nutritional Information Per Serving: Calories: 294; Fat: 7.3g; Carbs: 49.2g; Protein: 7g

Ninja Foodi Salmon

Prep Time: 5-6 minutes | Cook Time: 4-5 minutes | Serves: 4

Ingredients:

2 salmon fillets
1 cup water
Juice from 1 lemon, about ½ cup
Lemon slices
4-5 sprigs of fresh dill (or rosemary)
Salt and pepper to taste

Directions:

1. Pour water and lemon juice into the Ninja Foodi. 2. Add lemon slices and dill. 3. Add the fillets. 4. Add the lemon slices on top of the salmon. 5. Sprinkle with salt and pepper. 6. Secure the Ninja Foodi Pressure Lid. 7. Make sure the valve is set to Seal, use the manual settings and cook on High Pressure for 4 minutes. Add an additional minute if the fillet is frozen. 8. Once done, release the valve to Vent (quick release) and then open the lid. 9. Serve the salmon immediately or store in fridge.

Nutritional Information Per Serving: Calories: 273; Fat: 14g; Carbs: 10g; Protein: 25g

Ninja Foodi Asparagus Scallops

Prep Time: 10 minutes | Cook Time: 10 minutes | Serves: 8

Ingredients:

1½ pounds scallops
2 tbsp coconut oil
2 tsp lemon zest, finely grated
¼ cup shallots, chopped
1½ pounds asparagus, chopped
2 garlic cloves, minced
2 tbsp fresh lemon juice
2 tbsp fresh rosemary, chopped
Salt and black pepper, to taste

Directions:

1. Add oil in Ninja Foodi and set the unit on Sear/Sauté mode. Then sauté shallots in it at MD for about 2 minutes. 2. Add in garlic and rosemary and sauté for about 1 minute. 3. Stir in asparagus and lemon zest and cook for about 2 minutes. 4. Add in scallops, lemon juice, salt, and pepper and cook for about 5 minutes. 5. Take out and serve hot.

Nutritional Information Per Serving: Calories: 375; Fat: 6.3g; Carbs: 21.3g; Protein: 59.5g

Spicy Shrimps

Prep Time: 8-10 minutes | Cook Time: 13-15 minutes | Serves: 2

Ingredients:

1 pound shrimps
Salt to taste
Pepper to taste
½ tsp cumin powder
1 tsp coriander powder
½ tsp red chili powder
1 tbsp lemon juice
1 cup mixed vegetables
Foil (3 to 4 sheets)
Cooking oil spray (olive or coconut)

Directions:

1. Spray the foil sheets with olive oil. Do this on about a maximum of four sheets. 2. Season it up with salt, pepper, red chili powder, cumin, and coriander powder. Pour in some lemon juice and coat all the shrimps well. 3. Again, spray another coat of olive oil on foil sheets and put the shrimps on the foil. 4. Using the Bake/Roast function, preheat the Ninja Foodi Deluxe XL Pressure Cooker at 375°F for 5 minutes. 5. Cook it using a Bake function at 375°F for 13 to 15 minutes. Do this by placing foil sheets in it.

Nutritional Information Per Serving: Calories: 188; Fat: 10g; Carbs: 10.1g; Protein: 37.3g

Ninja Foodi Ginger Salmon

Prep Time: 10 minutes | Cook Time: 18 minutes | Serves: 3

Ingredients:

¼ pound salmon fillets
½ tsp fresh ginger, minced
½ tbsp sesame seeds
½ tbsp coconut aminos
½ tbsp fresh lime juice
Salt and black pepper, to taste

Directions:

1. Add all the ingredients to a large bowl and mix well. 2. Dredge salmon fillets in the mixture and transfer them to the Ninja Foodi cooking pot. Close the 3. Crisping Lid and set the unit on Bake/Roast function. 4. Bake for about 18 minutes at 325°F. 5. Open the Crisping Lid and take out. 6. Serve and enjoy!

Nutritional Information Per Serving: Calories: 64; Fat: 3.1g; Carbs: 1.7g; Protein: 7.7g

Ninja Foodi Air Crisp Herbed Salmon

Prep Time: 1 minutes | Cook Time: 4-5 minutes | Serves: 6

Ingredients:

8 ounces sizzle fish salmon fillets, I used two, 4 ounces sizzle fish sockeye salmon fillets
1 tsp Herbes de Provence
¼ tsp natural ancient sea salt
¼ tsp black pepper
¼ tsp smoked paprika
2 tbsp olive oil
1 tbsp Medlee Seasoned Butter

Directions:

1. Dry your filets with a paper towel and run the surface gently to ensure that there are no bones. 2. Drizzle the olive oil on the fish and rub it in on both sides of the fish. 3. Mix the seasonings and sprinkle them on both sides of the fish. 4. Turn your Air Crisp on 390°F and set the cook time for 5 to 8 minutes and cook. I recommend starting with 5 minutes, checking the fish, and increasing the time by one additional minute until it flakes easily with a fork. 5. Melt the seasoned butter for 30 seconds in the microwave and pour it over the fish before eating.

Nutritional Information Per Serving: Calories: 338; Fat: 27g; Carbs:s 1g; Protein: 23g

Mixed Seafood Platter

Prep Time: 9 minutes | Cook Time: 6 minutes | Serves: 6

Ingredients:

1 pound peeled and devein fresh shrimps
1 pound mussels
1 potato (coarsely cut)
½ cup fresh corn
12 oz. Sausage (2-inch pieces)
2-3 cups water
2 tbsp old bay seasoning
2 tsp oil flakes
¼ cup fresh chopped parsley
1 cup butter, melted
1 tsp garlic powder

Directions:

1. Add potatoes, corn, sausages, water, and oil flakes in the Ninja Foodi cooking pot. Give it a good stir. Close the Pressure Lid and turn the valve to Seal position. 2. Now on the Pressure Cook mode, cook it at HI for 4 minutes and do a quick release. 3. Once the timer is completed and pressure is released, open the lid carefully. 4. Now add shrimps, mussels, and old bay seasoning. Mix it well and cook it on Pressure Cook setting at HI in Ninja Foodi for 1 minute. Allow for natural release of pressure for 2 minutes, after 1 minute of cooking in Ninja Foodi on Pressure Cook mode at HI. 5. Then add butter and garlic powder to a small bowl. Mix it well and top up with parsley. Drizzle all over the platter.

Nutritional Information Per Serving: Calories: 521; Fat: 39.9g; Carbs: 22.6g; Protein: 19.3g

Fish Skewers

Prep Time: 3 minutes | Cook Time: 8-10 minutes | Serves: 4

Ingredients:

- 1 pound frozen fish cubes
- 6-8 skewers
- Salt to taste
- Pepper to taste
- 2 tbsp ginger garlic paste
- ½ tsp paprika
- 1 tbsp lemon juice
- 1 tsp oregano
- ½ tsp liquid charcoal
- 1 tbsp olive oil

Directions:

1. Oil spray the Ninja Foodi Cook & Crisp Basket. Combine the fish cubes with all the seasonings in a bowl. Set aside for 1-2 hours. 2. Align the cubes on the skewers. Now place the fish sticks in an even manner into the Ninja Foodi Cook & Crisp Basket. 3. For 10 minutes, cook at 390°F on Air Crisp Mode. Flip it if needed and the skewers are ready to be served!

Nutritional Information Per Serving: Calories: 182; Fat: 8.5g; Carbs: 3g; Protein: 23.3g

Crumbed Tilapia

Prep Time: 12 minutes | Cook Time: 6 minutes | Serves: 4

Ingredients:

- 4 frozen tilapia fillets
- 1 cup bread crumbs
- 2 tbsp seafood seasoning
- 1 egg
- Olive oil spray

Directions:

1. At 390°F, preheat the Ninja Foodi at Air Crisp Mode for 5 minutes. 2. To pat dry the fillet, use paper towels and dry the moisture. 3. Add salt and pepper to the egg in a bowl and whisk it well. First, dip the fillet in the whisked egg. 4. Combine bread crumbs with seafood seasoning on a plate and press the fillet from both sides into that mixture to coat generously. 5. Place the fillets in the Ninja Foodi Cook & Crisp Basket and close the lid and cook depending on the thickness of the tilapia and in most cases, 4 minutes have been a good amount of time for a good result. Take out the golden crispy fillets and eat a proteinaceous meal!

Nutritional Information Per Serving: Calories: 212; Fat: 4.5g; Carbs: 15.9g; Protein: 27.5g

Lemon Garlic Scallops

Prep Time: 8-10 minutes | Cook Time: 15-20 minutes | Serves: 2

Ingredients:

- 1 pound scallops
- ½ tsp pepper
- ½ tsp salt
- 1 tbsp extra-virgin olive oil
- 2 tbsp chopped parsley
- ¼ tsp lemon zest
- 1 tsp chopped garlic

Directions:

1. Season scallops with pepper and salt. Give the Ninja Foodi Cook & Crisp Basket a generous oil spray. 2. Set the Ninja Foodi at Air Crisp at 390°F, cook the scallops for about 6 minutes. 3. Now take a small bowl and add oil, parsley, lemon zest, and garlic. 4. Once scallops are seared well, drizzle this mixture over the scallops!

Nutritional Information Per Serving: Calories: 320; Fat: 10.2g; Carbs: 14.4g; Protein: 35.4g

Chapter 6 Vegetable Recipes

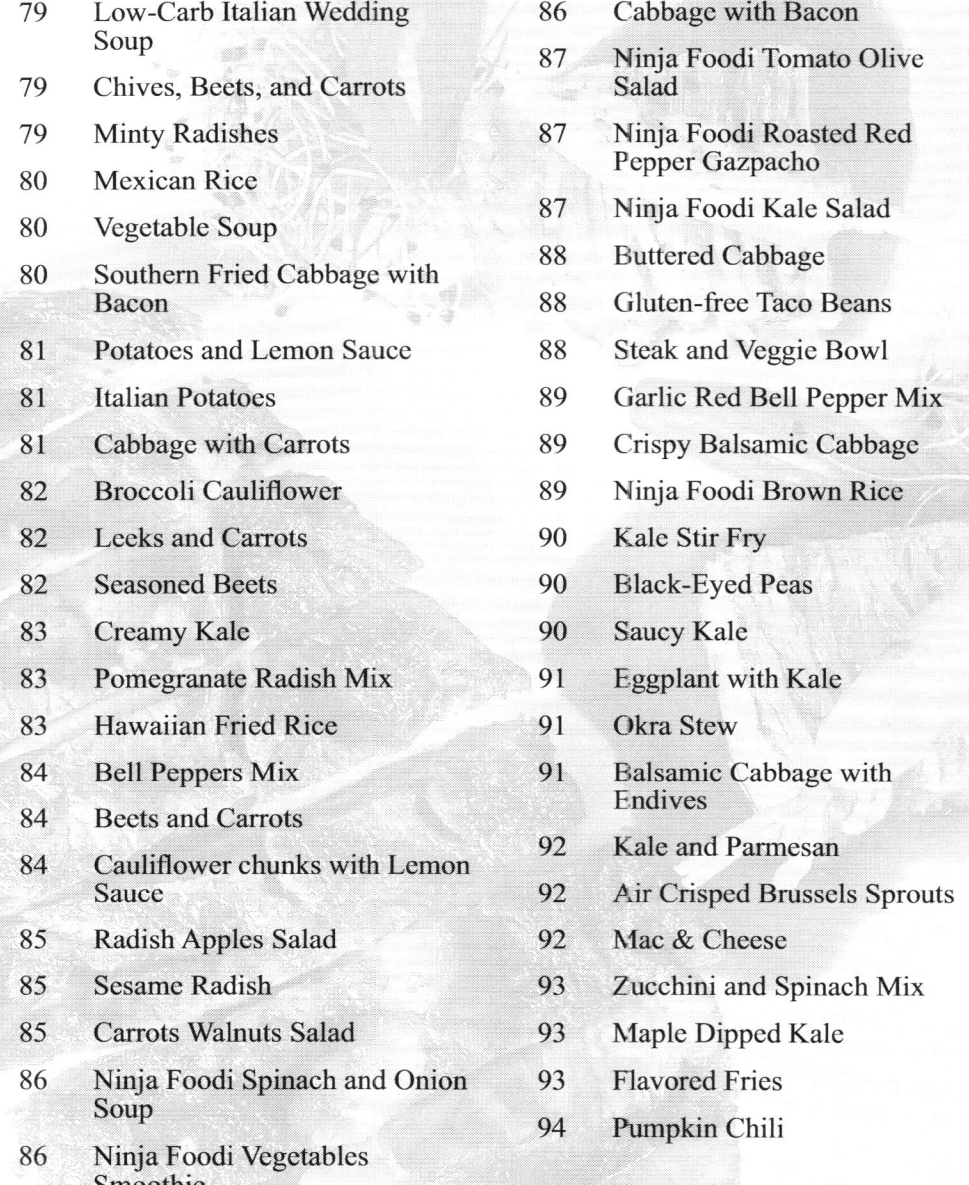

79	Low-Carb Italian Wedding Soup
79	Chives, Beets, and Carrots
79	Minty Radishes
80	Mexican Rice
80	Vegetable Soup
80	Southern Fried Cabbage with Bacon
81	Potatoes and Lemon Sauce
81	Italian Potatoes
81	Cabbage with Carrots
82	Broccoli Cauliflower
82	Leeks and Carrots
82	Seasoned Beets
83	Creamy Kale
83	Pomegranate Radish Mix
83	Hawaiian Fried Rice
84	Bell Peppers Mix
84	Beets and Carrots
84	Cauliflower chunks with Lemon Sauce
85	Radish Apples Salad
85	Sesame Radish
85	Carrots Walnuts Salad
86	Ninja Foodi Spinach and Onion Soup
86	Ninja Foodi Vegetables Smoothie
86	Cabbage with Bacon
87	Ninja Foodi Tomato Olive Salad
87	Ninja Foodi Roasted Red Pepper Gazpacho
87	Ninja Foodi Kale Salad
88	Buttered Cabbage
88	Gluten-free Taco Beans
88	Steak and Veggie Bowl
89	Garlic Red Bell Pepper Mix
89	Crispy Balsamic Cabbage
89	Ninja Foodi Brown Rice
90	Kale Stir Fry
90	Black-Eyed Peas
90	Saucy Kale
91	Eggplant with Kale
91	Okra Stew
91	Balsamic Cabbage with Endives
92	Kale and Parmesan
92	Air Crisped Brussels Sprouts
92	Mac & Cheese
93	Zucchini and Spinach Mix
93	Maple Dipped Kale
93	Flavored Fries
94	Pumpkin Chili

Low-Carb Italian Wedding Soup

Prep Time: 13 minutes | Cook Time: 15 minutes | Serves: 6

Ingredients:

Meatballs

1 lb. ground sausage
¼ cup parmesan cheese, shredded
½ cup pork rinds, crushed
¼ cup heavy cream

1 egg, beaten
½ tbsp Italian seasoning
Salt and pepper, to taste

Soup

6 cups chicken broth
1 garlic, minced
1 tbsp Italian seasoning
1 carrot, chopped
3 green onions, chopped

3 ribs celery, chopped
10 oz frozen riced cauliflower
3 oz baby spinach
Parmesan cheese, shredded, for garnish

Directions:

1. Mix the meatball ingredients together in a bowl. Form into 12 meatballs and spread them across the base of the Ninja Foodi cooking pot. Close the Crisping Lid. 2. Select the unit on Air Crisp mode at 350°F for 13 minutes. 3. When done, open the lid, pour the broth over the top of the meatballs, and gently stir. 4. Add all the remaining ingredients except the spinach and garnish. Close the Pressure lid and turn the pressure release valve to SEAL position. 5. Select Pressure Cook mode. Pressure cook at HI for 15 minutes and then do a quick release. Stir in the spinach.

Nutritional Information Per Serving: Calories: 345; Fat: 27.9g; Carbs: 5g; Protein: 18g

Chives, Beets, and Carrots

Prep Time: 5 minutes | Cook Time: 20 minutes | Serves: 4

Ingredients:

1 lb. beets, peeled and roughly cubed
1 lb. baby carrots, peeled
Salt and black pepper, to taste

2 tbsp olive oil
1 tbsp chives, minced

Directions:

1. In a bowl, mix the beets with the carrots and the other ingredients and toss well. 2. Put the beets and carrots in the Cook & Crisp Basket and place it in the Ninja Foodi. Close the Crisping Lid and air crisp at 390°F for 20 minutes. Divide between plates and serve.

Nutritional Information Per Serving: Calories: 150; Fat: 4.5g; Carbs: 7.3 g; Protein: 3.6g

Minty Radishes

Prep Time: 5 minutes | Cook Time: 15 minutes | Serves: 4

Ingredients:

1-pound radishes, halved
black pepper and salt
2 tbsp balsamic vinegar

2 tbsp mint, chopped
2 tbsp olive oil

Directions:

1. In your Ninja Foodi Cook & Crisp Basket, combine the radishes with the vinegar and the other ingredients, and 2. Cook on Air Crisp at 380°F for 15 minutes. 3. Divide the radishes between plates and serve.

Nutritional Information Per Serving: Calories: 170; Fat: 4.5g; Carbs: 7.4g; Protein: 4.6g

Mexican Rice

Prep Time: 5 minutes | Cook Time: 3 minutes | Serves: 6

Ingredients:

2 tbsp canola or vegetable oil
1 cup basmati rice
½ green peppers, diced into ¼-inch
1 onion (about 1cup), diced into ¼-inch
1 carrot, diced into ¼-inch
Spice blend
1½ tsp fine-grind sea salt
1½ tsp cumin

½ red bell pepper, diced into ¼-inch
1 jalapeño pepper, diced into ¼-inch
2 tbsp tomato paste
2 cups water

1½ tsp smoked paprika

Directions:

1. Place the oil in the Ninja Foodi cooking pot. Select Sear/Sauté mode and put it on HI. 2. When the oil is hot, add the rice and sauté for 3–5 minutes, stirring constantly. 3. When the rice starts to brown, add in the vegetables and the spice blend. Stir and sauté for 3–5 minutes. Add in the tomato paste and stir to combine. 4. Pour in the 2 cups of water and put the Pressure Lid on. Turn the seal to VENT and select the Steam function. Steam together for 8 minutes. 5. When finished, remove the lid and stir the rice.

Nutritional Information Per Serving: Calories: 178; Fat: 5g; Carbs: 30g; Protein: 3g

Vegetable Soup

Prep Time: 20 minutes | Cook Time: 4 minutes | Serves: 8

Ingredients:

1 lb. ground turkey
1 (14½ oz) can of beef broth
4 cups water
1 (15 oz) can tomato sauce
1 cup frozen corn
2 potatoes, halved and quartered
2 large carrots, sliced

2 stalks celery, diced
1 medium tomato, sliced
½ cup white onion, diced
½ cup white cooking wine
½ tsp parsley
1 cup elbow macaroni

Directions:

1. Set the Ninja Foodi to Sear/Sauté mode on MD temperature setting. Cook the meat in the cooking pot, then add in the remaining ingredients. Close the Pressure Lid and turn the pressure release valve to SEAL position. 2. Set the unit on Pressure Cook mode. 3. Pressure cook at HI for 4 minutes. 4. Quick-release the steam and remove the lid.

Nutritional Information Per Serving: Calories: 314; Fat: 13g; Carbs: 26g; Protein: 20g

Southern Fried Cabbage with Bacon

Prep Time: 5 minutes | Cook Time: 20 minutes | Serves: 4

Ingredients:

4 cups red cabbage, shredded
¼ cup veggie stock
A pinch of salt and black pepper
1 tbsp olive oil

1 cup crushed canned tomatoes
1 lime, grated zest
2 oz cooked bacon, crumbled

Directions:

1. Put the reversible rack in the Ninja Foodi, add the baking pan, and grease it with the oil. 2. Add the cabbage, the stock, and the other ingredients to the pan. 3. Set the Ninja Foodi to Bake/Roast mode at 380°F for 20 minutes. 4. When done, divide the mixture between plates and serve.

Nutritional Information Per Serving: Calories: 144; Fat: 3g; Carbs: 4.5g; Protein: 4.4g

Potatoes and Lemon Sauce

Prep Time: 5 minutes | Cook Time: 15 minutes | Serves: 4

Ingredients:

1 lb. Yukon Gold potatoes, peeled and cut into wedges
1 tbsp fresh dill, chopped
1 tbsp grated lemon zest
½ lemon, juiced
2 tbsp butter, melted
Salt and black pepper, to the taste

Directions:

1. Set the Ninja Foodi to Sear/Sauté mode on MD: HI temperature setting. Add the butter, melt it, then add the potatoes and brown for 5 minutes. 2. Add the lemon zest and the other ingredients. Stir to combine. Close the Crisping Lid. 3. Set the Ninja Foodi to Air Crisp mode and cook at 390°F for 10 minutes. 4. Divide everything between plates and serve.

Nutritional Information Per Serving: Calories: 122; Fat: 3.3g; Carbs: 3g; Protein: 2g

Italian Potatoes

Prep Time: 6 minutes | Cook Time: 10-12 minutes | Serves: 4

Ingredients:

4 potatoes
1 tbsp olive oil
2 lemons
½ tsp salt
1 tbsp Italian Seasoning
1 tsp mixed herbs

Directions:

1. Wash off the potatoes and cut them into wedges. 2. In the Ninja Foodi, set the inner pot and then pour in half a cup of water. Now add the Ninja Foodi Cook & Crisp Basket into the cooking pot and dump in wedges to it. Close the Pressure Lid and turn the pressure release valve to SEAL position. 3. Preheat Ninja Foodi, Pressure Cook at LO for 20 minutes. 4. Pressure Cook potatoes at HI for 4 minutes. 5. Meanwhile, prepare your seasoning mixture by combining Italian seasoning, lemon juice, herbs, salt, and olive oil in a mixing bowl and put its side. 6. Once the potatoes are cooked, release the pressure by setting the valve to vent. After the pressure has been released remove the lid, take 1 tbsp of olive oil, and spread evenly on the potatoes. 7. Now for an additional 3 to 5 minutes, cook wedges in the Ninja Foodi, until the desired crispiness is achieved. Sprinkle some more seasoning and serve!

Nutrition Information per Serving: Calories: 70; Fat: 4.1g; Carbs: 11g; Protein: 1.2g

Cabbage with Carrots

Prep Time: 5 minutes | Cook Time: 20 minutes | Serves: 4

Ingredients:

1 Napa cabbage, shredded
2 carrots, sliced
2 tbsp olive oil
1 red onion, chopped
Black pepper and salt to the taste
2 tbsp sweet paprika
½ cup tomato sauce

Directions:

1. Set the Ninja Foodi on Sear/Sauté mode, stir in the oil, heat it up, add the onion and sauté for 5 minutes. 2. Add the carrots, the cabbage, and the other ingredients, toss. 3. Close the pressure Lid and turn the pressure release valve to VENT position. Sear on HI for 15 minutes. 4. Release the pressure quickly for 5 minutes, divide everything between plates and serve.

Nutritional Information Per Serving: Calories: 140; Fat: 3.4g; Carbs: 1.2g; Protein: 3.5 g

Broccoli Cauliflower

Prep Time: 10 minutes | Cook Time: 15 minutes | Serves: 4

Ingredients:

2 cups broccoli florets
1 cup cauliflower florets
2 tbsp lime juice
1 tbsp avocado oil
⅓ cup tomato sauce
2 tsp ginger, grated
2 tsp garlic, minced
1 tbsp chives, chopped

Directions:

1. Set the Ninja Foodi on Sear/Sauté mode at MD, stir in the oil, heat it up, add the garlic and the ginger and sauté for 2 minutes. 2. Stir in the broccoli, cauliflower, and the rest of the ingredients. 3. Close the Pressure Lid and turn the pressure release valve to VENT position. Sear at HI for 13 minutes. 4. Divide everything between plates and serve.
Nutritional Information Per Serving: Calories: 118; Fat: 1.5g; Carbs: 4.3g; Protein: 6g

Leeks and Carrots

Prep Time: 5 minutes | Cook Time: 15 minutes | Serves: 4

Ingredients:

2 leeks, roughly sliced
2 carrots, sliced
1 tsp ginger powder
1 tsp garlic powder
½ cup chicken stock
Black pepper and salt to the taste
2 tbsp lemon juice
2 tbsp olive oil
½ tbsp balsamic vinegar

Directions:

1. In your Ninja Foodi, combine the leeks with the carrots and the other ingredients. Select the unit to Sear/Sauté mode. 2. Close the Pressure Lid and turn the pressure release valve to SEAL position. Sauté at High for 15 minutes. 3. Divide the mix between plates and serve.
Nutritional Information Per Serving: Calories: 133; Fat: 3.4g; Carbs: 5g; Protein: 2.1g

Seasoned Beets

Prep Time: 5 minutes | Cook Time: 25-30 minutes | Serves: 2

Ingredients:

5-6 beets
¼ cup water
Salt to taste
Black pepper to taste
½ tsp paprika

Directions:

1. Trim the beets well. It's suggested to leave about half an inch of stem and roots, this way these can easily be peeled after cooking and then wash and scrub the beets thoroughly. Pour in the water and place the rack in the Ninja Foodi cooking pot. Align the prepared beets on the rack. 2. Now in place, close the Pressure Lid and turn the pressure release valve to SEAL position. 3. Set the unit on Pressure Cook mode and pressure cook at HI for 30 minutes. After the time, release pressure and take it out. 4. Use a sharp knife to pierce the beets. If the knife easily pierces the flesh without much resistance, it means they are done, and if the beets seem a little hard or firm, cook for another two to 5 minutes on Pressure Cook mode at HI. 5. Now let the beets cool down to handle them easily. Once they are cool, trim off both of its ends to peel off, use your hands under running water, slice it up, season it with salt, pepper, paprika, and serve!
Nutritional Information Per Serving: Calories: 74; Fat: 0.4g; Carbs: 16.6g; Protein: 2.8g

Creamy Kale

Prep Time: 5 minutes | Cook Time: 15 minutes | Serves: 4

Ingredients:

1 tbsp lemon juice
2 tbsp balsamic vinegar
1-pound kale, torn
1 tbsp ginger, grated
1 garlic clove, minced

2 tbsp olive oil
1 cup heavy cream
A pinch of black pepper and salt
2 tbsp chives, chopped

Directions:

1. Set the Ninja Foodi on Sear/Sauté mode, stir in the oil, heat it up, add the garlic and the ginger and sauté at HI for 2 minutes. 2. Stir in the kale, lemon juice and the other ingredients. 3. Close the Pressure Lid and turn the pressure release valve to VENT position. Sauté at HI for 13 minutes. 4. Divide between plates and serve.
Nutritional Information Per Serving: Calories: 130; Fat: 2g; Carbs: 3.4g; Protein: 2g

Pomegranate Radish Mix

Prep Time: 5 minutes | Cook Time: 8 minutes | Serves: 4

Ingredients:

1-pound radishes, roughly cubed
Black pepper and salt to the taste
2 garlic cloves, minced

½ cup chicken stock
2 tbsp pomegranate juice
¼ cup pomegranate seeds

Directions:

1. In your Ninja Foodi, combine the radishes with the stock and the other ingredients. Select the unit on Sear/Sauté mode. 2. Close the Pressure Lid and turn the pressure release valve to VENT position. Sauté at HI for 8 minutes. 3. Divide everything between plates and serve.
Nutritional Information Per Serving: Calories: 133; Fat: 2.3g; Carbs: 2.4g; Protein: 2g

Hawaiian Fried Rice

Prep Time: 6 minutes | Cook Time: 12-15 minutes | Serves: 3-4

Ingredients:

½ cup rice
1 cup water
1 tbsp cooking oil
½ cup frozen peas
½ cup corn
½ cup diced carrots

1 tbsp soya sauce
¼ cup chopped green onions
1 scrambled egg
1 cup shredded chicken
Salt according to taste

Directions:

1. Combine rice, water, and oil in the Ninja Foodi cooking pot. Close the unit with Pressure Lid and turn the steam valve to Seal position. Select the unit to Pressure Cook mode. 2. Pressure cook at HI for 1 minute. 3. Cut the vegetables while the rice is being cooked. Then except for the eggs and green onions, add all the remaining ingredients. 4. Put on the Ninja Foodi Crisping Lid. Set the unit on Air Crisp mode and set temperature to 390°F. Adjust the cook time for 10 minutes. Keep stirring occasionally. 5. Make a well in the center pushing the rice to the edges, pour the egg, and scramble it. 6. Select the unit to Sear/Sauté mode at MD and add the green onion to it. Cook it for 2 to 3 minutes and dish out the refreshing rice!
Nutrition Information per Serving: Calories: 187; Fat: 10.5g; Carbs: 14.6g; Protein: 9.3.

Bell Peppers Mix

Prep Time: 5 minutes | Cook Time: 16 minutes | Serves: 4

Ingredients:

1-pound red bell peppers, cut into wedges

½ tsp curry powder

½ cup tomato sauce

Black pepper and salt to the taste

1 tbsp olive oil

2 garlic cloves, minced

1 tbsp parsley, chopped

Directions:

1. Put the reversible rack in the Ninja Foodi, add the baking pan inside and grease it with the oil. 2. Add the peppers, curry powder, and the other ingredients except for the parsley, toss a bit. 3. Close the Crisping Lid. Cook on Bake/Roast mode at 380°F for 16 minutes. 4. Divide cooked peppers between plates and serve with the parsley sprinkled on top.

Nutritional Information Per Serving: Calories: 150; Fat: 3.5g; Carbs: 3.1g; Protein: 1.2g

Beets and Carrots

Prep Time: 5 minutes | Cook Time: 20 minutes | Serves: 4

Ingredients:

1-pound beets, peeled and roughly cubed

1-pound baby carrots, peeled

Black pepper and salt to the taste

2 tbsp olive oil

1 tbsp chives, minced

Directions:

1. In a suitable bowl, mix the beets with the carrots and the other ingredients and toss. 2. Put the beets and carrots in the Foodi Cook & Crisp Basket. 3. Cook on Air Crisp at 390°F for 20 minutes, divide between plates and serve.

Nutritional Information Per Serving: Calories: 150; Fat: 4.5g; Carbs: 7.3g; Protein: 3.6g

Cauliflower chunks with Lemon Sauce

Prep Time: 5 minutes | Cook Time: 15 minutes | Serves: 4

Ingredients:

1-pound cauliflower, cut into chunks

1 tbsp dill, chopped

1 tbsp lemon zest, grated

Juice of ½ lemon

2 tbsp butter, melted

Black pepper and salt to the taste

Directions:

1. Set the Ninja Foodi on Sear/Sauté mode at MD, stir in the butter, melt it, add the cauliflower chunks and brown for 5 minutes. 2. Add the lemon zest and the other ingredients. Close the Crisping Lid and set the machine on Air Crisp and cook at 390°F for 10 minutes. 3. Divide everything between plates and serve.

Nutritional Information Per Serving: Calories: 122; Fat: 3.3g; Carbs: 3g; Protein: 2g

Radish Apples Salad

Prep Time: 5 minutes | Cook Time: 15 minutes | Serves: 4

Ingredients:

1-pound radishes, roughly cubed
2 apples, cored and cut into wedges
¼ cup chicken stock
2 spring onions, chopped
3 tbsp tomato paste
Juice of 1 lime
Cooking spray
1 tbsp cilantro, chopped

Directions:

1. In your Ninja Foodi, combine the radishes with the apples and the other ingredients. Close the Pressure Lid and turn the pressure release valve to SEAL position. Set the unit on Pressure Cook mode. 2. Pressure cook at HI for 15 minutes. 3. Release the pressure quickly for 5 minutes, divide everything between plates and serve.
Nutritional Information Per Serving: Calories: 122; Fat: 5g; Carbs: 4.5g; Protein: 3g

Sesame Radish

Prep Time: 5 minutes | Cook Time: 15 minutes | Serves: 4

Ingredients:

2 leeks, sliced
½ pound radishes, sliced
2 scallions, chopped
2 tbsp black sesame seeds
⅓ cup chicken stock
1 tbsp ginger, grated
1 tbsp chives, minced

Directions:

1. In your Ninja Foodi, combine the leeks with the radishes and the other ingredients. 2. Close the unit with Pressure Lid. Turn the pressure release valve to Seal position. Select to Pressure Cook mode and cook at HI for 15 minutes more. 3. Release the pressure quickly for 5 minutes, divide everything between plates and serve.
Nutritional Information Per Serving: Calories: 112; Fat: 2g; Carbs: 4.2g; Protein: 2g

Carrots Walnuts Salad

Prep Time: 5 minutes | Cook Time: 15 minutes | Serves: 4

Ingredients:

4 carrots, roughly shredded
½ cup walnuts, sliced
3 tbsp balsamic vinegar
1 cup chicken stock
Black pepper and salt to the taste
1 tbsp olive oil

Directions:

1. In your Ninja Foodi, mix the carrots with the vinegar and the other ingredients except for the walnuts 2. Close the Pressure Lid and turn the pressure release valve to SEAL position. Set the unit on Pressure Cook mode. Pressure cook at HI for 15 minutes. 3. Release the pressure quickly for 5 minutes, divide the mix between plates and serve with the walnuts sprinkled on top.
Nutritional Information Per Serving: Calories: 120; Fat: 4.5g; Carbs: 5.3g; Protein: 1.3g

Ninja Foodi Spinach and Onion Soup

Prep Time: 10 minutes | Cook Time: 20 minutes | Serves: 6

Ingredients:

4 chicken bouillon cubes
6 celery stalks, chopped
½ cup spinach, chopped
½ cup chopped onion
1 cup water
Salt and black pepper, to taste

Directions:

1. Add water and chicken bouillon cubes in the Ninja Foodi cooking pot. Close the Crisping Lid and set the unit on Broil mode. 2. Cook for about 5 minutes and open the lid. 3. Stir in vegetables and simmer the mixture for 15 minutes. 4. Take out, serve and enjoy!
Nutritional Information Per Serving: Calories: 13; Fat: 0.3g; Carbs: 2.1g; Protein: 0.7g

Ninja Foodi Vegetables Smoothie

Prep Time: 10 minutes | Cook Time: 5 minutes | Serves: 4

Ingredients:

½ cup chopped spinach
1 cup broccoli florets, chopped
1 cup chopped green bell peppers
3 cups chilled water
1 cup green cabbage, chopped
2 tsp sugar

Directions:

1. Add spinach, broccoli, bell peppers, cabbage, sugar and water in the Ninja Foodi cooking pot. 2. Close the Pressure Lid and turn the pressure release valve to SEAL position. Set the unit on Pressure Cook mode. 3. Pressure cook at LO for 5 minutes. 4. Open the lid, take out and refrigerate for 2 to 3 hours. 5. Pour in serving glasses and serve.
Nutritional Information Per Serving: Calories: 30; Fat: 0.2g; Carbs: 6.9g; Protein: 1.3g

Cabbage with Bacon

Prep Time: 5 minutes | Cook Time: 20 minutes | Serves: 4

Ingredients:

4 cups red cabbage, shredded
¼ cup veggie stock
A pinch of black pepper and salt
1 tbsp olive oil
1 cup canned tomatoes, crushed
Zest of 1 lime, grated
2 ounces bacon, cooked and crumbled

Directions:

1. Put the reversible rack in the Ninja Foodi, add the baking pan inside and grease it with the oil. 2. Add the cabbage, the stock, and the other ingredients into the pan. 3. Close the Crisping Lid. 4. Cook on Bake/Roast mode at 380°F for 20 minutes. 5. Divide the mix between plates and serve.
Nutritional Information Per Serving: Calories: 144; Fat: 3g; Carbs: 4.5g; Protein: 4.4g

Ninja Foodi Tomato Olive Salad

Prep Time: 10 minutes | Cook Time: 2 minutes | Serves: 4

Ingredients:

4 tbsp red wine vinegar
5 cucumbers, chopped
½ red onion, thinly sliced
5 tomatoes, chopped
½ cup green olives, chopped
1 cup black olives, halved

Directions:

1. Add every ingredient in the Ninja Foodi cooking pot. Close the Pressure Lid and turn the pressure release valve to VENT position. Set the unit on "Steam" mode. 2. Cook for 2 minutes and open the lid. 3. Take out and toss to coat well. 4. Serve and enjoy!

Nutritional Information Per Serving: Calories: 133; Fat: 4.5g; Carbs: 23.3g; Protein: 4.3g

Ninja Foodi Roasted Red Pepper Gazpacho

Prep Time: 10 minutes | Cook Time: 5 minutes | Serves: 2

Ingredients:

1 cup cherry tomatoes
2 roasted red sweet peppers
½ red onion, chopped
1 garlic clove, minced
1 cucumber, chopped
2 tbsp diced mild green chilies
1 tbsp apple cider vinegar
1 tbsp olive oil

Directions:

1. Add everything in the Ninja Foodi. Close the Pressure Lid and turn the pressure release valve to SEAL position. Set the unit on Pressure Cook mode. 2. Pressure cook at HI for 5 minutes and open the lid. 3. Take out, serve and enjoy!

Nutritional Information Per Serving: Calories: 131; Fat: 7.5g; Carbs: 15.7g; Protein: 2.7g

Ninja Foodi Kale Salad

Prep Time: 10 minutes | Cook Time: 5 minutes | Serves: 4

Ingredients:

2 tomatoes, sliced
2 tbsp fresh lemon juice
2 red onions, sliced
2 scallions, chopped
8 cups fresh kale, trimmed and chopped
4 tbsp fresh orange juice

Directions:

1. Add all the ingredients in the Ninja Foodi cooking pot. Close the Pressure Lid and turn the pressure release valve to VENT position. Set the unit on "Steam" mode. 2. Cook for 5 minutes in the Ninja Foodi and open the lid. 3. Take out and refrigerate for about 8 hours. 4. Serve and enjoy!

Nutritional Information Per Serving: Calories: 110; Fat: 0.3g; Carbs: 23.9g; Protein: 5.5g

Buttered Cabbage

Prep Time: 5 minutes | Cook Time: 12-15 minutes | Serves: 4

Ingredients:

1 finely cut cabbage head
½ cup unsalted butter
1 cup chicken broth
Salt to taste
Pepper to taste
½ tsp chili flakes

Directions:

1. Take the Ninja Foodi cooking pot and add chicken broth and butter to it. Then add chopped cabbage and make sure the lid is closed tightly and set the pressure lid on the Seal. Cook on High Pressure for 6 minutes. 2. Slowly move the valve to the Vent for a quick release. Open the lid once the pressure is released. 3. Stir the cabbage and sprinkle salt, pepper, and chili flakes to season it!

Nutritional Information Per Serving: Calories: 291; Fat: 22.3g; Carbs: 10.5g; Protein: 5.3g

Gluten-free Taco Beans

Prep Time: 5 minutes | Cook Time: 20-25 minutes | Serves: 1

Ingredients:

½ cup Albi beans
2 cloves minced garlic
1 diced onion
½ tsp of salt and pepper
1 tbsp taco seasoning mix
5-7 cups water

Directions:

1. In the pot of Ninja Foodi, place your beans, garlic, onions, and the seasonings together. 2. Add water and secure with Pressure Lid and set its valve to Seal. 3. Let it cook for 25 minutes on Pressure Cook mode at HI, but keep in mind if the beans have been soaked already, then cook for 3 minutes only. 4. When the cooking is over do nothing for 10 minutes and let them naturally release and your taco beans are ready!

Nutritional Information Per Serving: Calories: 126; Fat: 0.5g; Carbs: 20.9g; Protein: 6.6g

Steak and Veggie Bowl

Prep Time: 6 minutes | Cook Time: 12-15 minutes | Serves: 1

Ingredients:

2 steak strips
½ coarsely cut red bell pepper
½ coarsely cut green bell pepper
½ coarsely cut summer squash
10 sliced olives
½ cup diced onion
2 tbsp barbecue sauce
Salt to taste
Black pepper to taste
Olive oil spray

Directions:

1. Start by cutting the steak into smaller chunks. Spray olive oil in the Ninja Foodi Cook & Crisp Basket. 2. Now put the steak chunks and cut vegetables in Cook & Crisp Basket. Sprinkle salt, pepper, and barbecue sauce evenly and make sure the seasoning is sprinkled generously. 3. Again, spray with olive oil. Close the unit with Crisping Lid and cook for 7 minutes at 375°F on Bake/Roast mode. Open the lid carefully and toss the ingredients. 4. Spray some more olive oil and cook for an additional 8 minutes. Serve it in a bowl!

Nutritional Information Per Serving: Calories: 19.4g; Fat: 5.2g; Carbs: 12g; Protein: 21g.

Garlic Red Bell Pepper Mix

Prep Time: 5 minutes | Cook Time: 16 minutes | Serves: 4

Ingredients:

1 lb. red bell peppers, cut into wedges
½ tsp curry powder
½ cup tomato sauce
Salt and black pepper, to the taste

1 tbsp olive oil
2 garlic cloves, minced
1 tbsp parsley, chopped

Directions:

1. Put the reversible rack in the Ninja Foodi. Place the baking dish on top, and grease it with the oil. 2. Add the peppers, curry powder, and the other ingredients except for the parsley to a dish. Toss to combine. Close the Crisping Lid. Cook them on Bake/Roast mode at 380°F for 16 minutes. 3. When done, divide between plates and serve with the parsley sprinkled on top.
Nutritional Information Per Serving: Calories: 150; Fat: 3.5g; Carbs: 3.1g; Protein: 1.2g

Crispy Balsamic Cabbage

Prep Time: 5 minutes | Cook Time: 15 minutes | Serves: 4

Ingredients:

1 green cabbage head, shredded
2 endives, trimmed and sliced lengthwise
Salt and black pepper, to taste
1 tbsp olive oil

2 shallots, chopped
½ cup chicken stock
1 tbsp sweet paprika
1 tbsp balsamic vinegar

Directions:

1. Set the Ninja Foodi to Sear/Sauté mode on MD: HI temperature setting. Add the oil, heat it up, then add the shallots and sauté for 2 minutes. 2. Add the cabbage, endives, and the other ingredients. Stir to combine. 3. Put the Pressure Lid on. Turn the pressure release valve to Seal position. Set to Pressure Cook mode and cook on HI for 13 minutes. 4. Quick-release the pressure for 5 minutes, then divide the mixture between plates and serve.
Nutritional Information Per Serving: Calories: 120; Fat: 2g; Carbs: 3.3g; Protein: 4g

Ninja Foodi Brown Rice

Prep Time: 5 minutes | Cook Time: 15 minutes | Serves: 4

Ingredients:

2 cups brown rice
1 tsp salt
1 tsp cumin

Cooked chicken chunks (optional)
Cooked veggies (optional)

Directions:

1. Add 2 cups of brown rice along with the salt and cumin to your Ninja Foodi. 2. Add 2¼ cups water. Put the Pressure Lid on and turn the steam valve to the Seal position. 3. Select Pressure Cook mode, set it to HI, and adjust the cook time to 15 minutes. 4. When done, allow it to naturally release pressure for 5 minutes, and then release the rest quickly.
Nutritional Information Per Serving: Calories: 337; Fat: 12g; Carbs: 73g; Protein: 6g

Kale Stir Fry

Prep Time: 5 minutes | Cook Time: 15 minutes | Serves: 4

Ingredients:

- 1 lb. kale, torn
- 2 leeks, sliced
- 2 tbsp balsamic vinegar
- 1 tbsp fresh parsley, chopped
- Salt and black pepper, to the taste
- 2 shallots, chopped
- ½ cup tomato sauce

Directions:

1. Combine the kale with the leeks and the other ingredients in the Ninja Foodi cooking pot. 2. Put the Pressure Lid on, turn the pressure release valve to SEAL position, and set the unit on Pressure Cook mode. Pressure cook at HI for 15 minutes. 3. Quick-release the pressure for 5 minutes, divide the mix between plates, and serve.

Nutritional Information Per Serving: Calories: 100; Fat: 2g; Carbs: 3.4g; Protein: 4g

Black-Eyed Peas

Prep Time: 5 minutes | Cook Time: 35 minutes | Serves: 10

Ingredients:

- 1 tsp olive oil
- 1 cup white onion, chopped
- 3 garlic cloves
- 6 cups chicken broth
- 1 lb. bag dried black-eyed peas, rinsed
- 1 fully-cooked smoked turkey leg (about 1–1½ lbs.)
- 1 tsp Creole seasoning
- 1 bay leaf

Directions:

1. Set the Ninja Foodi to Sear/Sauté mode on MD: HI temperature setting and add the olive oil. 2. When hot, add the onions and garlic. Sauté until translucent and fragrant. 3. Add the chicken broth, black-eyed peas, smoked turkey leg, Creole seasoning, and bay leaf. Stir. 4. Place on the Pressure Lid and turn the pressure release valve to SEAL position. Select Pressure Cook mode and cook for 30 minutes on HI. 5. When the pot indicates that the cooking time is over, allow the steam to release naturally for 10 minutes. 6. Open the pot and remove the bay leaf and smoked turkey leg. Use 2 forks to shred the turkey. Return it to the pot. Taste it and add salt and pepper if needed. 7. Serve the black-eyed peas using a slotted spoon.

Nutritional Information Per Serving: Calories: 248; Fat: 10.8g; Carbs: 40.7g; Protein: 2.5g

Saucy Kale

Prep Time: 5 minutes | Cook Time: 15 minutes | Serves: 4

Ingredients:

- 1-pound kale, torn
- 2 leeks, sliced
- 2 tbsp balsamic vinegar
- 1 tbsp parsley, chopped
- Black pepper and salt to the taste
- 2 shallots, chopped
- ½ cup tomato sauce

Directions:

1. In your Ninja Foodi, combine the kale with the leeks and the other ingredients. 2. Close the Pressure Lid and turn the pressure release valve to SEAL position. Pressure cook at HI for 15 minutes. 3. Release the pressure quickly for 5 minutes, divide the mix between plates and serve.

Nutritional Values Per Serving: Calories: 100; Fat: 2g; Carbs: 3.4g; Protein: 4g

Eggplant with Kale

Prep Time: 5 minutes | Cook Time: 15 minutes | Serves: 4

Ingredients:

Juice of 1 lime
1-pound eggplant, roughly cubed
1 cup kale, torn
A pinch of black pepper and salt
½ tsp chili powder
½ cup chicken stock
3 tbsp olive oil

Directions:

1. Set the Ninja Foodi on Sear/Sauté mode, stir in the oil, heat it up, add the eggplant and sauté for 2 minutes at HI. 2. Stir in the kale and the rest of the ingredients. 3. Close the Pressure Lid and turn the pressure release valve to VENT position. Sear at HI for 13 minutes. 4. Divide the mix between plates and serve.
Nutritional Values Per Serving: Calories: 110; Fat: 3g; Carbs: 4.3g; Protein: 1.1g

Okra Stew

Prep Time: 5 minutes | Cook Time: 12 minutes | Serves: 4

Ingredients:

1-pound okra, trimmed
2 leeks, sliced
Black pepper and salt to the taste
1 cup tomato sauce
¼ cup pine nuts, toasted
1 tbsp cilantro, chopped

Directions:

1. In your Ninja Foodi, mix the okra with the leeks and the other ingredients except the cilantro. 2. Close the unit with Pressure Lid and turn the pressure release valve to SEAL position. Set the unit on Pressure Cook. Pressure cook at HI for 12 minutes. 3. Release the pressure quickly for 5 minutes, divide the okra mix into bowls and serve with the cilantro sprinkled on top.
Nutritional Values Per Serving: Calories: 146; Fat: 3g; Carbs: 4g; Protein: 3g

Balsamic Cabbage with Endives

Prep Time: 5 minutes | Cook Time: 15 minutes | Serves: 4

Ingredients:

1 green cabbage head, shredded
2 endives, trimmed and sliced lengthwise
Black pepper and salt to the taste
1 tbsp olive oil
2 shallots, chopped
½ cup chicken stock
1 tbsp sweet paprika
1 tbsp balsamic vinegar

Directions:

1. Set the Foodi on Sear/Sauté mode, stir in the oil, heat it up, add the shallots and sauté at MD for 2 minutes. 2. Add the cabbage, the endives, and the other ingredients. 3. Close the Pressure Lid and turn the pressure release valve to SEAL position. Set the unit on Pressure Cook mode. Pressure cook at HI for 13 minutes. 4. Release the pressure quickly for 5 minutes, divide the mix between plates and serve.
Nutritional Values Per Serving: Calories: 120; Fat: 2g; Carbs: 3.3g; Protein: 4

Kale and Parmesan

Prep Time: 5 minutes | Cook Time: 15 minutes | Serves: 4

Ingredients:

- 1-pound kale, torn
- 2 tbsp parmesan, grated
- 1 red onion, sliced
- 1 cup bacon, cooked and chopped
- ½ cup chicken stock
- 1 tbsp olive oil
- A pinch of black pepper and salt
- 1 tbsp balsamic vinegar

Directions:

1. Set the Ninja Foodi on Sear/Sauté mode, stir in the oil, heat it up, add the onion and sauté for 2 minutes. 2. Stir in the kale and the other ingredients except the parmesan. 3. Sprinkle the cheese at the end. Close the Crisping Lid. Set the machine on Air Crisp mode. 4. Air crisp at 380°F for about 12 minutes. 5. Divide everything into bowls and serve.

Nutritional Values Per Serving: Calories: 130; Fat: 5g; Carbs: 3.4g; Protein: 6g

Air Crisped Brussels Sprouts

Prep Time: 6 minutes | Cook Time: 12-15 minutes | Serves: 2-3

Ingredients:

- ¼ pound brussels sprouts
- 2 slices of bacon
- 1 onion
- Salt to taste
- Pepper to taste

Directions:

1. Preheat the Ninja Foodi by selecting Air Crisp Mode at 390°F for about 5 minutes. 2. Cut off the ends of Brussels sprouts and slice them in half. Cut the bacon into small pieces and cut the onions into slices. 3. Put all the ingredients including Brussels sprouts, onions, and bacon in Ninja Foodi. 4. Season it with salt and pepper. Close the Crisping Lid. Set the unit on Air Crisp mode. Let it air crisp at 390°F for 15 minutes and mix occasionally. Keep a check and make sure it does not burn!

Nutritional Values Per Serving: Calories: 90; Fat: 2.3g; Carbs: 14.5g; Protein: 7.1g

Mac & Cheese

Prep Time: 4-5 minutes | Cook Time: 3-4 minutes | Serves: 4

Ingredients:

- 1 tbsp salted and melted butter
- 1 tbsp flour
- 4 ounces milk
- 1 cup water
- 4 ounces elbow macaroni
- 2 ounces cheddar cheese

Directions:

1. In a pan combine butter and flour and keep stirring until a smooth paste is formed. 2. Now add milk and stir continuously to avoid the lumps. 3. Add one cup water and macaroni to the Ninja Foodi cooking pot and stir to mix well. 4. Make sure pasta is fully drenched in the water. Place the wrap in Ninja Foodi and seal the pressure lid. Cook for 3 minutes on Pressure Cook mode at HI. When time is up, naturally release pressure for 2 minutes and then manually release the leftover pressure. 5. Meanwhile, grate the cheese. After that remove the rack and stir that mixture and pour into the macaroni and mix well. 6. Add grated cheese and stir to melt it!

Nutritional Values Per Serving: Calories: 297; Fat: 17.7g; Carbs: 22.4g; Protein: 12g

Zucchini and Spinach Mix

Prep Time: 5 minutes | Cook Time: 17 minutes | Serves: 4

Ingredients:

2 zucchinis, sliced
1 lb. baby spinach
½ cup tomato sauce
Salt and black pepper
1 tbsp avocado oil
1 red onion, chopped
1 tbsp sweet paprika
½ tsp garlic powder
½ tsp chili powder

Directions:

1. Set the Ninja Foodi to Sear/Sauté mode on MD: HI temperature setting. Add the oil, heat it up, and then add the onion and sauté for 2 minutes. 2. Add the zucchinis, spinach, and other ingredients. Stir to combine. Close the Pressure Lid. Turn the pressure release valve to Seal position. 3. Set the unit on Pressure Cook mode. Pressure cook the mixture at HI for 15 minutes. 4. Quick-release the pressure for 5 minutes, then divide everything between plates and serve.
Nutritional Information Per Serving: Calories: 130; Fat: 5.5g; Carbs: 3.3g; Protein: 1g

Maple Dipped Kale

Prep Time: 5 minutes | Cook Time: 15 minutes | Serves: 4

Ingredients:

2 pounds kale, torn
½ cup soy sauce
1 tsp choc zero maple syrup
2 tsp olive oil
½ tsp garlic powder
Black pepper and salt

Directions:

1. In your Ninja Foodi, combine the kale with the soy sauce and the other ingredients. 2. Close the Pressure Lid and turn the pressure release valve to SEAL position. Set the unit on Pressure Cook mode. Pressure cook the kale for 15 minutes. 3. Release the pressure quickly for 5 minutes, divide everything between plates and serve.
Nutritional Values Per Serving: Calories: 120; Fat: 3.5g; Carbs: 3.3g; Protein: 1.1g

Flavored Fries

Prep Time: 12 minutes | Cook Time: 15 minutes | Serves: 2

Ingredients:

2 medium-sized sweet potatoes
1 tbsp butter
1 tsp salt
1 tsp cinnamon
2 tsp brown sugar
½ tsp chili flakes

Directions:

1. Preheat the Ninja Foodi at Air Crisp Mode at 390°F for 5 minutes. Cut sweet potatoes into thick strips. Rinse the fries, then let them dry. 2. Take a bowl and add fries, butter, cinnamon, salt, and chili flakes in it. Mix it well. 3. In the Ninja Foodi, place fries in a single layer, it is recommended to work in batches. Close the Crisping Lid. Set the unit on Air Crisp mode. 4. Cook it at 390°F for 3 to 7 minutes and then shake the Ninja Foodi Cook & Crisp Basket. 5. Again, cook it for another 7 minutes and sprinkle brown sugar on top of it.
Nutritional Values Per Serving: Calories: 89; Fat: 6.1g; Carbs: 4.2g; Protein: 4.4g.

Pumpkin Chili

Prep Time: 10 minutes | Cook Time: 4 minutes | Serves: 8

Ingredients:

- 1 lb. lean ground beef
- 2 (16 oz each) cans chili beans
- 1 (14½ oz) can beef broth
- 1 (10 oz) can diced tomatoes
- 1 cup pureed pumpkin
- 2 tsp pumpkin pie spice
- ¼ cup yellow or white onion, chopped
- 1 clove garlic, crushed
- 1 tsp chili powder
- ½ cup natural ketchup
- Toppings (optional)
- Cornbread
- Fritos
- Shredded cheese
- Sour cream
- Green onions

Directions:

1. Set the Ninja Foodi to Sear/Sauté mode on MD: HI temperature setting. Add the ground beef and brown it. 2. Drain the ground beef if necessary and then return it to the pot. 3. Add in all the remaining chili ingredients, then stir. 4. Close the Pressure Lid securely, ensuring the steam vent is closed. 5. Select Pressure Cook mode and cook on HI for 4 minutes. 6. Quickly release the steam.

Nutritional Information Per Serving: Calories: 345; Fat: 12g; Carbs: 35g; Protein: 25g

Chapter 7 Dessert Recipes

96	Raspberry Cobbler	101	Lime Blueberry Cheesecake
96	Double Chocolate Cake	102	Mini Chocolate Cheesecakes
97	Mocha Cake	102	Chocolate Brownie Cake
97	Vanilla Cheesecake	102	Banana Bread
98	Blackberry Cake	103	Mini Vanilla Cheesecakes
98	Chocolate Lava Cake	103	Chocolate Walnut Cake
98	Yogurt Cheesecake	103	Pineapple Chunks
99	Chocolate Cheesecake	104	Ninja Foodi Blackberry Crumble
99	Ninja Foodi Yogurt Cheesecake	104	Rocky Road Fudge
100	Chocolate Blackberry Cake	105	Honey Almond Scones
100	Strawberry Crumble	105	Air Crisped Cake
100	Ninja Foodi Banana Custard	105	Crispy Apple Delight
101	Lemon Cheesecake	106	Blueberry Buttermilk Cake

Raspberry Cobbler

Prep Time: 15 minutes. | Cook Time: 2 hours | Serves: 8

Ingredients:

- 1 cup almond flour
- ¼ cup coconut flour
- ¾ cup Erythritol
- 1 tsp baking soda
- ¼ tsp ground cinnamon
- ⅛ tsp salt
- ¼ cup unsweetened coconut milk
- 2 tbsp coconut oil
- 1 large egg, beaten lightly
- 4 cups fresh raspberries

Directions:

1. Grease the Ninja Foodi cooking pot. 2. In a large bowl, mix together flours, Erythritol, baking soda, cinnamon, and salt. 3. In another bowl, stir in the coconut milk, coconut oil, and egg and beat until well combined. 4. Add the prepared egg mixture into the flour mixture and mix until just combined. 5. In the Ninja Foodi cooking pot, add the mixture evenly and top with raspberries. 6. Close the Pressure Lid and turn the pressure release valve to VENT position. Set the unit on "Slow Cook" mode. 7. Slow cook at LO for 2 hours. 8. Place the pot onto a wire rack to cool slightly. 9. Serve warm.

Nutritional Values Per Serving: Calories: 164; Fats: 12.5g; Carbs: 10.9g; Proteins: 4.7

Double Chocolate Cake

Prep Time: 15 minutes. | Cook Time: 1 hour | Serves: 12

Ingredients:

- ½ cup coconut flour
- 1½ cups Erythritol
- 5 tbsp cacao powder
- 1 tsp baking powder
- ½ tsp salt
- 3 eggs
- 3 egg yolks
- ½ cup butter, melted and cooled
- 1 tsp vanilla extract
- ½ tsp liquid stevia
- 4 ounces 70% dark chocolate chips
- 2 cups hot water

Directions:

1. Grease the Ninja Foodi's insert. 2. In a large bowl, stir in the flour, 1¼ cups of Erythritol, 3 tbsp of cacao powder, baking powder, and salt. 3. In a suitable bowl, add the eggs, egg yolks, butter, vanilla extract, and liquid stevia and beat until well combined. 4. Stir in the egg mixture into the flour mixture and mix until just combined. 5. In a small bowl, add hot water, remaining cacao powder and Erythritol and beat until well combined. 6. In the prepared Ninja Foodi cooking pot, stir in the mixture evenly and top with chocolate chips, followed by the water mixture. 7. Close the Ninja Foodi with Pressure Lid. Turn the pressure release valve to the VENT position. Then select "Slow Cook" function. 8. Slow cook at LO for 3 hours. 9. Transfer the pot onto a wire rack for about 10 minutes. 10. Flip the baked and cooled cake onto the wire rack to cool completely. 11. Cut into desired-sized slices and serve.

Nutritional Values Per Serving: Calories: 169; Fats: 15.4g; Carbs: 4.4g; Proteins: 3.9g

Mocha Cake

Prep Time: 15 minutes. | Cook Time: 3 hours 37 minutes | Serves: 6

Ingredients:

- 2 ounces 70% dark chocolate, chopped
- ¾ cup butter, chopped S
- ½ cup heavy cream
- 2 tbsp instant coffee crystals
- 1 tsp vanilla extract
- ⅓ cup almond flour
- ¼ cup unsweetened cacao powder
- ⅛ tsp salt
- 5 large eggs
- ⅔ cup Erythritol

Directions:

Grease the Ninja Foodi's insert.
1. In a microwave-safe bowl, stir in the chocolate and butter and microwave on High for about 2 minutes or until melted completely, stirring after every 30 seconds. 2. Remove from the microwave and stir well. 3. Set aside to cool. 4. In a small bowl, stir in the heavy cream, coffee crystals, and vanilla extract and beat until well combined. 5. In a suitable bowl, mix the flour, cacao powder, and salt. 6. In a large bowl, stir in the eggs and with an electric mixer, beat on high speed until slightly thickened. 7. Slowly, stir in the Erythritol and beat on high speed until thick and pale yellow. 8. Stir in the chocolate mixture and beat on low speed until well combined. 9. Stir in the dry flour mixture and mix until just combined. 10. Slowly stir in the cream mixture and beat on medium speed until well combined. 11. In the prepared Ninja Foodi's insert, add the mixture. 12. Close the Pressure Lid, turn the pressure release valve to VENT position, and then set the unit on "Slow Cook" mode. 13. Slow cook at LO for 2½-3½ hours. 14. Transfer the pan onto a wire rack for about 10 minutes. 15. Flip the baked and cooled cake onto the wire rack to cool completely. 16. Cut into desired-sized slices and serve.

Nutritional Values Per Serving: Calories: 407; Fats: 39.7g; Carbs: 6.2g; Proteins: 9g

Vanilla Cheesecake

Prep Time: 15 minutes. | Cook Time: 2 hours | Serves: 6

Ingredients:

For Crust:
- 1 cup almonds, toasted
- 1 egg
- 2 tbsp butter
- 4-6 drops liquid stevia

For Filling:
- 2 8-ounce packages of cream cheese, softened
- 4 tbsp heavy cream
- 2 eggs
- 1 tbsp coconut flour
- 1 tsp liquid stevia
- 1 tsp vanilla extract

Directions:

1. For the crust: in a high-speed food processor, stir in almonds and pulse until a flour-like consistency is achieved. 2. In a suitable bowl, add ground almond, egg, butter and stevia and mix until well combined. 3. In the bottom of a suitable oval pan, place the crust mixture and press to smooth the top surface, leaving a little room on each side. 4. For the filling: in a suitable bowl, stir in all ingredients and with an immersion blender, blend until well combined. 5. Place the prepared filling mixture over the crust evenly. 6. In the Ninja Foodi cooking pot place 1 cup of water. 7. Carefully set the pan in the Ninja Foodi's insert. 8. Close the Ninja Foodi with a pressure lid, turn the pressure release valve to VENT position, and select "Slow Cook". 9. Slow cook on "LO" for 2 hours. 10. Place the pan onto a wire rack to cool. 11. Refrigerate to chill for at least 6-8 hours before serving.

Nutritional Information Per Serving: Calories: 446; Fats: 42.9g; Carbs: 7.2g; Proteins: 10.6g

Blackberry Cake

Prep Time: 15 minutes | Cook Time: 3 hours | Serves: 10

Ingredients:

- 2 cups almond flour
- 1 cup unsweetened coconut, shredded
- ½ cup erythritol
- ¼ cup unsweetened protein powder
- 2 tsp baking soda
- ¼ tsp salt
- 4 large eggs
- ½ cup heavy cream
- ½ cup unsalted butter, melted
- 1 cup fresh blackberries
- ⅓ cup 70% dark chocolate chips

Directions:

1. Grease the Ninja Foodi pot. 2. Mix together the flour, coconut, erythritol, protein powder, baking soda, and salt in a bowl. 3. In another large bowl, add the eggs, cream, and butter and beat until well combined. 4. Add the flour mixture to the wet mixture and mix until well combined. 5. Fold in the blackberries and chocolate chips. 6. Place the mixture in the prepared pot of the Ninja Foodi. 7. Close the Foodi with Pressure Lid and turn the pressure release valve to VENT position. 8. Set the unit on Slow Cook mode. Slow cook at LO for 3 hours. 9. When done, transfer the pot onto a wire rack to cool for about 10 minutes. 10. Carefully invert the cake onto the wire rack to cool completely.

Nutritional Information Per Serving: Calories: 305; Fat: 27.9g; Carbs: 7.7g; Protein: 10.6g

Chocolate Lava Cake

Prep Time: 10 minutes | Cook Time: 10 minutes | Serves: 4

Ingredients:

- 7 tbsp butter
- 1 cup chocolate chips
- 2 eggs
- 3½ tbsp sugar
- 1½ tbsp self-rising flour

Directions:

1. Melt the chocolate chips and butter together in the microwave. (Put in for 30 seconds, stir, then heat for another 30 seconds until it's melted and smooth.) 2. Whisk together the eggs and sugar in a separate bowl. Then whisk the egg mixture and chocolate together until combined and smooth. 3. Then mix in the flour until smooth. 4. Pour the batter equally into 4 oven-safe ramekins. Fill each ¾ full. 5. Put in the ramekins in the Ninja Foodi cooking pot. Close the Crisping Lid. Set the unit on Air Crisp mode for 10 minutes at 370°F. 6. Allow the ramekins to cool for 2 minutes before flipping over onto plates.

Nutritional Information Per Serving: Calories: 297| Fat 33g; Carbs: 43g; Protein: 5g

Yogurt Cheesecake

Prep Time: 10 minutes. | Cook Time: 40 minutes | Serves: 8

Ingredients:

- 4 cups plain Greek Yogurt
- 1 cup Erythritol
- ½ tsp vanilla extract

Directions:

1. Line a cake pans with parchment paper. 2. In a suitable bowl, stir in the yogurt and Erythritol and with a hand mixer, mix well. 3. Stir in vanilla extract and mix to combine. 4. Add the mixture into the prepared pan and cover with a paper kitchen towel. 5. Then with a piece of foil, cover the pan tightly. 6. In the Ninja Foodi' cooking pot, place 1 cup of water. 7. Set a "Reversible Rack" in the Ninja Foodi cooking pot. 8. Place the ramekins over the "Reversible Rack". 9. Close with Pressure Lid and place the pressure valve to the "Seal" position. 10. Select "Pressure Cook" mode. Pressure cook at "HI" for 40 minutes. 11. Switch the pressure valve to "Vent" and do a "Quick" release. 12. Place the pan onto a wire rack and remove the foil and paper towel. 13. Again, cover the pan with a new paper towel and refrigerate to cool overnight.

Nutritional Information Per Serving: Calories: 88; Fats: 1.5g; Carbs: 8.7g; Proteins: 7g

Chocolate Cheesecake

Prep Time: 15 minutes. | Cook Time: 20 minutes | Serves: 10

Ingredients:

For Crust

¼ cup coconut flour
¼ cup almond flour
2½ tbsp cacao powder

1½ tbsp Erythritol
2 tbsp butter, melted

For Filling

16 ounces cream cheese, softened
⅓ cup cacao powder
½ tsp powdered Erythritol
½ tsp stevia powder
1 large egg

2 large egg yolks
6 ounces unsweetened dark chocolate, melted
¾ cup heavy cream
¼ cup sour cream
1 tsp vanilla extract

Directions:

1. For the crust: in a suitable bowl, mix together flours, cacao powder, and Erythritol. 2. Stir in the melted butter and mix until well combined. 3. Stir in the mixture into a parchment paper-lined 7-inch springform pan evenly, and with your fingers, press evenly. 4. For filling: in a food processor, add the cream cheese, cacao powder, monk fruit powder, and stevia and pulse until smooth. 5. Stir in the egg and egg yolks and pulse until well combined. 6. Add the rest of the ingredients and pulse until well combined. 7. Place the prepared filling mixture on top of the crust evenly and with a rubber spatula, smooth the surface. 8. With a piece of foil, cover the springform pan loosely. 9. In the Ninja Foodi cooking pot, place 2 cups of water. 10. Set a "Reversible Rack" in the Ninja Foodi cocking pot. 11. Place the springform pan over the "Reversible Rack". 12. Close the Pressure Lid and place the pressure valve in the "Seal" position. 13. Select "Pressure Cook" mode and pressure cook at HI for 20 minutes. 14. Switch the pressure valve to "Vent" and do a "Natural" release. 15. Place the pan onto a wire rack to cool completely. 16. Refrigerate for about 6-8 hours before serving.

Nutritional Information Per Serving: Calories: 385; Fats: 35.6g; Carbs: 9.8g; Proteins: 8.9g

Ninja Foodi Yogurt Cheesecake

Prep Time: 15 minutes | Cook Time: 30 minutes | Serves: 10

Ingredients:

6 drops liquid stevia
1 tsp vanilla extract
4 egg whites
½ cup cocoa powder

3 cups low-fat Greek yogurt
¼ cup arrowroot starch
Pinch of salt

Crust

¼ cup white sugar
7 graham crackers
¼ cup brown sugar

1 pinch salt
6 tbsp butter, melted

Directions:

1. Gather all the crust ingredients and dump into the blender. 2. Blend until all the ingredients are well combined and form the sand like consistency. 3. Combine all crust ingredients in a blender and blend until mixture becomes the consistency of damp sand. 4. Shift the crust mixture into a 7-inch springform pan and pat it down with spatula. 5. Add all the ingredients of cheesecake filling in a large bowl and mix well. 6. Pour the mixture in the springform pan over the top of the crust and place it in Ninja Foodi cooking pot. 7. Close the Crisping Lid and set the unit on Bake/Roast mode. 8. Bake for about 30 minutes at 350°F. 9. Open the lid and take out. 10. Slice and serve.

Nutritional Information Per Serving: Calories: 236; Fat: 9.3g; Carbs: 35.1g; Protein: 5.9g

Chocolate Blackberry Cake

Prep Time: 15 minutes. | Cook Time: 3 hours | Serves: 10

Ingredients:

- 2 cups almond flour
- 1 cup unsweetened coconut, shredded
- ½ cup Erythritol
- ¼ cup unsweetened protein powder
- 2 tsp baking soda
- ¼ tsp salt
- 4 large eggs
- ½ cup heavy cream
- ½ cup unsalted butter, melted
- 1 cup fresh blackberries
- ⅓ cup 70% dark chocolate chips

Directions:

1. Grease the Ninja Foodi's insert. 2. In a suitable, mix together the flour, coconut, Erythritol protein powder, baking soda, and salt. 3. In another large bowl, stir in the eggs, cream, and butter and beat until well combined. 4. Stir in the dry flour mixture and mix until well combined. 5. Fold in the blackberries and chocolate chips. 6. In the prepared Ninja Foodi's insert, add the mixture. 7. Close the Pressure Lid, turn the pressure release valve to VENT position, and set the unit on "Slow Cook" mode. 8. Slow cook on "LO" for 3 hours. 9. Transfer the pot onto a wire rack about 10 minutes. 10. Flip the baked and cooled cake onto the wire rack to cool completely. 11. Cut into desired-sized slices and serve.

Nutritional Information Per Serving: Calories: 305; Fats: 27.5g; Carbs: 7.7g; Proteins: 10.6g

Strawberry Crumble

Prep Time: 15 minutes. | Cook Time: 2 hours | Serves: 5

Ingredients:

- 1 cup almond flour
- 2 tbsp butter, melted
- 10 drops liquid stevia
- 4 cups fresh strawberries, hulled and sliced
- 1 tbsp butter, chopped

Directions:

1. Lightly, grease the Ninja Foodi cooking pot. 2. In a suitable bowl, stir in the flour, melted butter and stevia and mix until a crumbly mixture form. 3. In the pot of the prepared Ninja Foodi, place the strawberry slices and dot with chopped butter. 4. Spread the flour mixture on top evenly. 5. Close the Ninja Foodi's lid with a pressure lid. Turn the pressure release valve to VENT position and select "Slow Cook". 6. Cook the crumble on LO for 2 hours. 7. Place the pan onto a wire rack to cool slightly. 8. Serve warm.

Nutritional Information Per Serving: Calories: 233; Fats: 19.2g; Carbs: 10.7g; Proteins: 0.7g

Ninja Foodi Banana Custard

Prep Time: 10 minutes | Cook Time: 25 minutes | Serves: 4

Ingredients:

- 1 banana, mashed
- 1 cup almond milk
- ¼ tsp vanilla extract
- 2 eggs

Directions:

1. Add all the ingredients in a large bowl and mix well. 2. Pour the batter evenly in custard cups and place them in Ninja Foodi cooking pot. 3. Close the Crisping Lid and set the unit on Bake/Roast mode. 4. Bake for 25 minutes at 350°F. 5. Open the lid and take out. 6. Serve and enjoy!

Nutritional Information Per Serving: Calories: 196; Fat: 16.6g; Carbs: 10.3g; Protein: 4.5g

Lemon Cheesecake

Prep Time: 15 minutes. | Cook Time: 4 hours | Serves: 12

Ingredients:

For Crust:

1½ cups almond flour

4 tbsp butter, melted

3 tbsp sugar-free peanut butter

3 tbsp Erythritol

1 large egg, beaten

For Filling:

1 cup ricotta cheese

24 ounces cream cheese, softened

1½ cups Erythritol

2 tsp liquid stevia

⅓ cup heavy cream

2 large eggs

3 large egg yolks

1 tbsp fresh lemon juice

1 tbsp vanilla extract

Directions:

1. Grease the Ninja Foodi's insert. 2. For crust: in a suitable bowl, add all the ingredients and mix until well combined. 3. In the pot of prepared of Ninja Foodi, place the crust mixture and press to smooth the top surface. 4. With a fork, prick the crust at many places. 5. For filling: in a food processor, stir in the ricotta cheese and pulse until smooth. 6. In a large bowl, add the ricotta, cream cheese, Erythritol, and stevia and with an electric mixer, beat over medium speed until smooth. 7. In another bowl, stir in the heavy cream, eggs, egg yolks, lemon juice, and vanilla extract and beat until well combined. 8. Stir in the egg mixture into cream cheese mixture and beat over medium speed until just combined. 9. Place the prepared filling mixture over the crust evenly. 10. Close the Ninja Foodi with a pressure lid, turn the pressure release valve to VENT position, and select "Slow Cook". 11. Slow cook at LO for 3-4 hours. 12. Place the pan onto a wire rack to cool. 13. Refrigerate to chill for at least 6-8 hours before serving.

Nutritional Information Per Serving: Calories: 410; Fats: 37.9g; Carbs: 6.9g; Proteins: 13g

Lime Blueberry Cheesecake

Prep Time: 15 minutes. | Cook Time: 30 minutes | Serves: 6

Ingredients:

¼ cup plus 1 tsp Erythritol

8 ounces cream cheese, softened

⅓ cup Ricotta cheese

1 tsp fresh lime zest, grated

2 tbsp fresh lime juice

½ tsp vanilla extract

1 cup blueberries

2 eggs

2 tbsp sour cream

Directions:

1. In a suitable bowl, stir in ¼ cup of Erythritol and remaining ingredients except for eggs and sour cream and with a hand mixer, beat on high speed until smooth. 2. Stir in the eggs and beat on low speed until well combined, then fold in blueberries. 3. Transfer the mixture into a 6-inch greased springform pan evenly. 4. With a piece of foil, cover the pan. 5. In the Ninja Foodi's insert, place 2 cups of water. 6. Set a "Reversible Rack" in the Ninja Foodi's insert. 7. Place the springform pan over the "Reversible Rack". 8. Close the Ninja Foodi's lid with a pressure lid and place the pressure valve in the "Seal" position. 9. Select "Pressure Cook" mode and pressure cook it to "HI" for 30 minutes. 10. Switch the pressure valve to "Vent" and do a "Natural" release. 11. Place the pan onto a wire rack to cool slightly. 12. Meanwhile, in a small bowl, stir in the sour cream and remaining erythritol and beat until well combined. 13. Spread the cream mixture on the warm cake evenly. 14. Refrigerate for about 6-8 hours before serving.

Nutritional Information Per Serving: Calories: 182; Fats: 16.6g; Carbs: 2.1g; Proteins: 6.4g

Mini Chocolate Cheesecakes

Prep Time: 15 minutes. | Cook Time: 18 minutes | Serves: 4

Ingredients:

1 egg
8 ounces cream cheese, softened
¼ cup Erythritol
1 tbsp powdered peanut butter
¾ tbsp cacao powder

Directions:

1. Grease the Ninja Foodi's insert. 2. In a blender, stir in the eggs and cream cheese and pulse until smooth. 3. Add the rest of the ingredients and pulse until well combined. 4. Transfer the mixture into 2 8-ounce mason jars evenly. 5. In the Ninja Foodi's insert, place 1 cup of water. 6. Set a "Reversible Rack" in the Ninja Foodi's insert. 7. Place the mason jars over the "Reversible Rack". 8. Close with Pressure Lid and place the pressure valve in the "Seal" position. 9. Select "Pressure Cook" mode and set temperature to "HI" and the cook time for 18 minutes. 10. Switch the pressure valve to "Vent" and do a "Natural" release. 11. Open the Ninja Foodi's lid and place the ramekins onto a wire rack to cool. 12. Refrigerate to chill for at least 6-8 hours before serving.
Nutritional Information Per Serving: Calories: 222; Fats: 28.4g; Carbs: 2.9g; Proteins: 6.5g

Chocolate Brownie Cake

Prep Time: 15 minutes. | Cook Time: 35 minutes. | Serves: 6

Ingredients:

½ cup 70% dark chocolate chips
½ cup butter
3 eggs
¼ cup Erythritol
1 tsp vanilla extract

Directions:

1. In a microwave-safe bowl, stir in the chocolate chips and butter and microwave for about 1 minute, stirring after every 20 seconds. 2. Remove from the microwave and stir well. 3. Set a "Reversible Rack" in the pot of the Ninja Foodi. 4. Close the Crisping Lid and select "Air Crisp". 5. Set its cooking temperature to 350°F and the cook time for 5 minutes. 6. Press the "Start/Stop" button to initiate preheating. 7. In a suitable bowl, add the eggs, Erythritol, and vanilla extract and blend until light and frothy. 8. Slowly add in the chocolate mixture and beat again until well combined. 9. Add the mixture into a lightly greased springform pan. 10. After preheating, open the Ninja Foodi's lid. 11. Place the springform pan into the Cook & Crisp Basket. 12. Close the Ninja Foodi with Crisping Lid and select "Air Crisp". 13. Set its cooking temperature to 350°F and the cook time for 35 minutes. 14. Press the "Start/Stop" button to initiate cooking. 15. Place the hot pan onto a wire rack to cool for about 10 minutes. 16. Flip the baked and cooled cake onto the wire rack to cool completely. 17. Cut into desired-sized slices and serve.
Nutritional Information Per Serving: Calories: 302; Fats: 28.2g; Carbs: 5.6g; Proteins: 5.6g

Banana Bread

Prep Time: 10 minutes | Cook Time: 30 minutes | Serves: 4

Ingredients:

2 large ripe bananas
¾ cup all-purpose flour
1 egg
3 tsp brown sugar
2 tsp butter
¼ cup sour cream
½ tsp baking soda
½ tsp salt

Directions:

1. Preheat the Ninja Foodi at Bake/Roast function at 190°C/375°F for 5 minutes. 2. Now grease the mini loaf and set it aside. 3. Take all ingredients in a medium bowl and combine them and stir until combined well. 4. Put the batter evenly in a butter paper-lined loaf pan. Dump the pan in the cooking pot. Close the unit with Crisping Lid and Bake it for 25 to 30 minutes. 5. To check the doneness, make sure that when a toothpick is inserted in the center, it comes out clean. Check the banana bread with a toothpick and serve it warm!
Nutritional Information Per Serving: Calories: 271; Fat: 10.4g; Carbs: 40.8g; Protein: 4.8g

Mini Vanilla Cheesecakes

Prep Time: 15 minutes. | Cook Time: 10 minutes | Serves: 4

Ingredients:

¾ cup Erythritol
2 eggs
1 tsp vanilla extract
½ tsp fresh lemon juice
16 ounces cream cheese, softened
2 tbsp sour cream

Directions:

1. Preheat the Ninja Foodi by selecting Air Crisp function, setting the temperature to 175°C/350°F, and setting time to 5 minutes. Press Start/Stop to begin. 2. In a blender, stir in the Erythritol, eggs, vanilla extract, and lemon juice and pulse until smooth. 3. Stir in the cream cheese along with sour cream and pulse until smooth. 4. Stir in the mixture into 2- 4-inch springform pans evenly. 5. After preheating, open the lid. 6. Place the pans into the Cook & Crisp Basket. 7. Close the Crisping Lid and select "Air Crisp". 8. Set its cooking temperature to 175°C/350°F and cook time for 10 minutes. 9. Press the "Start/Stop" button to initiate cooking. 10. Place the pan onto a wire rack for 10 minutes. 11. Refrigerator overnight before serving.

Nutritional Information Per Serving: Calories: 436; Fats: 21g; Carbs: 3.2g; Proteins: 13.1g

Chocolate Walnut Cake

Prep Time: 15 minutes. | Cook Time: 20 minutes | Serves: 6

Ingredients:

3 eggs
1 cup almond flour
⅔ cup Erythritol
⅓ cup heavy whipping cream
¼ cup butter softened
¼ cup cacao powder
¼ cup walnuts, chopped
1 tsp baking powder

Directions:

1. In a suitable bowl, mix all the ingredients and with a mixer, beat until fluffy. 2. Add the mixture into a greased Bundt pan. 3. With a piece of foil, cover the pan. 4. In the Ninja Foodi's insert, place 2 cups of water. 5. Set a "Reversible Rack" in the Ninja Foodi's insert. 6. Place the Bundt pan over the "Reversible Rack". 7. Close the Ninja Foodi with a pressure lid and place the pressure valve to the "Seal" position. 8. Select "Pressure Cook" mode and pressure cook it at HI for 20 minutes. 9. Switch the pressure valve to "Vent" and do a "Quick" release. 10. Place the pan onto a wire rack to cool for about 10 minutes. 11. Flip the baked and cooled cake onto the wire rack to cool completely. 12. Cut into desired-sized slices and serve.

Nutritional Information Per Serving: Calories: 270; Fats: 25.4g; Carbs: 7g; Proteins: 8.9g

Pineapple Chunks

Prep Time: 3 minutes | Cook Time: 10-12 minutes | Serves: 6

Ingredients:

1 stick melted butter
½ cup brown sugar
½ tsp cinnamon
1 sliced pineapple

Directions:

1. Combine melted butter, cinnamon, and brown sugar in a low-sided dish. Mix it well. 2. Put in your pineapple pieces to allow it to soak in the flavors for a bit. 3. Add the pineapple pieces in the Ninja Foodi cooking pot. Close the unit with Crisping Lid. Select the Bake/Roast function, and set the temperature to 375°F. Bake for 12 minutes. 4. Flip the pineapple slices gently halfway through. 5. Serve immediately when ready!

Nutritional Information Per Serving: Calories: 455; Fat: 22.4g; Carbs: 39g; Protein: 4.5g

Ninja Foodi Blackberry Crumble

Prep Time: 10 minutes | Cook Time: 45 minutes | Serves: 6

Ingredients:

Blackberries Filling:

- ¼ cup coconut flour
- 3 tbsp water
- ¼ cup arrowroot flour
- 2 tbsp melted butter
- ¼ cup mashed banana
- 1½ cups fresh blackberries
- ¾ tsp baking soda
- ½ tbsp lemon juice

Crumble Topping

- ½ cup old fashioned oats
- ½ cup coconut flour
- ½ cup brown sugar, packed
- ⅛ tsp baking powder
- ⅛ tsp baking soda
- ¼ cup butter, softened

Directions:

1. Add all the ingredients for filling except blackberries in a bowl and mix well. 2. Combine the ingredients for crumble topping in another bowl. 3. Arrange blackberries in the bottom of Ninja Foodi cooking pot and pour the filling batter on them. 4. Top with the crumble topping. 5. Close the Crisping Lid and set the unit on Bake/Roast mode. 6. Bake the crumble for 40 minutes at 300°F. 7. Open the lid and take out. 8. Serve and enjoy!

Nutritional Information Per Serving: Calories: 292; Fat: 10.7g; Carbs: 45.7g; Protein: 5.9g

Rocky Road Fudge

Prep Time: 5 minutes | Cook Time: 5 hours | Serves: 6

Ingredients:

- 8 ounces pretend condensed milk
- 9 ounces chocolate chips
- 1 tsp vanilla extract
- ¼ tsp sea salt
- ½ cup almonds
- 2 ounces marshmallows

Directions:

1. On Broil mode, preheat the Ninja Foodi for 10 minutes with the Cook & Crisp Basket inside. Now add almonds to the basket and broil it for 3 to 5 minutes. Take out the almonds and let them cool. 2. Line the square pan with parchment paper, add in chocolate chips and sweetened condensed milk, and then cover it again with the foil. 3. Place the pan in Ninja Foodi. Add 2 cups of water in it. Place the pan in Ninja Foodi deluxe reversible rack on the lower position. Close the unit with the Pressure Lid. Turn the pressure release valve to the VENT position. Cook at Steam setting for 5 minutes. 4. Meanwhile, crush the almonds coarsely and cut marshmallows if you're using large ones. 5. Remove the pan from Ninja Foodi and add vanilla, marshmallows, salt, and chopped almonds. Give it a good mix. 6. Then the fudge will start to thicken up as it cools down. Let it cool down for two to four hours in the refrigerator and cut it into bite-size squares!

Nutritional Information Per Serving: Calories: 328; Fat: 18.7g; Carbs: 38.1g; Protein: 7.1g

Honey Almond Scones

Prep Time: 5 minutes | Cook Time: 6 minutes | Serves: 6

Ingredients:

2 cups all-purpose flour
3 tbsp brown sugar
1 egg
1 tsp baking powder
½ tsp salt

1 cup milk
1 tsp almond extract
¼ cup butter
Cinnamon to sprinkle

Directions:

1. Combine the dried ingredients in a large bowl. Melt butter in a pan, then adds it to dry ingredients. 2. Now combine all the wet ingredients with the dry ones and stir it. Make sure to not overwork with the dough mixture. 3. Place on parchment paper in Cook & Crisp Basket. Scoop out the dough with a rounded spoon on the basket. Set your Ninja Foodi to Air Crisp function and set the temperature at 390°F for 8 minutes until it's golden brown. 4. Let the cones cool down and then sprinkle a little bit of cinnamon!

Nutritional Information Per Serving: Calories: 267; Fat: 9.9g; Carbs: 37.4g; Protein: 6.5g

Air Crisped Cake

Prep Time: 10 minutes | Cook Time: 20 minutes | Serves: 6

Ingredients:

4 tbsp self-rising flour
7 tbsp butter
1 cup chocolate chips

3 tbsp sugar
2 eggs

Directions:

1. Melt the butter and chocolate chips. Mix until the chocolate is completely melted. 2. Beat eggs and sugar together in a bowl for 2 minutes. Make sure that sugar is beaten well. Pour this egg mixture into the chocolate mix and fold it to make a smooth batter. 3. Then mix in flour until smooth. Fold it well. 4. Take 4 oven-safe ramekins, and pour the batter equally in them. Fill it ¾th of the ramekin and Air Crisp it for 10 minutes at 390°F in Ninja Foodi. 5. Let it cool for 2 minutes before you flip it onto the plate!

Nutritional Information Per Serving: Calories: 370; Fat: 25.8g; Carbs: 34g; Protein: 5.3g

Crispy Apple Delight

Prep Time: 6 minutes | Cook Time: 10 minutes | Serves: 4

Ingredients:

5 medium-sized apples
½ cup water
½ tsp nutmeg powder
1 tsp cinnamon
4 tbsp butter

¼ cup flour
¾ cup rolled oats
¼ cup brown sugar
½ tsp salt
1 tsp maple syrup

Directions:

1. Cut apples in bite sizes and place them on the bottom of your Ninja Foodi. 2. Now sprinkle cinnamon, maple syrup, and nutmeg on it. Then pour water over this mixture. 3. Melt butter in a separate bowl then adds flour, brown sugar, butter, oats, and salt to the bowl. Mix it well. 4. Pour this butter mix over the apple layer. 5. Seal the Pressure Lid and secure the valve to SEAL position. Cook for 10 minutes on Pressure 6. Cook mode at HI. Then manually release pressure for 5 minutes. 6. Lower the Crisping Lid and then let this combination sit for a few minutes before serving!

Nutritional Information Per Serving: Calories: 322; Fat: 12.5g; Carbs: 54.2g; Protein: 2g

Blueberry Buttermilk Cake

Prep Time: 10 minutes | Cook Time: 15-20 minutes | Serves: 8

Ingredients:

- 8 tbsp unsalted butter
- 1 cup sugar (keep 1 tbsp aside)
- 1 egg
- 1 tsp vanilla
- 2 cups all-purpose flour (¼ cup aside)
- 1 tsp baking powder
- ¼ tsp salt
- ½ cup buttermilk
- 2 cups blueberries

Directions:

1. Beat the butter with 1 cup of sugar for 4 to 5 minutes, until it's light and fluffy. 2. Now add vanilla and eggs into it and beat it well. 3. Put in ¼ cup of flour, 1 tbsp sugar, and blueberries together in a bowl to coat them and set aside. 4. Mix the remaining flour, salt, and baking powder in another bowl. 5. Add this dry mixture to batter and mix it with a spatula, then add buttermilk. 6. Beat until flour is mixed in and add remaining flour. Now fold in the blueberries and remove the excess flour from the blueberry bowl behind it. 7. Spray the Ninja Foodi cooking pot with canola oil. Pour this batter into the Ninja Foodi cooking pot. Close the Crisping Lid and set the unit on Air Crisp mode. Adjust the temperature to 390°F and time for 25 minutes. 8. Let it cook. Check it with a toothpick and extend the time if it's raw. Enjoy!

Nutritional Information Per Serving: Calories: 344; Fat: 12.4g; Carbs: 33.4g; Protein: 4.5g

Conclusion

The Ninja Foodi Smart XL Pressure Cooker Steam Fryer gives you a whole new experience of convenient cooking by bringing a variety of cooking styles into a single appliance. While the Ninja Foodi guarantees effective cooking with minimal supervision, this cookbook ensures that you get the most out of your Ninja Foodi Smart XL Pressure Cooker Steam Fryer by developing its better understanding and by trying all sorts of recipes including breakfasts, poultry, meat, snacks, seafood, and desserts, which are all shared in different chapters of this cookbook. With its single read, all the Ninja Foodi Smart XL Pressure Cooker Steam Fryer beginners can readily learn basic techniques to steam, pressure cook, air fry, bake and cook like a pro.

Appendix 1 Measurement Conversion Chart

WEIGHT EQUIVALENTS

US STANDARD	METRIC (APPROXIMATE)
1 ounce	28 g
2 ounces	57 g
5 ounces	142 g
10 ounces	284 g
15 ounces	425 g
16 ounces (1 pound)	455 g
1.5 pounds	680 g
2 pounds	907 g

VOLUME EQUIVALENTS (LIQUID)

US STANDARD	US STANDARD (OUNCES)	METRIC (APPROXIMATE)
2 tablespoons	1 fl.oz	30 mL
¼ cup	2 fl.oz	60 mL
½ cup	4 fl.oz	120 mL
1 cup	8 fl.oz	240 mL
1½ cup	12 fl.oz	355 mL
2 cups or 1 pint	16 fl.oz	475 mL
4 cups or 1 quart	32 fl.oz	1 L
1 gallon	128 fl.oz	4 L

VOLUME EQUIVALENTS (DRY)

US STANDARD	METRIC (APPROXIMATE)
⅛ teaspoon	0.5 mL
¼ teaspoon	1 mL
½ teaspoon	2 mL
¾ teaspoon	4 mL
1 teaspoon	5 mL
1 tablespoon	15 mL
¼ cup	59 mL
½ cup	118 mL
¾ cup	177 mL
1 cup	235 mL
2 cups	475 mL
3 cups	700 mL
4 cups	1 L

TEMPERATURES EQUIVALENTS

FAHRENHEIT(F)	CELSIUS(C) (APPROXIMATE)
225 °F	107 °C
250 °F	120 °C
275 °F	135 °C
300 °F	150 °C
325 °F	160 °C
350 °F	180 °C
375 °F	190 °C
400 °F	205 °C
425 °F	220 °C
450 °F	235 °C
475 °F	245 °C
500 °F	260 °C

Appendix 2 Air Fryer Cooking Chart

Chicken	Temp(°F)	Time(min)
Chicken Whole (3.5 lbs)	350	45-60
Chicken Breast (boneless)	380	12-15
Chicken Breast (bone-in)	350	22-25
Chicken Drumsticks	380	23-25
Chicken Thighs (bone-in)	380	23-25
Chicken Tenders	350	8-12
Chicken Wings	380	22-25

Beef	Temp(°F)	Time (min)
Burgers (1/4 Pound)	350	8-12
Filet Mignon (4 oz.)	370	15-20
Flank Steak (1.5 lbs)	400	10-14
Meatballs (1 inch)	380	7-10
London Broil (2.5 lbs.)	400	22-28
Round Roast (4 lbs)	390	45-55
Sirloin Steak (12oz)	390	9-14

Pork & Lamb	Temp(°F)	Time
Bacon	350	8-12
Lamb Chops	400	8-12
Pork Chops (1" boneless)	400	8-10
Pork Loin (2 lbs.)	360	18-21
Rack of Lamb (24-32 oz.)	375	22-25
Ribs	400	10-15
Sausages	380	10-15

Fish & Seafood	Temp(°F)	Time
Calamari	400	4-5
Fish Fillets	400	10-12
Salmon Fillets	350	8-12
Scallops	400	5-7
Shrimp	370	5-7
Lobster Tails	370	5-7
Tuna Steaks	400	7-10

Vegetables	Temp(°F)	Time
Asparagus (1" slices)	400	5
Beets (whole)	400	40
Broccoli Florets	400	6
Brussel Sprouts (halved)	380	12-15
Carrots (1/2" slices)	360	12-15
Cauliflower Florets	400	10-12
Corn on the Cob	390	6-7
Eggplant (1 1/2" cubes)	400	12-15
Green Beans	400	4-6
Kale Leaves	250	12
Mushrooms (1/4" slices)	400	4-5
Onions (pearl)	400	10
Peppers (1" chunks)	380	8-15
Potatoes (whole)	400	30-40
Potatoes (wedges)	390	15-18
Potatoes (1" cubes)	390	12-15
Potatoes (baby, 1.5 lbs.)	400	15
Squash (1" cubes)	390	15
Sweet Potato (whole)	380	30-35
Tomatoes (cherry)	400	5
Zucchini (1/2" sticks)	400	10-12

Frozen Foods	Temp(°F)	Time
Breaded Shrimp	400	8-9
Chicken Burger	360	12
Chicken Nuggets	370	10-12
Chicken Strips	380	12-15
Corn Dogs	400	7-9
Fish Fillets (1-2 lbs.)	400	10-12
Fish Sticks	390	12-15
French Fries	380	12-17
Hash Brown Patties	380	10-12
Meatballs (1-inch)	350	10-12
Mozzarella Sticks (11 oz.)	400	8
Meat Pies (1-2 pies)	370	23-25
Mozzarella Sticks	390	7-9
Onion Rings	400	10-12
Pizza	390	5-10
Tater Tots	380	15-17

Appendix 3 Recipes Index

A
Adobo Steak   49
Air Crisped Brussels Sprouts   92
Air Crisped Cake   105
Air Crisped Chicken Nuggets   30
Air Fried Scallops   71
Almond Quinoa Porridge   15
Apricot Oatmeal   15
Avocado Cups   18
Avocado Deviled Eggs   24
Awesome Shrimp Roast   65

B
Bacon Strips   55
Bagel Chicken Tenders   38
Balsamic Cabbage with Endives   91
Banana Bread   102
Bay Crab Legs   67
Beef Bourguignon   56
Beef Enchiladas   57
Beef Jerky   49
Beef Onion Pattie Burgers   61
Beef Stew   58
Beer Battered Fish   73
Beets and Carrots   84
Bell Pepper Frittata   14
Bell Peppers Mix   84
Blackberry Cake   98
Black-Eyed Peas   90
Blueberry Buttermilk Cake   106
Braised Lamb Shanks   56
Breadsticks   24
Breakfast Oats Bowl   22
Broccoli Cauliflower   82
Broccoli Egg Scramble   12
Buffalo Cauliflower Platter   29
Butter Lime Salmon   66
Buttered Cabbage   88
Buttered Fish   70
Buttery Potatoes   31
Buttery Scallops   72

C
Cabbage with Bacon   86
Cabbage with Carrots   81
Cajun Shrimp   71
Carrots Walnuts Salad   85
Cashew Cream   32
Cauliflower chunks with Lemon Sauce   84
Cauliflower Meal   16

Char Siu Pork   52
Cheese Stuffed Dates   32
Chicken Bruschetta   38
Chicken Omelet   13
Chicken Pasta with Dried Tomatoes   45
Chicken Potato Stew   40
Chicken Saltimbocca   47
Chicken Vegetable Soup   46
Chicken Wings   31
Chives, Beets, and Carrots   79
Chocolate Blackberry Cake   100
Chocolate Brownie Cake   102
Chocolate Cheesecake   99
Chocolate Lava Cake   98
Chocolate Walnut Cake   103
Chorizo Omelet   18
Coated Onion Rings   31
Coconut Curry Salmon with Zucchini Noodles   68
Corned Beef   55
Corned Cabbage Beef   55
Cowboy Casserole   11
Creamy Kale   83
Crispy Apple Delight   105
Crispy Balsamic Cabbage   89
Crispy Spiced Broccoli   13
Crumbed Tilapia   77
Crusted Pork Chops   53

D
Deviled Eggs   12
Double Chocolate Cake   96
Dried Tomatoes   25

E
Eastern Lamb Stew   54
Egg Bites   21
Eggplant with Kale   91
Eggs in Avocado Cups   11

F
Fish Broccoli Stew   70
Fish Skewers   77
Fish Stew   69
Flavored Fries   93
Flaxseeds Granola   16
French Toast Bites   11
Fruit Pancakes   16

G
Garlic Pretzels with Ranch

Dressing   30
Garlic Red Bell Pepper Mix   89
Garlicky Pork Chops   49
Garlicky Tomato   32
Glazed Carrots   17
Glazed Chicken & Vegetables   44
Glazed Coho Salmon   68
Gluten-free fish tacos   74
Gluten-free Taco Beans   88

H
Hainanese Chicken   37
Ham Breakfast Casserole   17
Ham-Stuffed Turkey Rolls   42
Hassel Back Chicken   42
Hawaiian Fried Rice   83
Herbed Cauliflower Fritters   34
Honey Almond Scones   105
Honey Garlic Chicken   40

I
Instant Cheesy Broccoli   33
Instant Lamb Steaks   57
Italian Potatoes   81

J
Jalapeno Chicken Nachos   39
Japanese Eggs   25
Juicy Sesame and Garlic Chicken Wings   41

K
Kale and Parmesan   92
Kale Stir Fry   90

L
Lamb Balls   63
Lamb Curry   50
Lamb Shanks   59
Leeks and Carrots   82
Lemon and Chicken Extravaganza   37
Lemon Cheesecake   101
Lemon Garlic Scallops   77
Lime Blueberry Cheesecake   101
Loaded Zucchini Chips   29
Lobster Tail   72
Lobster with Fried Rice   70
Low-Carb Crab Soup   65
Low-Carb Italian Wedding Soup   79

M
Mac & Cheese   92
Mahi-Mahi with Citrus Sauce   69

Maple Dipped Kale 93
Maple Glazed Pork Chops 54
Maple Lamb Chops 62
Mexican Chicken Soup 37
Mexican Chicken with Rice 47
Mexican Rice 80
Mini Chocolate Cheesecakes 102
Mini Vanilla Cheesecakes 103
Minty Radishes 79
Mixed Seafood Platter 76
Mocha Cake 97
Mongolian Beef 53

N

Ninja Foodi Air Crisp Herbed Salmon 76
Ninja Foodi Arugula Omelet 10
Ninja Foodi Asparagus Scallops 75
Ninja Foodi Baked Eggs 20
Ninja Foodi Banana Cookies 35
Ninja Foodi Banana Custard 100
Ninja Foodi Barbeque Chicken Drumsticks 45
Ninja Foodi Basil Pesto Chicken 44
Ninja Foodi Beef Casserole 58
Ninja Foodi Beef Chili 51
Ninja Foodi Blackberry Crumble 104
Ninja Foodi Broccoli Pancakes 21
Ninja Foodi Broiled Mahi-Mahi 74
Ninja Foodi Brown Rice 89
Ninja Foodi Carrot & Pork Stew 50
Ninja Foodi Cheddar Biscuits 26
Ninja Foodi Chicken & Carrot Stew 43
Ninja Foodi Chicken & Salsa Chili 43
Ninja Foodi Chicken Broth 46
Ninja Foodi Chickpea Crackers 28
Ninja Foodi Cinnamon Tea 20
Ninja Foodi Coconut Cereal 19
Ninja Foodi Cod Sticks 26
Ninja Foodi Duck Broth 39
Ninja Foodi Duck Fajita Platter 44
Ninja Foodi Ginger Cod 74
Ninja Foodi Ginger Salmon 76
Ninja Foodi Ground Beef Soup 61
Ninja Foodi Ham Muffins 20
Ninja Foodi Hard-Boiled Eggs 19
Ninja Foodi Herb Crackers 30
Ninja Foodi Kale Salad 87
Ninja Foodi Lamb & Carrot Stew 59
Ninja Foodi Lamb & Kale Stew 50
Ninja Foodi Lamb Chops with Tomatoes 60
Ninja Foodi Lemon Scones 29
Ninja Foodi Lime Chicken Soup 39
Ninja Foodi Minced Beef with Tomatoes 58
Ninja Foodi Mushroom & Beef Stew 52
Ninja Foodi Pancakes 21
Ninja Foodi Parsley Baked Salmon 66
Ninja Foodi Plum & Beef Salad 60
Ninja Foodi Popcorn 27
Ninja Foodi Pork Shoulder Roast 57
Ninja Foodi Roasted Red Pepper Gazpacho 87
Ninja Foodi Salmon 75
Ninja Foodi Salmon with Sweet Potatoes 66
Ninja Foodi Spiced Almonds 28
Ninja Foodi Spicy Cashews 28
Ninja Foodi Spicy Peanuts 35
Ninja Foodi Spicy Popcorns 27
Ninja Foodi Spinach and Onion Soup 86
Ninja Foodi Spinach Beef Soup 51
Ninja Foodi Spinach Chicken 38
Ninja Foodi Spinach Chips 27
Ninja Foodi Steak Fajitas 59
Ninja Foodi Stir-Fried Shrimp 73
Ninja Foodi Tomato Olive Salad 87
Ninja Foodi Turkey & Beans Wrap 43
Ninja Foodi Vegetables Smoothie 86
Ninja Foodi Yogurt Cheesecake 99
Nutmeg Peanuts 34
Nutmeg Pumpkin Porridge 14
Nut-Packed Porridge 13

O

Okra Stew 91
Omelets in the Jar 17

P

Panko Crusted Cod 72
Parmesan Breadsticks 26
Pepperoni Omelets 19
Pineapple Chicken 46
Pineapple Chunks 103
Pomegranate Radish Mix 83
Pork Chili Verde 52
Pork Meatballs 53
Pork Shank 33
Pork Tenderloin 62
Potatoes and Lemon Sauce 81
Pulled Barbecue Chicken 45
Pumpkin Chili 94

R

Radish Apples Salad 85
Raspberry Cobbler 96
Roasted BBQ Shrimp 65
Roasted Beef 51
Roasted Chickpeas 33
Roasted Lamb 62
Rocky Road Fudge 104

S

Saucy Kale 90
Seasoned Beets 82
Sesame Chicken Wings 42
Sesame Radish 85
Shredded Chicken Salsa 40
Shrimp Scampi Linguini 71
Shrimp Zoodles 73
Southern Fried Cabbage with Bacon 80
Spicy Crispy Shrimp 68
Spicy Indian Shrimp Curry 67
Spicy Shrimps 75
Spinach and Turkey Cups 10
Spinach Casserole 10
Spinach Turkey Cups 15
Steak and Veggie Bowl 88
Strawberry Crumble 100
Stuffed Whole Chicken 41
Sweet and Sour Fish 69
Sweet and Sour Pork 60
Swiss Bacon Frittata 18

T

Taco Meatballs 54
Tomahawk Rib-Eye Steak 61
Tortilla Crackers 34
Turkey Meatballs 41

V

Vanilla Banana Bread 12
Vanilla Cheesecake 97
Vegetable Soup 80
Veggies & Beef Stew 56

W

Western Omelet 14
White Fish with Garlic Lemon Pepper Seasoning 67

Y

Yogurt Cheesecake 98

Z

Zucchini and Spinach Mix 93
Zucchini Egg Tots 25
Zucchini Muffins 24

Made in the USA
Las Vegas, NV
26 March 2023

69714656R00067